The Medieval Siege

THEME AND IMAGE
IN MIDDLE
ENGLISH ROMANCE

MALCOLM HEBRON

CLARENDON PRESS · OXFORD
1997

Oxford University Press, Great Clarendon Street, Oxford OX2 6DP

Oxford New York
Athens Auckland Bangkok Bombay
Calcutta Cape Town Dar es Salaam Delhi
Florence Hong Kong Istanbul Karachi
Kuala Lumpur Madras Madrid Melbourne
Mexico City Nairobi Paris Singapore
Taipei Tokyo Toronto
and associated companies in
Berlin Ibadan

Oxford is a trade mark of Oxford University Press

Published in the United States
by Oxford University Press Inc., New York

British Library Cataloguing in Publication Data
Data available

Library of Congress Cataloging in Publication Data
Hebron, Malcolm.
The medieval siege: theme and image in Middle English romance /
Malcolm Hebron.
(Oxford English monographs)
Includes bibliographical references (p.   ) and index.
1. Romances, English—History and criticism. 2. Sieges in
literature. 3. English literature—Middle English, 1100–1500—
History and criticism. 4. Military history, Medieval, in
literature. 5. Civilization, Medieval—14th century. 6. Siege
warfare—History. 7. Allegory. I. Title. II. Series.
PR317.S53H43 1997
820.9'358—dc21   97–2024
ISBN 0–19–818620–7

1 3 5 7 9 10 8 6 4 2

Typeset by Alliance Phototypesetters, Pondicherry
Printed in Great Britain
on acid-free paper by
Bookcraft Ltd.,
Midsomer Norton, Somerset

Acknowledgements

A grant from the British Academy allowed me to complete the research for the doctoral thesis on which this book is based. I am especially grateful to Douglas Gray for his patient supervision, and to my examiners, Maldwyn Mills and Richard Hamer, for their corrections and suggestions for improvement. At Winchester, I have been fortunate in being able to call on Stephen Anderson for help with translations from Latin. Elsewhere, translations are my own unless otherwise indicated. Thorn and yogh have been modernized throughout.

Winchester 1996   M. H.

Contents

Abbreviations

AHS	*Archives Héraldiques Suisses*
AJA	*American Journal of Archaeology*
AM	*Annuale Mediaevale*
ANTS	Anglo-Norman Text Society
Archiv	*Archiv für das Studium der neueren Sprachen und Literaturen*
BEC	*Bibliothèque de l'École des Chartes*
BHR	*Bibliothèque d'Humanisme et Renaissance*
BMQ	*British Museum Quarterly*
BN	Bibliothèque Nationale
BRABLB	*Boletín de la Real Academia de Buenas Letras de Barcelona*
Cahiers	*Cahiers de Civilisation Médiévale*
CCSL	*Corpus Christianorum. Series Latina*
CFMA	Classiques Français du Moyen Age
CHF	Classiques de l'Histoire de France
CHFMA	Les Classiques de l'Histoire de France au Moyen Age
ChRev	*Chaucer Review*
CLS	*Comparative Literature Studies*
CSEL	*Corpus Scriptorum Ecclesiasticorum Latinorum*
E&S	*Essays and Studies*
EETS, OS, ES, SS	Early English Text Society, Ordinary Series, Extra Series, Special Series
EHD	*English Historical Documents*
EHR	*English Historical Review*
ELN	*English Language Notes*
Eng. Stud.	*Englische Studien*
ER	*Estudis Romànics*
EUC	*Estudis Universitaris Catalans*
HZ	*Historische Zeitschrift*
JEGP	*Journal of English and Germanic Philology*
LMA	*Le Moyen Age*
LSE	*Leeds Studies in English*
MÆ	*Medium Ævum*
MFR	*Mississippi Folklore Register*
MGH	Monumenta Germaniae Historica
MLN	*Modern Language Notes*
MLR	*Modern Language Review*
MP	*Modern Philology*
MS	*Mediaeval Studies*

Neu.Mitt.	*Neuphilologische Mitteilungen*
NHQ	*New Hungarian Quarterly*
NMS	*Nottingham Medieval Studies*
N&Q	*Notes and Queries*
PBA	*Proceedings of the British Academy*
PL	*Patrologiae cursus completus,* Series Latina, ed. J.-P. Migne (Paris, 1844-)
PMLA	*Publications of the Modern Language Association of America*
PQ	*Philological Quarterly*
RES	*Review of English Studies*
Rev	*Revue des langues romanes*
RPh	*Romance Philology*
RSSCW	*Research Studies of the State College of Washington*
SATF	Société des Anciens Textes Français
SHF	Société de l'Histoire de France
SN	*Studia Neophilologia*
SP	*Studies in Philology*
SSL	*Studies in Scottish Literature*
STS	Scottish Text Society
TSL	*Tennessee Studies in Literature*
WBEP	*Wiener Beitrage zur englischen Philologie*
ZRP	*Zeitschrift für romanische Philologie*

Introduction

IN the Preface to his translation of Boethius' *Consolation of Philosophy*, the thirteenth-century poet and translator Jean de Meun says he has previously, 'ou rommant de la Rose, puis que Jalousie ot mis en prison Bel Acueil, enseignai la maniere du chastel prendre et de la rose cueillir, et translatay de latin en françois le livre Vegece de chevalerie' ('in the Romance of the Rose, since Jealousy had put Warm Welcome in prison, I showed how to capture the castle and to pluck the rose, and I translated from Latin into French the book of Vegetius on chivalry').[1] The comment refers to the siege of Love in *Le Roman de la rose*, which, while allegorical, employs much realistic imagery: it does indeed show us how a real castle may be won as well as how the rose-bushes of love may be plucked and the beloved possessed. The mention of Vegetius reminds us of another kind of siege description, the military treatise on the methods of defending and attacking a fortress. Jean de Meun was evidently as interested in the purely technical side of siegecraft as he was in the opportunities it provided for symbolism. His knowledge of Vegetius can be detected in the unusually detailed description of battle in the romance.

The types of siege brought to mind by Jean de Meun's phrasing are abundant in medieval literature. Writers of manuals on warfare, often following Vegetius, describe exemplary or hypothetical cases. Chroniclers report on, and dramatize, the siege as the most common kind of military engagement of the time. The authors of the romances re-create the great sieges of the past—Troy and Thebes from ancient history, Jerusalem from the Roman age, and the cities won by Charlemagne and the crusaders. At times, these ancient sieges seem to suggest truths about the movement of history itself, through the cyclical rise and fall of cities and dynasties. Commentators on the scriptures employ extended siege imagery of their own in explicating a variety of passages. Preachers and authors of homilies use the siege as a picture of the soul endangerd by sin, a device also employed frequently in religious poetry and moral dramas. The symbolic properties of sieges are further

---

[1] Jean de Meun, *Li Livres de confort de philosophie*, 168. Full details of texts mentioned are given in the Bibliography.

explored by poets writing allegories and love lyrics, in their descriptions of the travails of the lover, and the beloved beleaguered by his advances.

Sieges thus featured extensively in the medieval imagination, illustrating and in turn affecting attitudes to such subjects as chivalry, history, and spiritual growth. Of course it would be mistaken to claim that this fascination is specific to the Middle Ages. As a particular form of warfare, the siege has a special hold on the imagination. From at least the time of Homer to the present day, writers have been inspired to reshape historical conflicts as literature and to invent imaginary scenarios of their own. Like any form of battle, the siege is associated with individual and communal acts of courage and with other extremes of human behaviour during war. It is a focus for the depiction of the horror and the spectacle of fighting, for the literary exploration of subjects such as chivalry and the military arts, the suffering and resilience of those under attack, and the actions and attitudes of the victorious. Warfare of all kinds also lends itself to the symbolic representation of the battle between good and evil, a theme that runs from medieval allegory to the cosmic struggles of modern science fiction.

As literary themes, the siege and open battle are very similar and will have numerous elements in common. The siege may be distinguished from general battle, however, partly in the sheer range of subjects with which it is associated: as has been suggested, it can illustrate the shape of history, evoke the state of embattled nations and cultures, and express the temptations and tribulations of the soul. The theme of the siege is also distinct from that of pitched battle in the importance of the central element of a definite, enclosed space which is assailed and defended. Again, this element gives rise to a great richness of suggested ideas: the besieged city or castle is used to illustrate national solidarity and personal heroism, and the strength of religious faith in crusading romance; or it may symbolize female beauty and sexuality, enclosing the pure spirit and the heart of the beloved in allegorical writings. Concepts of the identity of nations and the private self are more fully explored in writings on sieges than in descriptions of open battles, and, though the two themes are closely related, it is this complex of associations which separates the siege from open battle as a theme and image in literature.

The appeal of the siege as a subject for writers is thus not difficult to explain: at a realistic level it provides an opportunity for the description of cowardice, guile, technical ingenuity, and heroism. At the same time, a literary account of a siege can serve to dramatize wider conflicts of a historical, cultural, or moral kind. Given the frequency of sieges in Western history, their occurrence in literature and the other arts is unsurprising. Sieges interest modern readers as they did their medieval ancestors. From the defence of the Alamo, to Gordon at Khartoum, to modern Sarajevo, sieges translate easily from actual event into popular legend and myth. Last stands and valiant defences inevitably arouse an interest in human resilience and endurance; the particularly exposed nature of a siege reveals human conduct at various extremes, from cruelty to compassion, mutual endeavour to betrayal, intrepidity to stupidity. Journalists' descriptions of Sarajevo and other towns in Bosnia have much in common with the descriptions of medieval chronicles: the physical conditions of the besieged, the strategies of the besieging army, and individual tragedies and acts of heroism are topics of perpetual interest. Images from illuminated chronicle accounts of sieges are not entirely dissimilar to contemporary photographs, and the medieval chronicler and modern film-maker approach the task of shaping and ordering the narrative of a siege in a comparable manner. While concepts and legislation of warfare have changed, the basic interest in the events and emotions of sieges has hardly altered. Popular literature, journalism, television, and films provide a rich iconography of sieges for the modern reader and viewer. With this easy availability of ideas and images there is perhaps a danger of our becoming inured to the theme and incurious about the ways in which it is represented to us. Sieges remain part of the common language of everyday experience.

Yet it is worth pausing to see what further analysis of the treatment of contemporary sieges might reveal. Journalistic reports of the events in Bosnia or, to take an example of a siege which spawned much 'instant' analytical writing, the FBI siege of David Koresh and his followers at Waco in Texas, include first-hand descriptions of individual tragedies and memorable acts, together with an attempt at more general reflection, with which a medieval chronicler would sympathize. After the shock of the immediacy of articles, photos, and television footage has worn off, their construction and style would surely repay close attention, as examples of the way in which historical event is transformed into literary and dramatic forms. The emphases and details of writings and documentary programmes provide evidence of what aspects of sieges—moral, technological, or human—are of most interest to modern readers. Certainly there is no lack of analysis of the wider significance of such events: in films, in magazine features and newspaper editorials these events are taken as emblematic of the state of Europe or the state of America. The response by European states to the siege of Sarajevo has induced debate in the West which will tell the future historian much of contemporary attitudes to war and governmental responsibility. The siege of Koresh's Branch Davidian sect induced a spate of writing on the increase in fundamentalism and religious belief in the United States and its social and political consequences. Taken together, a study of the way in which real events are depicted, and the types of sieges in various art forms which are invented, would reveal much of the anxieties and interests of the present age in Western Europe to a future historian.

The aim of this book is to conduct a similar exercise with regard to some writings on sieges from the medieval period, and to follow Jeun de Meun in considering the capture both of the real castle and the symbolic rose. Literary treatments of real sieges from history tell us much about prevailing ideas on important themes such as the just war, the ethics as well as the practical expertise expected of a commander, the definition of heroism, and even the perceived logic of history itself. Non-historical sieges appear most frequently in allegorical romances, or in spiritual writings, and are used as models for the trials of the soul or the state of mind of the courtly lover. Examination of various writings on the different kinds of siege, from the historical to the allegorical, can lead us to a better understanding of a range of ideas and preoccupations of the medieval period.

It has been calculated by a military historian that, from the eleventh century, 'warfare consisted of perhaps one per cent battles and ninety-nine per cent sieges'.[2] The number of texts which would be relevant to the present study is consequently very great indeed. Chroniclers often show an interest in sieges which goes beyond the simple recording of facts: Anna Comnena's account of the siege of Antioch in the First Crusade in her *Alexiad*, for example, shows a deep interest in character as well as the politics and machinery of war. Froissart's chronicles contain numerous descriptions of sieges, some of them, such as that of Calais, taking up considerable space: his treatment of siege warfare constitutes an examination of personalities, customs, and the code of chivalry in addition to a pure record of events. Together with those of many other chroniclers, the treatment of sieges by these writers provides valuable material for the historian of literature and ideas as well as for military and political historians.

---

[2] J. Bradbury, *The Medieval Siege* (Woodbridge, 1992), 71. Referred to hereafter as 'Bradbury'.

Besides the chronicles of crusading campaigns and sieges in Western Europe, poetic treatments of the sieges of history are also frequent from an early period. Two works of the Carolingian period exemplify many of the themes which will interest later medieval writers. Abbo's *Bella Parisiciae urbis* (c.887–96), on a Danish attack on Paris in 885–6, combines praise of Paris and its defenders, Count Odo and Bishop Gozlin, with a sporadically detailed record of the events of the siege and the weapons and tactics employed, expressed in epic verse of Virgilian pretensions. Ermoldus Nigellus' description of the capture of Barcelona by Louis in *In honorem Hludowici* (826–8) also embellishes realistic reportage with literary effect and stresses throughout the great qualities of King Louis, to whom the work is dedicated.

Literary topics present in the epic accounts of sieges of the Carolingian period are continued in the epic poems dealing with the early part of the reconquest of cities in Northern Spain in the late eleventh century. Perhaps the most famous of these works is the Spanish *Poem of the Cid*, which contains a lengthy account of the siege of Valencia by the hero, Rodrigo Díaz de Vivar, in 1093–4. Another example is the twelfth-century French epic, *Le Siège de Barbastre*, which describes at great length the recapture of Barbastro in 1063 by the Duke of Aquitaine, in alliance with the Catalans and Aragonese. Here dynastic and political issues figure largely in the treatment of the event. The subjects involved in the epic description of sieges appear also in chronicle treatments: texts such as the *De expugnatione Lyxbonensi* (1148), describing the capture of Lisbon from the Moors in 1147, or an account of the siege and capture of Damietta in the Fifth Crusade, *La Prise de Damiette*, both of probable clerical authorship, share with Carolingian and French epic an emphasis on aristocratic virtues, on divine aid and the bravery of individuals. Another common element in all these works is an interest in a particular town, the most usual type of place to be besieged before the spread of castles in Europe in the twelfth-century. The description of siege warfare and other types of battle fought for the reconquest of a town or city in these poems reveals much about twelfth- and thirteenth-century attitudes not only towards war strategy and heroism but also towards the city as a symbol of wealth and culture and place of habitation and trade as well as a refuge.[3]

[3] For a discussion of this theme in Old French epic, see J. Le Goff, 'Warriors and Conquering Bourgeois: The Image of the City in Twelfth-Century French Literature', in *The Medieval Imagination*, trans. A. Goldhammer (Chicago and London, 1988), 151–76.

The main themes arising from treatments of the conquest or re-capture of cities from the Moors, as well as the literary techniques employed, also appear in crusading epics. The conduct of commanders and nobles, the strategy employed and qualities exhibited, together with assertions of the moral justice of the campaign, are some of the main subjects explored in such works as the epic of the First Crusade, *La Chanson d'Antioche*, and the long verse account of the Third Crusade by Ambroise, *L'Estoire de la Guerre Sainte*. The latter contains a long and detailed description of the siege of Acre by Richard the Lionheart, similar in tone and spirit to Ermoldus' epic homage to Louis. Considerable attention is given to strategy and to close description of the methods used in attack and defence. This is interspersed with moral commentaries on the divine sanction of the crusade and the cowardice of the enemy, together with descriptions of individual incidents generally chosen to reveal the superiority of the besieging crusading army. The devices and emphases of the French epics had an important influence on later chroniclers, such as Villehardouin and Jordan Fantosme, both of whom show a strong awareness of the opportunities for dramatic excitement offered by their subjects.[4]

Literary treatments of sieges in the fourteenth and fifteenth centuries include re-creations of crusading conflicts, such as the Middle English romance *Richard Coeur de Lion* and the various French and English accounts of the victories of Godfrey de Bouillon. The strong and lasting interest in the sieges of the great cities of antiquity, Troy and Thebes, runs from French courtly epics to Lydgate's vast works *The Siege of Thebes* and *The Troy Book*. Great military commanders were admired for their expertise at siegecraft, both in attack and defence: instructive examples were found from ancient history, such as Alexander the Great's siege of Tyre, or from more recent times. Detailed realistic description also appears in accounts of legendary sieges, reflecting a general interest in the conduct of siege warfare: Malory, for example, provides a realistic depiction in the episode of the siege of Benwick near the end of the *Morte Arthure*.[5] Some poets also had direct experience of this form of warfare. Chaucer unfortunately does not record his experience of being

M. Harney, 'Siege Warfare in Medieval Hispanic Epic and Romance', in I. A. Corfis and M. Wolfe (eds.), *The Medieval City under Siege* (Woodbridge, 1995), 177–90.

[4] On Villehardouin, see C. Morris, 'Geoffrey de Villehardouin and the Conquest of Constantinople', *History*, 53 (1968), 24–34, esp. 26. J. M. A. Beer, *Villehardouin: Epic Historian*, Études de philologie et d'histoire, 7 (Geneva, 1968).

[5] On the realism of this episode, see D. Bornstein, 'Military Strategy in Malory and Vegetius' *De re militari*', *CLS* 9 (1972), 123–9.

captured at the siege of Reims, but the poet and notary Jehan Maillart describes the conduct of a siege from the point of view of an administrative official in the *Roman du Comte d'Anjou* (*c.*1316). In addition to material drawn from ancient history, recent event, and legend, symbolic castles and their tribulations were developed from a long tradition of spiritual writing.

This brief account of literature on sieges in the medieval period is far from comprehensive. It does make it clear, though, that the present study will have to be highly selective. Emphasis throughout will be placed on Middle English texts, in particular the romances, which provide sufficient examples of different kinds of sieges to illustrate the themes with which we will be concerned. The popularity of this subject in medieval English literature is noted by John Burrow, who reminds us that the siege was a 'favourite topic for a History' in romances and observes that 'Middle English writers are as fond of allegorical sieges as they are of literal ones'.[6]

Some works in other languages will also be included for purposes of comparison; the siege of Rhodes in 1444 is recorded in two Catalan literary works, which provide a unique and intriguing contrast of approaches to the same siege. While certain chronicles will be referred to in passing, a full analysis of the approach of chroniclers to the description of sieges would need a separate study. Lydgate's depiction of a siege in *The Siege of Thebes* will be considered with reference to its later redaction in Chapter 1, but Lydgate's two long poems on sieges will not be treated as a separate subject here. Another exclusion will be a discussion of the legends of Thebes in medieval literature beyond Chapter 1, where the emphasis is on the description of the siege rather than the development or importance of the legend: as is suggested in Chapter 4 on Troy, many of the important aspects of the tradition of Troy in medieval literature are also relevant to the literature on Thebes, and therefore the subject of the siege of great cities of antiquity will be dealt with through a discussion on Troy alone.

Even given a high degree of selection, a study of sieges in medieval literature could be ordered in several different ways: a chronological study of various writings might reveal the development and persistence of certain ideas, for example, while a close reading of several pieces concentrating on a few specific events may illuminate some aspects of historiography or style. Our study will concentrate on themes shared by

[6] J. A. Burrow, *Medieval Writers and their Work* (Oxford, 1982), 69, 93.

writings on sieges, composed at various times. These range from practical counsel to spiritual reflection, and our study will broadly follow a
path from the realistic to the symbolic, starting with the practical and
local concerns of military advice and moving through treatments of ancient history to the more abstract and universal schemes of the sermon
and allegory.

We shall begin in the real world of medieval warfare. The anonymous redaction of Lydgate's poem on the siege of Thebes, considered
first, gives a memorable and detailed picture of a later medieval siege in
its treatment of a legendary event. The redactor's addition to his source
is instructive as an example of a siege being re-created and reworked by
an author evidently well versed in military terms. His text also serves as
a practical aid in following the writings next examined, which concentrate on the depiction of the siege commander in attack and defence.
The handling by a leader of either assault or resistance provided poets
with an opportunity to show exemplary skills and traits of character in
the context of an exciting story. One of the actions of a commander
may be an appeal to divine aid: miraculous interventions and the image
of an army or populace helped directly by God are common elements
of romance descriptions of sieges, and their occurrence in verse accounts of a real and an imagined battle against Saracens are considered
in Chapter 3.

The second half of this book is concerned with the use of the siege
as a vehicle for more general themes, in romances and in spiritual and
allegorical works. The popular subjects of the sieges of Troy and Jerusalem give rise to wider considerations concerning the nature of history
and revelations of God's will. In patristic commentaries, and in medieval
homilies, poems, and dramas, the siege is used as a model for the soul assailed by temptation. Finally the castle appears in allegory, love poetry,
and pageantry as an image of the heart or body of the beloved or, in a
frequent inversion of the topic, the lover, stormed by his own over-
powering feelings. In these works, the castle under attack, an image of
hostility and conflict, becomes an emblem of love and desire: the castle
is finally transformed into the rose.

The Prose Siege of Thebes, Military Manuals and the Conduct of Sieges in the Later Middle Ages

The Prose Siege of Thebes is a short account of the legendary story of the battle for Thebes by the two brothers Eteocles and Polyneices (the latter assisted by Adrastus, king of Argos). Essentially it is a summary of Lydgate's long poem on the same subject, itself based on various verse and prose treatments. Perhaps because of their secondary, derivative nature, the redactions of long verse works, which form a part of the corpus of late medieval romances, have received relatively little critical attention. This particular work rewards closer inspection and illustrates how individual such writings can be: in the description of the assault on Thebes and its defence, the redactor adds significantly to his source, interpolating many realistic details on the arms and tactics used by both sides. The resulting prose epitome constitutes a careful engagement with Lydgate's text, one which is far more creative and complex than its status as a convenient summary would imply. It has a further value for us as a guide to siege warfare of the medieval period: in this respect, *The Prose Siege of Thebes* is perhaps more useful for our purposes than a chronicle account of a specific siege, since the description includes most of the typical features of both ancient and modern methods, which may seldom have been used together in any single encounter.

The work appears with a companion piece on the siege of Troy and exists in only one manuscript, dated to the middle of the fifteenth century.[1] The two works, in the same Southern dialect and probably by the same author, provide readable synopses of Lydgate's *Siege of Thebes* and *Troy Book*, with the possible addition of material from Latin and French accounts of the two sieges, as well as details apparently drawn from

---

[1] Oxford, Bodleian Library, MS Rawlinson D. 82. *The Prose Siege of Thebes* on fos. 1–11r is followed by *The Prose Siege of Troy* on fos. 11v–25v. See R. M. Lumiansky, 'Legends of Troy', in J. B. Severs and A. E. Hartung (eds.), *A Manual of the Writings in Middle English* (New Haven, 1967–), i. 118–19. G. Guddat-Figge, *Catalogue of Manuscripts Containing Middle English Romances* (Munich, 1976), 96.

Chaucer's *Troilus and Criseyde*.[2] Both texts reflect a continuing interest
in the sieges of the cities of antiquity by English readers, especially perhaps among the aristocracy. They are comparable to the various French
prose accounts of the sieges of Thebes and Troy which were made in
the thirteenth and fourteenth centuries: Lydgate himself used some
French redactions of the *Roman de Thèbes* and other works in compos-
ing his long poem. The pairing of accounts of the fall of these two great
ancient cities also occurs elsewhere. Prose narratives of the two sieges
were often placed together in manuscript books, as, for example, in a
version of the *Histoire ancienne jusqu'à César* which appears in a beautifully illustrated French royal manuscript of the later fifteenth century.[3]

The English prose sieges of Thebes and Troy also reflect a taste for
concise retellings of longer works, and for versions of great sieges of the
past which give a fairly succinct account of the main events with limited
authorial commentary or independent material. *The Prose Siege of
Thebes* and *The Prose Siege of Troy* are similar in style and length to the
roughly contemporary translation by Kaye of the chronicle of the siege
of Rhodes of 1480, and to *The Prose Siege of Jerusalem*, both of which will
be considered later. It is evident from such writings that there was a de-
mand by some fifteenth-century readers for manageable accounts of
the sieges of great cities. The prose form might also have influenced a
reader's attitude to the subject: possibly the briefer prose romances were
viewed as historically more valid than the more long-winded and
elaborate poetic treatments of the subject. This would suggest a particular curiosity about the historical significance of the sieges of antiquity,
as key moments in the shaping of modern nations and dynasties.[4]

[2] On sources, see editions by Griffin, 158–72, and Brie, 40–7. C. R. B. Combellack, 'The
Composite Catalogue of *The Sege of Troye*', *Speculum*, 26 (1951), 624–34. C. D. Benson,
'Chaucer's Influence on the Prose "Sege of Troy"', *N&Q* 216, NS 18 (1971), 127–30.

[3] On the numerous French prose versions, and the relations between them, see:
K. Chesney, 'A Neglected Prose Version of the *Roman de Troie*', *MÆ* 11 (1942), 46–67;
G. Raynaud de Lage, 'Du *Roman de Troie* de Benoit au *Roman de Troie* en prose', in T. G. S.
Combe and P. Rickard (eds.), *The French Language: Studies Presented to Lewis Charles Harmer*
(London, 1970), 175–81; C. C. Williams, 'A Case of Mistaken Identity: Still Another Trojan
Narrative in Old French Prose', *MÆ* 53 (1984), 59–72. The manuscript referred to is Oxford,
Bodleian Library, MS Douce 353. On Lydgate's sources, see Lydgate, *Siege of Thebes*, ii. 6–10.

[4] For bibliography of French prose redactions, see B. Woledge and H. P. Clive, *Répertoire
des plus anciens textes en prose française* (Geneva, 1964), 27. For discussion of the form of the
redaction see Raynaud de Lage, 'Du Roman de Troie'. The issue of the relative veracity of
verse and prose is considered by G. Doutrepont, *Les Mises en prose des epopées et des romans
chevaleresques du xive au xvie siècle* (Brussels, 1939). See also R. Guiette, 'Chanson de geste,
chronique et mise en prose', *Cahiers*, 6 (1963), 423–40. English prose romances are discussed
by D. Pearsall, 'The English Romance in the Fifteenth Century', *E&S*, NS 29 (1976), 56–83.

The author of *The Prose Siege of Thebes* makes the most of his opportunity to describe siege warfare as fought by famous warriors of the past. The style of both this work and *The Prose Siege of Troy*, normally held to be of common authorship, has been variously praised for telling the story 'in simple, almost naive, language, and in a brisk, lively fashion' and as being 'reminiscent of Caxton's developed style in his later translations'.[5] In the description of the siege itself, however, the author departs from his usual more straightforward reporting method, in which a summary of events is supplemented with the occasional moral comment, and changes to a fuller, denser style, which contains a great deal of detail on the preparation for the siege and the battle for the city itself. In this, he departs extensively from the description in Lydgate, who makes little mention of the various arms and tactics of the assault. The illustrations of the manuscript mentioned earlier depict a besieging army with the arms and armour of the fifteenth century; the approach of our author is similar to this, but not identical. In common with other romance writers, he modernizes the warfare, giving it a contemporary setting, while incorporating some more old-fashioned elements perhaps expressing a nostalgia for the chivalry of the classical past.[6] Both the technical detail of sieges and some sense of an ideal military ethos of the past may be found in contemporary manuals on warfare. These writings may have played an important part in the composition of this text, as they certainly did in other fictional works. Before examining the description of the siege, therefore, it will be useful to consider some examples of the kinds of military treatise to which an English author of the middle of the fifteenth century could have had access.[7]

MILITARY TREATISES ON SIEGECRAFT

Technical manuals on siegecraft go back at least as far as that made by Aeneas the Tactician in the fourth century BC. In the first century AD, Hero of Alexandria writes on the subject, and Frontinus, copied and

[5] By, respectively, Griffin, 157; Pearsall, 'English Romance', 73.

[6] Oxford, Bodleian Library, MS Douce 353, fo. 1 shows Troy besieged by soldiers in plate armour using cannon: both features of later medieval warfare. See R. B. Ackerman, 'Armor and Weapons in the Middle English Romances', *RSSCW* 7/2 (June 1939), 104–18.

[7] For a fuller discussion of military books, see P. Contamine, *War in the Middle Ages*, trans. M. Jones (Oxford, 1984), 208–18. On their use in England, M. J. Cockle, *A Bibliography of English Military Books up to 1642*, ed. H. D. Cockle (London, 1900); D. Bornstein, 'Military Manuals in Fifteenth-Century England', *MS* 37 (1975), 469–77. A bibliography of siege manuals is also provided in J.-F. Finó, *Forteresses de la France médiévale* (Paris, 1967), 489–529.

translated in the Middle Ages, devotes the third of his four-volume *Stratagems* on the art of war to sieges.[8] The precepts of these works are repeated in translation in Antoine de la Sale's *La Salade* and Christine de Pisan's *Livre des fais d'armes et de chevalerie* (*c.*1410, translated into English by Caxton in 1489). Technical aspects of siegecraft, and defence against siege, are also considered in the first century AD by the Roman architect and military engineer Vitruvius, in his *De architectura*.[9]

Easily the most influential of the classical works dealing with sieges in the Middle Ages, however, was the treatise by Flavius Renatus Vegetius, *De re militari*, written in the late fourth or early fifth century AD. This appears to have been somewhat anachronistic in its picture of warfare even for the time in which it was written. Nevertheless, it was read avidly throughout the Middle Ages and there is evidence that several military commanders, Richard I among them, turned to Vegetius for practical advice.[10] This is not altogether surprising, since the conduct of sieges remained basically the same throughout the Middle Ages, and several Roman methods remained effective in medieval campaigns. One military historian has written that 'there is on the whole a greater continuity in the history of siegecraft and siege-machines through the whole Middle Ages down to the invention of gunpowder, than in the history of any other province of the military art'.[11]

At the same time as giving instructions on the best way both to mount a siege and to withstand one, Vegetius also presents a picture of Roman discipline and courage in warfare which became a pattern for later medieval conceptions of chivalry. Medieval literary treatments of siege warfare, such as *The Prose Siege of Thebes*, evoke a golden age of knightly conduct and strategic sophistication held up as models for contemporary military leaders. The popularity of Vegetius' treatise is illustrated by the wide dissemination of manuscript copies all over Europe and the large number of translations of the work into vernacular languages, some of which incorporate references to later battles and

---

[8] See R. Bossuat, 'Jean de Rouvroy, traducteur des *Stratagèmes* de Frontin', *BHR* 22 (1960), 273–86, 469–89.

[9] See Bibliography for details of editions.

[10] See W. Goffart, 'The Date and Purpose of Vegetius' *De re militari*', *Traditio*, 33 (1977), 65–100; Contamine, *War in the Middle Ages*, 211–12, on its diffusion and influence. On Richard I's use of Vegetius, see J. Gillingham, 'Richard I and the Science of War in the Middle Ages', in J. Gillingham and J. C. Holt (eds.), *War and Government in the Middle Ages: Essays in Honour of J. O. Prestwich* (London, 1984), 78–91. Reprinted in J. Gillingham, *Richard Coeur de Lion: Kingship, Chivalry and War in the Twelfth Century* (London, 1994), 211–26.

[11] C. Oman, *A History of the Art of War: The Middle Ages from the Fourth to the Fourteenth Century* (London, 1898), 131; ch. 6 on sieges, pp. 131–48.

developments.[12] At least five French translations were made in the thirteenth and fourteenth centuries.[13] The first English translation was made for Thomas, Lord Berkeley, in 1408. Other renderings include a verse treatment of *c.*1458 which was presented to Henry VI, and a Scottish redaction of some passages made towards the end of the fifteenth century.[14]

At the same time as the *De re militari* was copied and translated, portions of it were incorporated into other works on ecclesiastical and political topics. The variety of such texts suggests a widespread interest in the military disciplines by writers in many different subjects. Extracts from his work may be found in the section on military training (Book Six) in John of Salisbury's *Policraticus* (*c.*1159), and in Egidio Colonna's *De regimine principium* (*c.*1285). Christine de Pisan shows a familiarity with Vegetius in her *Livre du corps de policie* (*c.*1404) before translating and expanding his fourth book, on siege warfare, in the *Livre des fais d'armes et de chevalerie* (*c.*1410). Parts of this work appear in turn in William of Worcester's *Boke of Noblesse* (*c.*1450, revised 1475) and in the chapter on the art of siegecraft in Jean de Bueil's *Le Jouvencel* (1462–7).[15]

Jean de Bueil was not the only soldier of the later Middle Ages to write on modern developments in siegecraft. The invention of new weapons, particularly the cannon, and the development of existing ones, gave rise to numerous technical treatises.[16] In the fifteenth

[12] See C. R. Schrader, 'A Handlist of Extant Manuscripts containing the *De re militari* of Flavius Vegetius Renatus', *Scriptorium*, 33 (1979), 280–303.

[13] See L. Thorpe, 'Mastre Richard, a Thirteenth-Century Translator of the *De re militari* of Vegetius', *Scriptorium*, 6 (1952), 39–50. M. D. Legge, 'The Lord Edward's Vegetius', *Scriptorium*, 7 (1953), 262–5. See Bibliography under Jean de Meun and Jean Priorat. P. Meyer, 'Les Anciens Traducteurs français de Végèce et en particulier Jean de Vignai', *Romania*, 25 (1896), 401–23. C. Knowles, 'A 14th Century Imitator of Jean de Meung: Jean de Vignay's Translation of the *De re militari* of Vegetius', *SP* 53 (1956), 452–8. J. Camus, 'Notice d'une traduction française de Végèce faite en 1380', *Romania*, 25 (1896), 393–400. Jeun de Meun's method of translation from Vegetius is analysed by R. G. B. Mongeau, 'Thirteenth-Century Siege Weapons and Machines in *L'Art de chevalerie*', *Allegorica*, 7/2 (1982), 123–43.

[14] On English translations, see H. N. MacCracken, 'Vegetius in English: Notes on the Early Translations', in E. S. Sheldon *et al.* (eds.), *Anniversary Papers by Colleagues and Pupils of George Lyman Kittredge*, (Boston and London, 1913), 389–403. D. Bornstein, 'The Scottish Prose Version of Vegetius' *De re militari*', *SSL* 8 (1971), 174–83.

[15] See M. Springer, 'Vegetius im Mittelalter', *Philologus*, 123 (1979), 85–90. J. Wisman, 'L'*Epitoma rei militaris* de Végèce et sa fortune au Moyen Age', *LMA* 85 (1979), 13–29. Jean de Bueil, *Le Jouvencel*: Part II, chs. 16 and 17 on the art of war. On de Bueil's use of Christine de Pisan in the treatment of siege tactics, see G. W. Coopland, 'Le Jouvencel (Revisited)', *Symposium*, 5 (1951), 137–86.

[16] e.g. the *Art de l'artillerie et cannonerye* (Paris, BN, MSS frs. 2015 and 1244; MS lat. 4653, fos. 125–70) and *L'Art d'archerie: Publié avec notes d'après un manuscrit du xve siècle*, ed. H. Galice (Paris, 1901).

century, new manuals were written in response to major changes in siegecraft and fortifications, with less reliance on classical examples and more on actual experience. Treatises on warfare were written by those whose qualification to instruct was based on practical experience of campaigns rather than a reverence for antiquity. An example is the work known as *La Nef des princes* by Robert de Balsac, written between 1495 and 1499 and printed in Lyons in 1502. As Seneschal of Agenais, Balsac gained much practical experience of siege warfare in the Armagnac and Breton campaigns under Louis XI and in the Italian wars under Charles VIII. Detailed instructions on the most effective way to mount a siege based on these experiences are given in his treatise, which has been praised as 'the outstanding example of a work dealing with war in a soberly realistic spirit'.[17] This work was adapted later by Bérault or Béraud Stuart, Seigneur d'Aubigny (*c.*1447–1508), a Scottish nobleman in the service of the king of France. Stuart adds details of his own experience in the Italian wars while also embellishing and illustrating his points with classical allusions.[18]

Several other books of military instruction survive from the later medieval period, and the genre of the military treatise flourishes and develops in later centuries. It is not difficult to imagine a fifteenth-century author, commissioned to produce a version of the sieges of Thebes and Troy, turning to a copy of Vegetius, perhaps in translation, or to the records of a soldier of the time such as de Balsac, in order to enliven his narrative. Poets such as Lydgate and Hoccleve refer to Vegetius, and Malory's apparent familiarity with him in the episode of the siege at Benwick has already been mentioned.[19]

The popularity of Vegetius' work, and the growing number of military manuals based on direct experience of battles and sieges in modern Europe in the fifteenth-century, illustrate several important themes which should be borne in mind when reading *The Prose Siege of Thebes*.

[17] J. R. Hale, 'International Relations in the West: Diplomacy and War', ch. 9 of *The New Cambridge Modern History*, i, *The Renaissance 1493–1520*, ed. G. R. Potter (Cambridge, 1971), 259–91 (276).

[18] On Robert de Balsac, see P. Tamizey de Larroque (ed.), 'Notice sur Robert de Balsac: Le Chemin de l'ospital et ceulx qui en sont possesseurs', *Rev*, 3rd ser. 16 (1886), 276–300. See P. Contamine, 'The War Literature of the Late Middle Ages: The Treatises of Robert de Balsac and Béraud Stuart, Lord of Aubigny', in C. T. Allmand (ed.), *War, Literature and Politics in the Late Middle Ages* (Liverpool, 1976), 102–21. On Bérault or Béraud Stuart, see D. Gray, 'A Scottish "Flower of Chivalry" and his Book', *Words: Wai-te-ata Studies in English*, 4 (1973), 22–34.

[19] D. Bornstein, 'Military Strategy in Malory and Vegetius' *De re militari*', *CLS* 9 (1972), 123–9.

Technical information on both ancient and modern siegecraft was relatively easy to find: copies of Vegetius and other military books existed in the libraries of noblemen, who would be among the readers most likely to welcome an account of the sieges of antiquity of a comfortable length. The sieges of the classical past had a special interest as examples of the chivalric conduct and wisdom of the ancients. This is suggested by the continuing popularity of Vegetius even after the development of modern siege technology rendered his counsel old-fashioned. There was nothing unusual in presenting ancient warfare in modern dress; numerous versions of Vegetius had done just that, and, in any case, the essential elements of siege warfare did not change a great deal during most of the Middle Ages. In reading the description of the siege in *The Prose Siege of Thebes*, parallels and elucidation of details can be found in these manuals as well as in accounts of actual battles. In particular we shall refer to two of the manuals already mentioned: the 1408 translation of Vegetius, and *La Nef des princes*.[20] Although the latter was composed and printed after the English romance, the type of siege which it discusses is typical of the conduct of several sieges in Europe in the fifteenth century, of which Lydgate or his redactor may have had some knowledge. Thus the siege described may be read as a guide to the theory and practice of siegecraft of the later Middle Ages, and to the themes explored in romances and other writings on the subject.

THE SIEGE OF THEBES

The account of the siege in our text begins with a description of the army assembled and governed by Adrastus, king of Argos, about to march towards Thebes to capture the city from Ethiocles (to adopt the spelling of the author), on behalf of his brother Pollymet. The background to the siege, describing the causes, family quarrels, and political alliances leading to the conflict, while remaining generally faithful to the legend, is similar to the political machinations described by Froissart and other chroniclers. It reminds us that successful sieges depended as much on proven allies and secure deals as on technical and strategic superiority in battle. The author then describes the army, composed of 'the chivalry of Grece', gathered before Argos before setting out:

[20] References to 'Vegetius' are to Lester's edition of the 1408 English translation. References to de Balsac are to the 1502 print.

For as my Auctor seith, sith the world first bigon into that day, was never seyn
so faire a felde of peple And labour ynogh for many a herode for to distreve and
blase the Cates and baners of lordes, the brightnesse of which shone vp to
heven. This worthi king Adrastus ordeynyng ful worthely for the said peple and
principally for hem that come thider at theire owne cost and charge, And
gouerned him in suche wise that euery man of the said retenue, held him wel
content and plesed. (fo. 6b, p. 269)

The 'Auctor' alluded to is not Lydgate but 'Boas' or Boccaccio, although
the redactor does not appear to have direct knowledge of Boccaccio's
epic on Thebes. The redaction elaborates on Lydgate's fairly plain description of the gathered army, expanding in particular the theme of the
good general and adding realistic touches such as the heralds attempting to list everyone present.[21] Such alterations may have been influenced by wider reading. The description of a splendidly equipped army
beneath a city, for example, is a common feature of many medieval descriptions of sieges: Ambroise vividly describes the terrifying effect on
the enemy the crusading army has as it gathers near Acre, causing
Saladin and his relief force in the mountains to flee.[22] Jordan Fantosme
includes the topic in his description of the English army at the siege of
Carlisle:

> Or vëez, francs chevaliers, mult gentil appareil;
> Ne savez acunter le blanc ne le vermeil,
> Tant i ad gunfanuns cuntrement le soleil.

(Now behold, noble knights, a very splendid array; so many are the banners
gleaming in the sunshine that you cannot count the white and the red).[23]

Heralds, who are mentioned here trying to list all the many devices of
the Greek nobles, were given military responsibilities at sieges in the medieval period, which gradually declined as they took charge of funeral
ceremonies and chivalric displays.[24] In the next chapter we shall see the
heraldic banners and emblems on shields being carefully described by
the herald-author of *The Siege of Caerlaverok*; heralds also appear in one
of the accounts of Henry V's siege of Rouen in the English *Brut*, where
their function is again to list at least the nobles among those present.[25]

---

[21] *Lydgate's Siege of Thebes*, part iii, ll. 3544–60.
[22] Ambroise, *L'Estoire de la Guerre Sainte*, ll. 3973–8.
[23] J. Fantosme, *Jordan Fantosme's Chronicle*, ll. 1356–8.
[24] See P. Adam-Even, 'Les Fonctions militaires des hérauts d'armes', *AHS* 71 (1957), 2–33.
[25] *The Brut or the Chronicles of England*, ii. 395. A short prose account of the siege appears
on pp. 387–91. This is followed by a longer account, pp. 392–404, and John Page's poem
celebrating Henry V's victory, pp. 404–22.

Coloured emblems became a feature of armies in the later Middle Ages. Soldiers in crusading armies usually wore crosses, the colours denoting their country of origin. In Europe, armorial banners, shields, and coats of arms appeared from the middle of the twelfth century and were in general use from the middle of the thirteenth century.[26] The visual effect of a besieging army was clearly of great importance to the psychological dimension of siege warfare, and even when, as here, the army is not yet visible to the besieged, poets and chroniclers take care to tell us what a magnificent and daunting sight it was.

This passage also gives us a glimpse into the practical considerations surrounding the raising and payment of an army which may be needed for a long siege campaign. The exemplary Greek knights are praised for paying their own passage, which would allow the king to devote more resources to the provisions and payment of the foot-soldiers. This was not always the case: the chronicle of James I of Aragon, which gives a useful insight into the administrative challenges facing the commander of a besieging army since it is the king's own record of his victories, records numerous difficulties of payment during sieges. At one point his adviser Bernard Guillem is castigated for employing knights instead of buying provisions.[27] In 1418 Charles VI of France was forced by the costs of artillery and other expenses to abandon the siege of Senlis, 'si lui coûta tant en canons qu'en autre artillerie, avec autre dépense plus de deux cent mille francs', much to the chagrin of his men-at-arms, who were looking forward to the spoils of pillage.[28] Possibly the author of *The Prose Siege of Thebes* is indicating with this detail that the knights undertaking this siege conformed to the ideal picture as portrayed in a treatise on chivalry such as Geoffroy de Charny's *Livre de chevalerie* rather than the mercenaries who were increasingly visible in the sieges and battlefields of the fourteenth and fifteenth centuries.[29] Their loyalty is primarily to their commander, King Adrastus, rather than to a state. The army described is held together largely through personal loyalty to its leader (or employer) rather than by patriotic fervour or a belief in the ostensible cause and purpose of battle, a matter of which most of the combatants seem touchingly ignorant. The reference to money in the

---

[26] Contamine, *War in the Middle Ages* (1990 edn.), 190.

[27] Jaume I, *Crònica o llibre dels feits*. See Bradbury, 207–13.

[28] *Journal d'un bourgeois de Paris*, 106.

[29] For discussion of de Charny, see M. Keen, *Chivalry* (New Haven, 1984), 11–15. See also id., 'Chivalry, Nobility, and the Man-at-Arms', in Allmand (ed.), *War, Literature and Politics in the Late Middle Ages*, 32–45.

passage is a reminder of how important it was for a medieval commander to finance a siege or expedition properly. One of the first pieces
of advice which Robert de Balsac gives to the leader of a besieging
army is to see 'sil a assez argent pour fournir a ses gensdarmes & ce quil
fault au siege & pour le temps quil sera besoing & les bien payer' (58v)
('if he has enough money to provide for his men-at-arms and to pay
them well and what is required for the siege for as long as necessary').

King Adrastus is praised for the governance and ordinance of his
army, a topic to which the redactor draws our attention. This, too,
reflects contemporary reality. As armies increased in size and sieges increased in length and complexity, the establishment of discipline became especially important. A short Anglo-Norman life of Richard I
contains an account of the penalties for misconduct by soldiers.[30] Most
successful commanders of sieges were also extremely severe in dealing
with their own armies: at Caen, Edward III threatened arsonists, mur-
derers, and rapists with hanging. Henry V at Harfleur forbade arson,
rape, and pillage and buried deserters alive. Charles VII, preparing to recapture Harfleur, went even further and banned swearing, though with
what success is not recorded.[31] Robert de Balsac offers the following
advice:

Item mettre toute larmee a butin & deffendre le pillaige. E faire crier par toutes
les batailles que chascun ayt a tenir lordre que son chief de guerre luy ordon-
nera sur peine de estre pendu par la gorge. (57r)

Divide the spoils among all the army and forbid pillage. And have it announced
to all the orders of battle that each man must keep the place assigned to him by
his commander on pain of being hanged by the throat.

The description of the army assembled by Adrastus for the siege
shows us, then, a commander acting as any military leader contemplat-
ing a siege in the fifteenth century would have done: ensuring he has a
competent body of knights, checking his finances are in order and
establishing the discipline in his army which will be necessary for a successful blockade or assault. Adrastus is, in fact, following closely the
counsel with which de Balsac finishes his treatise:

Mais en somme le fait de la guerre gist principallement davoir assez argent pour
fournir a ce que len veult faire & a entrepris: aussi de tenir bon ordre & soy
gouverner pour loppinion & conseil des gens saiges & experimentez. & aussi

---

[30]　*The Crusade and Death of Richard I*, ch. 20.
[31]　Examples given by Bradbury, 306–7.

que la guerre se fait a leure & selon que gens saiges & experimentees cognoissent tant de leurs gens & force comme de leurs ennemys. (62r)

But in short the work of war consists principally in having enough money to provide for what one wants to do and has undertaken. Also in keeping good order and in letting oneself be governed by the opinion and advice of those who are wise and experienced. And war is waged at the right time and according to whether wise and experienced people know their own men and power as much as that of their enemy.

The Prose Siege of Thebes now turns from a description of the besieging army to one of the defending commander, Ethiocles in Thebes, preparing for the oncoming assault:

Ethiocles having knowlacche of this mighty purpose taken a yenst him; In al soden hast stuffed his Cite with vitaile and peple, waged fro many a contrey, purposingg fully to resist and withstond al theire malice. Repairing strongely his Cite in casting of diches, Enforcyng his wallis, contremunyng his depe diches, machecollyng his hie toures, Enbrayng his wacches abought the Cite, fortefying his bruges and barreris with many a mighty cheyne, purveying ful wisely his ordenaunce for his defence with bowes and balesteres, springaltes and tegrettes. And many a mighty bowe of brake and wyndeles, and many other cast of stone and of fire, sparing for no cost. Assignyng euery man fore the werre to his warde, where vppon, theire lyves most be plegge. (fos. 6v–7, p. 269)

Only the last sentence bears much resemblance to the equivalent passage in Lydgate; in the source text, Ethiocles appoints guards and tells those in the main tower to blow trumpets and clarions (Lydgate, iii. 3565–80). The redactor omits the last detail and adds the list of preparations for a siege given here. It is clear that he would have had little difficulty in passing an examination on the principles of siegecraft as expounded by writers of manuals following Vegetius. Ethiocles is seen following many of the instructions which the Roman author gives. Some details of the passage, however, belong to the conduct of sieges in the fourteenth and fifteenth centuries rather than to the Roman period. The description of a defending commander repays close analysis for what it tells us about both the theory and practice of this aspect of warfare in the later Middle Ages.

First we are told that Ethiocles has information about the approach of the army, perhaps an allusion to the system of spies and scouts on which military leaders relied. Spies are recommended by de Balsac and make an appearance in several of the sieges discussed in later chapters, such as the figure of the spy Master George who appears in the 1480

siege of Rhodes. Vegetius' advice to a commander in Ethiocles' position
is to 'drawe in to the alle the vitayles for man & for hors that is in the
contray about thi strengthe, that thou mowe haue plente withynne the
and thyn aduersarie scarste when he cometh. ffor there nys no thing that
may so sone lette the leggynge of a sege as skarste of vitailes' (IV. 7,
p. 163). Christine de Pisan elaborates on this with a long list of the essential food a besieged army should have. *La Nef des princes* also stresses the
need for a besieged place to be well provided for (59r). Ethiocles duly
gathers provisions from 'many a contrey', both stocking up the city and
rendering the outlying territories barren to the besieging army: this is
the reverse of the account given by Lydgate, who describes the besieging Greek army plundering Theban land and killing the livestock
(3587–600). The redactor appears to have a particular idea of what a
siege involves, which allows him to alter or correct and elaborate on his
source text. His idea of a siege may have been drawn from real experience: the bringing in to the city of 'peple' from outlying areas gives
a vivid image of a commander or governor calling on the services of
local allies, and at the same time sheltering the neighbouring population.

Ethiocles next turns his attention to preparing the defences of the
city. As Vegetius advises, he digs ditches of sufficient depth to hinder
miners from burrowing under the walls and firing them, hence the
reference to 'contremunyng'. Vegetius counsels:

How thou schalt make thi diches. Brode diches also & depe nede to ben imade
aboute walles of citees & castelles so brode that thilke that besege hem ne mowe
noght lightliche fille the diches; and also loke thei ben idikked so depe [that]
thei mowe holde good depnesse of water other of welle springes of here owne
or of ryuer rennynge into hem, for suche watery diches ben grete letters to
mynoures. (IV. 5, p. 162)

Robert de Balsac gives very similar advice to this in his *Nef des princes*,
in the chapter on defending a place against siege: he too suggests the
fortifying of ditches and countermining measures, and the reinforce-
ment of walls (60r).

Despite the several references to the 'Cite' of Thebes, the impression
we have when reading is rather of a castle: apart from the reference to
the many women of the city grieving for their dead at the end, there is
little indication of its size or of its function as anything other than a
military garrison. This is a reflection of one significant change in siege
warfare in the medieval period: in the early Middle Ages it was cities

and towns which were usually besieged, while from the thirteenth century castles were the most usual objects of attack. There were, of course,
many exceptions to this, such as the sieges of the great walled cities of
the Latin kingdom in the East, of Constantinople in 1453, of Rhodes in
1480 and 1522, or of Malta in 1565. Nevertheless, in Western Europe in
the later Middle Ages, sieges were usually of castles, and this had an important effect on literary descriptions, which often, as here, depict a city
or town as a fortress.

The description of the defences of Thebes consequently conforms
to later medieval castle architecture: high towers were a feature of
castle-building after 1250, built to hinder attempts at scaling. Ethiocles
adds to them machicolation, defined as 'a gallery or parapet projecting
on brackets and built on the outside of castle towers and walls, with
openings in the floor through which to drop molten lead, boiling oil,
and missiles'.[32] He also reinforces his walls, either by raising the curtain
or, as Vegetius suggests, by building double walls and reinforcing stone
walls with an earthen rampart behind (IV. 3). It was common practice in
medieval siege warfare to strengthen the bases of walls and add stone
paving to the scarps of ditches to counter mining. Ethiocles also reinforces his drawbridge and barbicans ('bruges and barreris'). All these
architectural features are present in, for example, the great castles built
in Wales for Edward I by the master architect James of St George at the
end of the thirteenth century, Conwy, Beaumaris and Caernarfon,
which incorporated all the most modern defences against siege.[33]

Various weapons are mentioned in the passage.[34] The first, 'bowes',
might refer either to the older type of bow, which retained its usefulness
in sieges throughout the Middle Ages, or to the crossbow, recorded as
being in use at a siege as early as the tenth century and in constant em-
ployment thereafter. Despite the invention of the primitive form of
handgun known as the culverin, and later the hacquebut, in the fifteenth century, the crossbow was still the most frequently used weapon
in sieges by the French army until the late sixteenth century when it was
finally superseded by the matchlock musket or 'arquebus'.[35]

[32] *The Penguin Dictionary of Architecture*, ed. J. Fleming *et al.* (Harmondsworth, 1966), 204.

[33] See A. Taylor, *The Welsh Castles of Edward I* (London, 1986).

[34] This discussion makes general use of Bradbury, ch. 9, 'Medieval Siege Weapons',
241–95. This work also contains a detailed bibliography of specialist studies of medieval siege
artillery. A useful shorter account is given in T. Newark, *Medieval Warfare* (London, 1979),
ch. 7, 'Sieges and Siege Machines', 99–112.

[35] M. Vale, *War and Chivalry: Warfare and Aristocratic Culture in England, France and Burgundy
at the End of the Middle Ages* (London, 1981), ch. 4, 'The Techniques of War', 100–46 (134–5).

The 'balester', or 'balista' to use the Latin term, was a larger version of the crossbow, used to shoot bolts or javelins against people. It employed 'a heavy framework to support the javelin; behind this a flexible strip of timber was hauled back by a windlass and then released, to fly back and strike the javelin to drive it forward'.[36] Balistas were operated either in this way, by drawing back a string on the same principle as a bow, sometimes using a winch, or by torsion, using twisted ropes to act as a spring. They are recorded in sieges in Hellenic and Roman conflicts and throughout the Middle Ages.

The 'springald' or 'espringale' was one of many terms, used with great inconsistency by medieval chroniclers, for various kinds of throwing machines. Here it probably refers to a smaller version of the mangonel, which has been defined thus: 'a long wooden arm with a spoon-shaped end, mounted in a heavy framework. The foot of the arm was lashed to a cross-beam, the lashing giving the required degree of spring to the arm's action; it was also supplemented in many cases by a cross-bar of flexible timber attached to the arm by ropes in the manner of a bow. The arm was then hauled back by the usual windlass, a stone placed on the spoon, and the arm released so as to fly forward flinging the stone a considerable distance into the air.'[37] The mangonel was a stone-throwing weapon used against walls, though it could also be used as a defensive weapon. Vegetius includes a springald in his list of weapons of defence against assault (IV. 29, p. 177).

The 'tegrette' probably refers to the 'target' or protective covering of an engine. It is conceivable that it is a corrupt form of the most important late medieval addition to siege artillery, the trebuchet. In the passage it follows a reference to another stone-throwing weapon and precedes another to a 'bowe of brake and windlass', which seems to be a vague description of numerous kinds of throwing engine which required a brake to stop the throwing arm in its course and a windlass to winch it back down again after firing. Other words for the trebuchet in medieval texts include 'trebus', 'triboke', 'trabuchetum', and 'trabocco', giving our speculation some substance.[38] The trebuchet was a missile-throwing engine based on a counterweight system: a heavy weight on the short end of a throwing arm laid across a cross-beam was brought down

---

[36] I. Hogg, 'Siege Techniques' and 'Siege and Siegecraft Fortifications', chs. 4 and 7 of H. W. Koch (ed.), *Medieval Warfare*, (London, 1978), 45–55, 77–85 (55).   [37] Ibid. 52.

[38] On the trebuchet see D. J. Cathcart-King, 'The Trebuchet and other Siege-Engines', *Chateau Gaillard Études de Castellologie médiévale*, 9–10, *Actes de Colloques internationaux tenus à Basel (1978) et à Durham (1980)* (Caen, 1982), 457–70.

suddenly to release the long arm, which flung a stone from a sling attached to its end a considerable distance to effect great damage on walls.
It was not known in ancient siegecraft in its counterweight form,
though an earlier traction model was of great antiquity. There is some
dispute as to its origins and the date of its appearance in the West,
though it is probable that it was of French provenance and that the name
is derived from the French verb 'trébucher', meaning 'to rock or tilt', a
good description of its action.[39] Whatever the details of its evolution,
the trebuchet was certainly in use in sieges in the West from the middle
of the thirteenth century, and its efficiency induced new developments
in the strengthening of castle walls. It continued to be in use after the
arrival of the cannon: at the siege of Orléans in 1420 it was still thought
to be the most effective piece of artillery for breaching walls, and as late
as 1480 it was used by the defenders of Rhodes, who found it extremely
effective against the guns of the Turks even though there was only one
mariner who knew how to build and operate one.[40]

Fire as well as stone is mentioned as a missile in this passage. Numerous incendiary devices were employed in medieval siege warfare, but
this is probably a reference to wild fire, also known as Greek fire. This
was an inflammatory substance which could be hurled from land or
from ships and which exploded on impact. It was first developed by the
Byzantines and was soon adopted in Western sieges: Geoffrey V of
Anjou used it to deal with a rebellious baron at the siege of Montreuil-
Bellay in 1151.[41] There are several descriptions of the use of Greek or
wild fire in *Richard Coeur de Lion*. Other fire weapons were developed
in the West, though Greek fire was more frequently, and perhaps more
expertly, used by the Greeks and the Turks.

The defences prepared by Ethiocles remind us that in a medieval
siege 'the overriding thought in castle strategy was not passive defence
but action and destruction'.[42] Thebes prepares for a battle in which
both sides will seek to destroy each other: the soldiers stationed around
the city are required by Ethiocles to pledge their lives to the defence of
Thebes. Ethiocles' conduct as a commander would win the approval of
de Balsac, who writes at some length on the subject of the duties of the
leader:

[39] Ibid. 461.
[40] E. Brockman, *The Two Sieges of Rhodes, 1480–1522* (London, 1969), 83.
[41] Bradbury, 85–6. See also id., 'Greek Fire in the West', *History Today*, 29 (1979), 326–31,
344.
[42] P. Warner, *Sieges of the Middle Ages* (London, 1968), 2.

Item que ledit prince ou chief parle en general aux gens de toutes ses batailles leur disant & demoustrant quilz le veillent bien servir a ce iour la & que ce sera service qui aura perpetuelle memoire de tous ceulx qui serviront bien & quilz luy veillent a ce iour garder son honneur & le leur de la nacion de la ou ilz sont & quil veult vivre & mourir avec eulx. (57r)

The prince or commander should speak publicly to men of all the orders of battle telling them and explaining to them that they should take care to serve him well on that day and that their service will have the perpetual memory of all those who shall serve well and that they should be careful on that day to guard their honour and that of the nation they come from and that he wishes to live and die with them.

The author of *The Prose Siege of Thebes*, closely following Lydgate, next goes on to describe Adrastus' search for Amphiorax, the prophet, as his counsellor. Amphiorax foresees his own fate in being swallowed up by the earth and hides, but he is revealed to Adrastus and his allies by his wife. He prophesies the extinction of Greek royal blood if the siege is pursued but is disbelieved. This may seem remote from the conduct of siege warfare in the Middle Ages, but it does serve as a reminder of the great importance placed by commanders of besieging armies on ex-perienced and knowledgeable advisers. A slightly unusual example of informed advice given to a besieging commander was that given by the monks of Marmoutier to Geoffrey, Count of Anjou, when he was besieging a castle in the Loire valley; apparently after consulting a modernized version of Vegetius, the monks told the Count how to make and use a small bomb.[43] It was common practice for defending and attacking leaders in a siege to consult with experts before battle: de Balsac advises a commander to take with him 'gens qui cognoissent le place' to be attacked and to have weak points in its defences detected by 'deux ou troyes hommes de bien cognoissans la guerre' (58v). In his capacity as adviser, Amphiorax the prophet has his real-life equivalents in the veteran counsellors at campaigns of the later Middle Ages.

Having secured the services of Amphiorax, Adrastus moves his army towards Thebes. We might imagine any besieging force of the four-teenth or fifteenth century being transported through friendly territory en route, with the king and the royal household suitably lodged, re-quisitioning the horses, timber, and provisions they will need to see them through a long siege:

---

[43] Contamine, *War in the Middle Ages*, 211.

So holding forth theire iournay, spreding al the contrey abought with bright baners and harneys, that hit was mervelouse to se, making theyre wey by the worthy king Ligurgius the which receyued Adrastus and al his ooste ful worthely, In whos lond, Adrastus and al his houge ooste were wel refresshed holding forth that iournay til they come bifore that worthi Cite of Thebes. (fo. 7v, p. 270)

Armies on the march, particularly those carrying the heavy artillery needed for siege warfare, needed to be well maintained and supplied. Skirmishes with the inhabitants even of allied countries where armies were briefly lodged were not infrequent, and sometimes could even lead to battles or sieges, as happened at Messina in the Third Crusade when a dispute arose between the French, the English, and the townspeople. Again the redactor is interested in showing some of the practicalities, as well as the splendour and romance, connected with his subject. The equivalent passage in Lydgate gives a picture of the Greeks surrounding the city and lighting fires through the night; the redaction replaces this with topics which emphasize the nobility and visual splendour of the besieging army.[44]

The army arrives at Thebes, sets up camp, blockades the city, and begins mining operations:

where they ful proudely lighten downe, settyng vp full many a riall pavilon and tent on euery side the Cite, closing the Cite all abought, making theire logges, and many a myghty warde on euery side; So that there might no man yssue oute of the Cite vnslayne or taken, A rering vp many a big bulwerk on euery side, setting mynours to the walles in full ferse wise. (fos. 7v-8, p. 270)

These preparations are very similar to those counselled by de Balsac:

Item que darrivee il face faire gros fossez endroit des portes de la place & ailleurs ou il sera besoing pour garder les saillies que pourroyent faire les enemis.

Et quil y ayt tousiours ung gros guet & puissant pour resister aux saillies quilz pourroyent faire.

Item faire fortifier darrivee leur champ & leur logis. (58v–59)

On arrival he should have great ditches made by the gates of the place and elsewhere where necessary to guard against the sallies that the enemies may make.

And there should always be a large and powerful watch to resist the sallies which they may make.

Their encampment and lodgings should be fortified on arrival.

---

[44] *Lydgate's Siege of Thebes*, part iii, ll. 3581–6.

Sealing off the surrounded place from outside aid and securing the besieging army against assaults from inside is an important factor in ancient and medieval siege warfare. It became even more essential in the later fourteenth and fifteenth centuries, when, owing to advances in defence technology, blockade was often the only way to capture a town. Splendid camps were a feature of medieval sieges, sometimes, as here, including special accommodation for the prince or king. An example from history similar to the scene depicted here is Edward III's siege of Calais. Edward decided not to attack the strongly fortified and heavily manned town but to reduce it by famine, exploiting the dunes and marshes surrounding it. The English camp soon became a small town with tents built for shops as well as for troops and provisions.[45] Bulwarks or 'boulevards', large mounds of earth with ditches below, were thrown up by both attackers and defenders at sieges in the Middle Ages to serve as gun emplacements (in the fifteenth century) and to restrict movement by the enemy.[46]

Adrastus sets 'mynours to the walles in full ferse wise'. Mining underneath walls to bring them down or to gain access to the fortress from within was a feature of siege practice in ancient times and continued throughout the Middle Ages. Adrastus' miners are attempting to defeat the countermining measures of Ethiocles and to accomplish the following operations, as described in the 1408 English version of Vegetius:

Another manere of takynge of citees and strengthes is by vndermynynge of the walles and so to entre into the citee vnder erthe priueliche vnwitynge of hem that be withinne; & somtyme thei that thus myne entreth be nyght thorgh the myne into the citee, and open the gates withynne & lete yn the oost, & thus thei take the citee. Somteyme thei undersette the wal that is vndermyned with drye poostes & tymber, & sette among drye fagot & strawe & suche thing that wole lightliche brenne. And when thei ben al redy to make assaut thei sette here myne postes on fyre, & when the tymber is brenned vnder the wal the wal cleue & falleth doun, & thanne haue the enemyes opoun entre to take the cite or the strengthe [place besieged]. (IV. 24, p. 174)

Ethiocles sees the preparations being made for the siege against him and reinforces his artillery and guard. There follows the negotiated settlement attempted by Queen Jocasta. The conventions of the

[45] J. Froissart, Œuvres: Chroniques, v. 145–222. In Lord Berners's translation, i, chs. 135–46, pp. 304–22. The Siege of Calais is included in Brereton's selection from Froissart, 97–112 (shops, 97). See J. Viard, 'Le Siège de Calais (4 septembre 1346–4 août 1347)', LMA 39 (1929), 129–89.

[46] See M. Vale, War and Chivalry, ch. 4, 'The Techniques of War', 100–46 (133).

conduct of sieges and the laws of war governing them will be more fully discussed in the next chapter with regard to the siege of Metz. It is worth noting here, however, that the classical legend is similar in some ways to medieval practice. Demands for surrender were normally made before a siege, and if these were refused, hostilities were regarded as formally commenced. Jocasta, speaking on behalf of Ethiocles, is received with courtesy by Adrastus and Pollymet, who shows her 'lowly obeysaunce' (p. 270). She asks Pollymet to be content with living on an allowance under Ethiocles, but the Greeks refuse to deal with Ethiocles 'but if he wold resigne crowne, septre, and all the dignite aftre the covenaunt and statutes made bifor tyme, of which they had the copies redy to shewe' (p. 270). The scene suggests both the niceties of conduct and the arguments over legal claims to a place which occur in several descriptions of medieval sieges. It also shows a royal woman in the role of peacemaker, a part sometimes played in life as well. Froissart's description of the Queen's plea for mercy to be shown to the six burghers of Calais is perhaps the most famous example of a supposedly historical incident of this kind.[47]

Jocasta returns to Thebes to let the war take its course. There is a brief skirmish outside the gates, in which Amphiorax descends to the earthly grave he had foreseen for himself and Adrastus and his lords are troubled enough by this to consider returning home. The veterans so valued by de Balsac contrast perhaps unfavourably here with the headstrong younger knights: while older and wiser voices counsel returning, the young lords disdainfully vow not to raise the siege 'while there were one left on lyve within the towne, or stone, stondyng on the wallis, but if hit were yolden at theire wil' (p. 271). In this, they have at least the conventions of medieval siege warfare on their side: having refused to renounce his governance of the city, Ethiocles has rendered his own life, and those of his army and people, forfeit in the event of a defeat by assault. We shall see examples of the ruthless massacre of defenders and inhabitants when a besieged city is stormed, in the sieges of Acre, Metz, Troy, and Jerusalem.

Seeing the defiant attitude of his knights, Adrastus orders a major assault on Thebes:

Charging al maner of men to be redi in aray, ordeynyng ladders, picos, and many other wepon, full cruelly assailing the Cite on euery side with skaling,

[47] J. Froissart, Œuvres: Chroniques, v. 214–16; trans. Berners, i, ch. 46, pp. 331–2; trans. Brereton, 108–9.

mynyng the wallys foynyng and sheting, hewyng downe of bruges and barreris.
They of within, in right manly wise, made theire defence in casting of stone &
wilde fire with brem stone, lede, picche molton, castyng on their hedes, beting
of bassenettis with axes, with ful many a mighty shotte outeward, foyned hem
fro the walles, filling ful her diches with slayn men. (fos. 8v–9, p. 271)

This passage constitutes another expansion of the source. Lydgate
provides a dramatic description of the battle, but with the exception of
a reference to cannon and arbalests, his version concentrates on hand-
to-hand fighting at the walls and within the city (4307–40). The redactor offers instead a detailed description of an assault. Three basic
manœuvres are involved: attempts to go over the walls (scaling), to go
under them and bring them down from beneath (mining), and to
breach them with engines ('shetyng'). 'Foynyng' or 'thrustyng' might
refer both to the projecting of missiles and to hand-to-hand fighting at
the walls. Mining has already been encountered in the text; the basic
principles of scaling and breaching should be briefly described.

The only method of scaling described here is that using ladders.
These were in use in sieges before the Romans, and continued to be
effective in the medieval period despite advances in fortification and the
increased height of walls. Sometimes ladders were made with claws to
grip the top of the wall; folding ladders of rope and leather were used as
well as wooden ones.[48] At the siege of Constantinople in 1453, the
Turks prepared to storm the city with 2,000 ladders. Vegetius gives instructions on measuring the height of walls before constructing scaling
equipment (IV. 30, p. 177). He also describes winding towers used for
scaling, and ladders with bridges which could be extended to the top of
the curtain wall (IV. 21, p. 172). One effect of the ladder was to create instant renown for whoever risked being the first in an assault. Any soldier
could attempt this, and thus 'the scaling ladder was the only means of
making an individual bid for victory; every other means of assault
meant teamwork'.[49]

For breaching the walls and other 'barreris' (perhaps the boulevards
mentioned earlier or the rampart recommended by de Balsac (60r)),
Adrastus uses engines for 'sheting' like the trebuchet and mangonel previously described. He also employs 'picos' or picks, 'and many other
wepon' to force an entry in the wall. Picks were used to undermine the

---

[48] There is a reference to leather and rope ladders, for example, in *The Siege of Jerusalem*,
l. 2953.

[49] Warner, *Sieges of the Middle Ages*, 71.

base of a wall, together with various other weapons for boring holes. Soldiers would operate these under cover of shields or more elaborate mobile defensive equipments, protecting the miners from the missiles of the defenders with reinforced roofs: these structures had various animal names, such as tortoises, cats, weasels, sows, and mice.[50] Mining in this fashion was an important part of siegecraft, especially before the invention of the trebuchet, though it continued in the later period. Christine de Pisan recommends the use of picks in her list of defensive munitions (II. xv, p. 141), as does de Balsac (60r). The latter, however, does not include mining in his advice on a successful assault, evidence of the decline of this method as gunpowder became more effective in the fifteenth century.

As Adrastus' soldiers attempt to penetrate the walls 'on euery side', the defenders respond by hurling stones and Greek fire from their engines at the outlying army, and by casting brimstone, lead, and molten pitch on those mining the base of the wall and scaling the tops of them. Boiling oil and water, rocks and other heavy substances, together with other items such as beehives, were used as defences against siege from at least as early as the ninth century. Boiling lead was a medieval development: the 1408 English translator of Vegetius adds the phrase 'hote meltyng leed' to Vegetius' description of defence from the walls:

Loke also that the wall of the arche ouer the inner gate be machekolud or so persed & holed that thou mowe hylde doun water to quenche the fire, if nede be, or hote meltyng leed on hem that stonde vnder. (IV. 4, p. 162)

Ethiocles, it will be remembered, had earlier ensured his walls were machicolated for this purpose.

With this description of an assault and valiant defence, the siege warfare in *The Prose Siege of Thebes* effectively ends. A battle in the open field before the city follows, in which both Pollymet and Ethiocles are slain, along with many thousands from both sides. Like Troy, Thebes was associated with tragedy and human disaster, which is the theme emphasized in the latter part of the redaction. The ladies grieve for their chivalrous menfolk, and Adrastus is moved by this to mourn the slaughter. Here too the redactor differs from Lydgate, who mentions only the mourning of Jocasta, Ismene, and Antigone for Ethiocles; in describing the general mourning of the ladies, the redactor again suggests something of the realities of contemporary experience and the real

---

[50] Vegetius, IV. 13–16, pp. 167–9. *Knyghthode and Bataile*, 87–9.

consequences of a siege in life as well as in literature.[51] Before considering further some of the general points suggested by this text, we should mention two important pieces of siege equipment in the Middle Ages which do not appear in it: the belfry and the cannon.

Belfries, or siege towers (also called 'somercastelles' in the 1408 English translation of Vegetius (IV. 22, p. 173)) were large mobile towers which could be moved to the walls of the place besieged. To be effective, they had to overlook the town or castle. Normally the towers would have different stages: at the lowest, miners, protected by a hide roof, would weaken the wall. Above, archers would fire at defenders, and assaults over the walls, sometimes using a bridge, could be effected. Siege towers were difficult to manœuvre, highly flammable, and demanded a great deal of material and skill to construct and operate successfully. They were, however, used both in Roman times and in the Middle Ages. As late as 1565, a siege tower was in use in the siege of Malta. The romance of *Richard Coeur de Lion* describes at some length the transportation of siege towers (which Richard assembled before the crusade, rather than having them made on arrival, the more usual practice) and their use in the siege of Acre.

The earliest illustration of a cannon in the West appears in Walter de Milemete's treatise on government in a manuscript of 1326, which also contains several illustrations of siege weapons and an allegorical siege of love.[52] Over the course of the fourteenth century, cannons were used in sieges by Edward III in his wars in Scotland and France, and they also appeared at sieges in other European countries, particularly in Italy. The advance in artillery soon produced its experts: a 'cannonier fort renommé' called Girault de Samien appears at the siege of Paris by the dukes of Berry and Brittany in 1465.[53] A study of the use of cannons in sieges in English Gascony in the fourteenth century has shown them to be highly effective even by this time. By the middle of the fifteenth century, when *The Prose Siege of Thebes* was written, cannons were commonplace at sieges. They were crucial in Charles VIII's Italian expedition of 1494–5, for example, and played a major part in the sieges of Rhodes in 1480 and 1522.[54]

[51] *Lydgate's Siege of Thebes*, part iii, ll. 4366–70.

[52] Oxford, Christ Church, MS 92. Illustrations referred to are: fo. 60v (cannon); fo. 68v (balista with winch); fo. 67r (trebuchet); fo. 75v (mining picks); fo. 73v (scaling ladder); fos. 3v–4r (siege of love). Reproduced in Bradbury (see pp. vii–xi). The siege of love is discussed in Ch. 6, below.

[53] Bradbury, 282–95. Siege of Paris: Philippe de Commynes, *Mémoires*, i. 40.

[54] Vale, *War and Chivalry*, ch. 4, 'The Techniques of War', pp. 100–46, esp. 130–46.

The shift from idealism towards greater realism in military manuals in the later Middle Ages has already been noted. The increasing use of cannons in sieges from the middle of the fourteenth century is thus reflected in the military treatises written at this time. Technical efficiency starts to take the place of individual heroism. Robert de Balsac, writing with the advantage of direct experience of the sieges of the Italian expedition, stresses the importance of artillery from cannons to hand-guns, and clearly imagines a siege as essentially a matter of blockade and battery rather than the more old-fashioned methods of storming as depicted in *The Prose Siege of Thebes*.[55] Both Christine de Pisan and Jean de Bueil (making use of Christine's text), augmenting Vegetius, give detailed information on the placing and usage of cannons at a siege.[56] Jean de Bueil advocates that the direction of siege-works should be left to masters of artillery; and the office of 'maître de l'artillerie' was often held by a nobleman.[57] The author of the 1408 English translation of Vegetius, who otherwise makes little effort to modernize his source, adds to the list of defences of walls the 'grete gunnes that schete now adayes [stoones] of so grete peys that no wall may withstonde hem, as hath ben wel schewed bothe in the north cuntrey and eke in the werres of Wales' (IV. 22, p. 173). The later verse paraphrase goes further, saying that cannons are now the main artillery weapon in a siege and that older siege engines have been superseded and are now 'unwiste'.[58]

Ancient cities were sometimes depicted being bombarded by cannon, as in the illustrations of Troy and Thebes in MS Douce 353 and other manuscripts and early prints.[59] The absence of cannons in *The Prose Siege of Thebes* is typical of many medieval literary treatments of sieges: though arms and armour are usually described in the modern fashion, a slightly more nostalgic approach to siege equipment seems to be favoured, similar to the copies of the manual of Vegetius still being made in the fifteenth century which retained its classical allusions without supplementing them with modern advances in technology. The appearance of 'grete gunnes' in Mordred's siege of Guinevere in the Tower of London towards the end of Malory's work seems to introduce a note of modernity and cold realism into the romance, though it is

---

[55] Rober de Balsac, 58v–59.

[56] *Le Jouvencel*, ii. 45–7. The textual relation is established by Coopland, 'Le Jouvencel (Revisited)', 137–86.

[57] Vale, *War and Chivalry*, 143–4. [58] *Knyghthode and Bataile*, IV. 2543, p. 93.

[59] See H. Buchthal, *Historia Troiana: Studies in the History of Mediaeval Secular Illustration*, Studies of the Warburg Institute, 32 (London, 1971).

likely that even here traditional engines rather than cannon are referred to.[60] Some authors, like Bérault Stuart, furnish their descriptions of warfare with examples from classical history and legend, as if deliberately avoiding the brutal realities of which they must have been aware. The contemporaneity, or lack of it, in descriptions of historical sieges in romances often seems to indicate a tension felt between the idealized conception of warfare and the experience of it in reality. In general, romance writers seemed to prefer a rather old-fashioned picture of siege warfare, fearing perhaps that the glow of antique chivalry would be obscured by the smoke of fifteenth-century cannon. The distinctively medieval features of *The Prose Siege of Thebes* are the banners of the army and the heralds listing them, Greek or wild fire, the apparent reference to a trebuchet, and, possibly, the boiling lead. All these elements, however, were present in the early Middle Ages, and some, such as the heralds and the trebuchet, were falling out of use at the time the piece was written. The author is fascinated by the drama and mechanics of a siege, but reluctant to omit the more dated elements which provide proper material for a chivalric tale of heroes.[61]

Redactions often minimize interpretative commentaries, but the treatment of the siege in *The Prose Siege of Thebes*, in addition to producing a swift and compelling narrative, also hints at a more universal moral point. The essential lesson of this particular battle is that evil can stem from incest and that slaughter results from internecine warfare. The piece begins with the story of Oedipus, dwells on the incest theme and the unnatural birth of the brothers, includes a reference to Tydeus' accidental murder of his brother, and ends with a reference to the later founding of Rome by Romulus and Remus (fo. 10v, p. 273). The message that battle between those of the same blood or nation always ends in catastrophe, starkly illustrated by the siege of brother against brother, would not be lost on an English audience at the time of the Wars of the Roses. The use of a siege description to point to or expound a more general aspect of human behaviour, perhaps involving an implied comment on current events, is another element encountered in other romances, particularly those on Troy and Jerusalem.

---

[60] See D. B. Mahoney, 'Malory's Great Guns', *Viator*, 20 (1989), 291–310. See also M. Vale, 'New Techniques and Old Ideals: The Impact of Artillery on War and Chivalry at the End of the Hundred Years War,' in Allmand (ed.), *War, Literature and Politics in the Late Middle Ages*, 57–60, 72.

[61] The implications for chivalric values are discussed by W. Wetherbee, 'Chivalry under Siege in Ricardian Romance', in I. A. Corfis and M. Wolfe (eds.), *The Medieval City under Siege* (Woodbridge, 1995), 207–26.

Because the siege of Thebes is one fought by Greeks on both sides and between two brothers, both sides are treated with equal sympathy or distance. The siege of Troy is similarly often described as a universal calamity rather than a victory for one side. In the sieges of literature, the way in which the enemy is described varies considerably, from the portrayal of heathens as comic or inhuman wretches in crusading romances and the Roman siege of Jerusalem, to the slightly more neutral characterization of the Roman enemy in the *Morte Arthure*. Sometimes the sympathies of the author are not easy to establish.

The Prose Siege of Thebes and other prose redactions written in the fifteenth century were presumably intended to be useful works, providing a concise epitome of the main events of much larger poems. They can still be useful to the modern reader, not only as summary accounts of legends or digestible versions of Lydgate, but also as illustrations of prevailing interests in a later medieval audience in particular subjects. *The Prose Siege of Thebes* tells us plainly that an interest in literary treatments of siege warfare in general, and in sieges of great cities of the past in particular, existed in England in the middle of the fifteenth century. Indeed, the chief interest of ancient cities to some readers would have been the military lessons that could be learned from their demise. Given the frequency of siege warfare in Europe at the time, such an interest is to be expected. Romances could also provide some idea of cause and reason that may have seemed absent in real life: witnesses to the campaigns in France, England, Wales, and Scotland looked to writers to give such events a shape and meaning, and perhaps an idealizing gloss. Heroic commanders were required, in literature as in life, to make sieges seem more dramatic and in some way more positive than they can have seemed at the time. The way in which some poets went about this task is the subject of the next chapter.

2

Historical Sieges in Fourteenth-Century Literature: The Siege Commander

A SIEGE like the one described in *The Prose Siege of Thebes* could have taken place in the thirteenth or early fourteenth century. The trebuchet was the key feature of this period, and remained the only significant medieval contribution to siege warfare, before advances in gunpowder during the fourteenth century. The basic elements of defence and attack in this account of the fall of Thebes, however, continued into the fourteenth and fifteenth centuries. This continuity in methods provides a context for the romances, which do not differ greatly in the basic description of siege techniques, unless an author wants to stress a particular aspect of his story, such as its exotic location or the skill of a commander. The romances are more notable for the variety and sophistication of literary themes surrounding a siege than for the technological terms they employ.

One of the most important themes is the depiction of the commander, and the ways in which his strategic and ethical approach to siege warfare is portrayed. The siege of Acre (1191) by the English and French crusading armies, as described in the Middle English romance *Richard Coeur de Lion* (*c*.1300), provides a good example of the siege techniques employed during the crusades. It also presents a striking portrait of a crusading commander in the figure of Richard I. The roughly contemporary Anglo-Norman poem known as *The Siege of Caerlaverok*, which describes an event of 1300 during Edward I's Scottish campaign, combines literary techniques derived from epic and romance writings with a list of heraldic motifs and some detailed descriptions of the conflict. Barbour's treatment in *The Bruce* (*c*.1375) of the siege of Berwick by the English in 1319 includes much realistic detail, and a perspective on this type of warfare from the point of view of the defenders. Finally, the siege of Metz in the alliterative *Morte Arthure* (*c*.1400), while probably not based on an actual historical episode, nevertheless includes many features typical of the sieges of the later fourteenth century fought by Edward III; in the figure of King Arthur, the poet presents an example of the various qualities shown in a siege by a leader, possibly including some negative attributes together with chivalric virtues. Our discussion will follow the chronological order of the events themselves rather than that of the texts: though siege warfare progressed slowly, some of the few developments which did occur over the period can be perceived by this approach.

The kings and commanders drawn in the romances belong to a long tradition. Portraits of soldier-emperors and kings exhibiting piety and prowess in battle and siegecraft exist in chronicles from an early date. Drawing on such sources as the campaigns of Caesar and the exploits of Old Testament and pagan heroes, royal biographers presented their subjects as heroic warriors: early examples are Einhard's biography of Charlemagne, and Widukind's presentation of Saxon emperors as the successors to Caesar. Often, religious devotion was added to skill as a crucial element of character. In his biography of Louis VI, for example, Suger emphasizes both Louis's piety and his expertise in laying sieges, adding detailed descriptions, as in the description of a moveable tower in use at the siege by Louis of the castle of Gournay in 1107. Spiritual fervour is of obvious importance in crusading commanders like Bohemond at the siege of Antioch and Simon de Montfort in the Albigensian crusade, whose feats were recorded in the visual arts as well as in chronicles.[1]

The praise of leaders at sieges also appears in the memoirs of kings and generals: examples are the chronicle, mentioned earlier, of the conquest of the Balearic islands by King James I of Aragon, in the composition of which the king played an important part (c.1244–74), the account of the Fourth Crusade by Villehardouin, or, from a later period, Jean de Bueil's own account of the siege of Orléans in 1428-9, where he fought alongside Joan of Arc. Chivalric biographies such as the Chandos Herald's life of the Black Prince continue the praise of leaders at sieges, and influence chronicle treatments of the subject;

[1] Suger, *Vie de Louis VI le Gros*, siege of castle of Gournay, pp. 71–7. Bohemond appears in *Gesta Francorum et aliorum Hierosolimitanorum*. *Chanson de la Croisade Albigeoise*. Siege of Carcassonne: i. 62–83. See also Peter of Vaux-de-Cernay, *Hystoria Albigensis*. The siege of Toulouse in 1218 is recorded in a detailed carving in the church of St Nazaire in Carcassonne, where Simon de Montfort is buried: reproduced in B. Smalley, *Historians in the Middle Ages* (London, 1974), 147. Another commander whose expertise at sieges is commented on is Roger de Flor, leader of the 14th-cent. Catalan company, in *The Chronicle of Muntaner*. See e.g. the siege of Messina, chs. 194–7. Muntaner's depiction of warfare is discussed by R. Sablonier, *Krieg und Kriegertum in der Crònica des Ramon Muntaner: Eine Studie zum spätmittelalterlichen Kriegswesen aufgrund Katalanischer Quellen*, Geist und Werk der Zeiten, 31 (Berne and Frankfurt, 1971).

Froissart's depiction of sieges often combines the praise of commanders such as the Black Prince with detailed description of weapons and strategy.[2]

The subject of the great leader conducting a siege is a popular one in epics and romances. The Carolingian epics of Abbo and Ermoldus are to a great extent elaborated eulogies of the captains whose deeds are described, and whose humility and courage contrasts with the wild savagery of the Moors.[3] French and Hispanic epics similarly focus on the martial and moral virtues of an individual, and victories are frequently presented as the result of an extraordinary leader's strategy and charisma rather than as a collective effort. Even invented or legendary heroes of romance sometimes prove themselves at real sieges, like William of Palerne, who fights in Spain, or the hero of *The Knight of Curtesy*, who serves in Rhodes, apparently in the real encounter which took place there in 1480. Beyond chronicle and romance are the forms of long verse description and popular song, such as the rhyming account of Henry V's siege of Rouen, which occurs in the English *Brut*, or the ballad recording the successful defence of Calais against Philip of Burgundy in 1436. Such pieces commonly commemorate individual acts of bravery, on the part of governors, soldiers, and ordinary citizens, giving us a colourful picture of late medieval conflicts. In all these genres, the decisions and actions of the commander attract particular attention.[4]

Hence by the fourteenth century the tradition of praising a leader at a siege, and the practice of combining an admiring portrait of a leader with detailed description of the events, was well established, both in chronicles and in other forms of narrative literature. It is against this background that we will look at four sieges as they are described in

[2] Jaume I (James I, King of Aragon), *Crònica o llibre dels feits*, siege of Majorca, Forster's translation, pp. 90–200. Sieges of Menorca and Ibiza, pp. 211–21. Jean de Bueil, *Le Jouvencel*: siege of Orléans, i, chs. 21–5. On Froissart's description of battles, see G. Jäger, *Aspekte des Krieges und der Chevalerie im XIV. Jahrhundert in Frankreich: Untersuchungen zu Jean Froissarts Chroniques*, Geist und Werk der Zeiten, 60 (Berne and Frankfurt, 1981), 194–207. His treatment of a specific siege is discussed by A. Artonne, 'Froissart Historien: Le Siège et la prise de la Roche-Vendeix', *BEC* 110 (1952), 89–107.

[3] Cultural implications are speculated upon by J. E. Ruiz Doménec, 'El asedio de Barcelona, según Ermoldo el Negro (Notas sobre el carácter de la guerra en la alta Edad Media)', *BRABLB* 37 (1977–8), 146–68. See also P. Godman, *Poets and Emperors: Frankish Politics and Carolingian Poetry* (Oxford, 1987), 114.

[4] *The Knight of Curtesy*: reference to siege of Rhodes, pp. 194–5. For poem on Henry V's siege of Rouen, see Bibliography under J. Page. See under 'Siege of Calais' for editions of ballad.

certain fourteenth-century texts, concentrating on the depiction of the leader and the details of the tactics and weapons used at the battle itself.

THE SIEGE OF ACRE AND OTHER SIEGES IN Richard Coeur de Lion

The Middle English romance of *Richard Coeur de Lion* was written in the beginning or first half of the fourteenth century, and is possibly a translation or adaptation of an earlier Anglo-Norman work. The existence of six manuscripts and an early print testify to its popularity. In the course of redaction, legendary episodes concerning Richard's birth and early life appear to have been added to an earlier, more plainly realistic, narrative account of the Third Crusade, though it is also probable that the shorter manuscripts also contain interpolated material. Despite such textual complications, it is clear that the main subject of the poem is King Richard I and his campaign; it includes a lengthy account of the siege of Acre and descriptions of other sieges, some of them apparently invented by the author.[5]

Richard Coeur de Lion is a biography of the English king, and the aspect of his character on which it concentrates is his effectiveness as a military commander, particularly in his direction of sieges. Two chronicles of the Third Crusade, Ambroise's verse account *L'Estoire de la Guerre Sainte* and the closely related anonymous *Itinerarium peregrinorum et gesta regis Ricardi*, also present heroic portraits of Richard conducting the siege of Acre, though the author of the romance does not seem to have drawn on any particular chronicle for his account.[6] Earlier writings describing Richard praise his fostering of the arts in Provence and his piety, while his famous duel against Saladin is represented in various artefacts. By the time the Middle English romance was composed,

---

[5] References are to Brunner's edition. On dating, manuscripts and sources, G. Paris, 'Le Roman de Richard Coeur de Lion', *Romania*, 26 (1897), 353–93, is still valuable, as is the review of Brunner's edition by R. S. Loomis, *JEGP* 15 (1916), 455–66. On the textual tradition, see W. C. Stokoe, 'The Work of the Redactors of *Sir Launfal, Richard Coeur de Lion* and *Sir Degaré*' (dissertation, Cornell University, 1947).

[6] See J. G. Edwards, 'The *Itinerarium Regis Ricardi* and the *Estoire de la Guerre Sainte*', in J. G. Edwards *et al.* (eds.), *Historical Essays in Honour of James Tate* (Manchester, 1933), 59–77. Their presentation of Richard is discussed by B. J. Levy, 'Pélerins rivaux de la 3ème croisade: Les Personnages des rois d'Angleterre et de France, d'après les chroniques d'Ambroise et d'"Ernoul" et le récit anglo-normand de la *Croisade et Mort Richard Coeur de Lion*', in D. Buschinger (ed.), *La Croisade: Réalités et fictions: Actes du Colloque d'Amiens 18–22 mars 1987*, Göppinger Arbeiten zur Germanistik, 503 (Göppingen, 1989), 143–55. F. Jentzsch, 'Die mittelenglische Romanze Richard Coeur de Lion und ihre Quellen', *Eng. Stud.* 15 (1891), 161–246, argues for the chronicles as a source, but this is persuasively refuted in Paris's article, mentioned above.

Richard had already become a legendary English hero, worthy to carry Excalibur; according to a Latin poem of the thirteenth century, he was the English equivalent of Charlemagne.[7] The theme of national pride is recurrent in the poem: the siege of Acre is depicted as a victory for Richard and the English rather than for the crusading army. Indeed, the French method of siegecraft under Philip Augustus comes in for a great deal of criticism: at the time of the Hundred Years War an English audience with a need for inspirational heroes 'could be expected to exult in Richard the Lion-Hearted's valiant deeds, his victories over the Saracens, and his frequent discomfiture of the French King'. It has been said that 'the feats which earned for Richard his place in legend were faults in a commander', but in the English romance his legendary qualities are illustrated by his management of the capture of Acre and by his mastery of the art of siegecraft in general.[8]

Acre had fallen to Saladin in July 1187 in a wave of attacks against the Latin kingdom, in which one Arab chronicler calculated that fifty-two towns and castles had been captured.[9] On 28 August 1189 Guy of Lusignan, recently defeated at Hattin, laid siege to Acre in an attempt to recapture this strategically vital town with its harbour open to communications from the West. A small, manifestly inadequate, initial force of 400 knights and 7,000 infantry was gradually augmented by reinforcements from Europe. This was sufficient to keep Saladin's relief force at bay, but Guy failed to blockade the city both by land and sea, and an Egyptian fleet managed to reach the Saracens in the besieged city. Efforts to capture Acre using siege towers and rams were thwarted by Greek fire. The besieging army was itself trapped by Saladin's force in

[7] On Richard in art and literature, see: G. H. Needler, *Richard Coeur de Lion in Literature* (Leipzig, 1890); B. B. Broughton, *The Legends of King Richard I Coeur de Lion: A Study of the Sources and Variations to the Year 1600*, Studies in English Literature, 25 (Paris and The Hague, 1966); J. Nelson (ed.), *Richard Coeur de Lion in History and Myth* (London, 1992); J. Gillingham, 'Some Legends of Richard the Lionheart: Their Development and their Influence', in *Ricardo Cuor di Leone nella storia e nella leggenda: Accademia Nazionale dei Lincei, colloquio italo-britannico*, Accademia Nazionale dei Lincei, Problemi attuali di scienza e di cultura, 253 (Rome, 1981), 35–50, repr. in J. Gillingham, *Richard Coeur de Lion: Kingship, Chivalry and War in the Twelfth Century* (London, 1994), 181–91; R. S. Loomis, 'Richard Coeur de Lion and the Pas Saladin in Medieval Art', *PMLA* 30 (1915), 509–28; poem comparing Richard to Charlemagne: *Poésies populaires latines du Moyen Age*, ed. E. du Méril (Paris, 1847), 277.

[8] Comments are, respectively, A. C. Baugh, 'The Middle English Romance: Some Questions of Creation, Presentation and Preservation', *Speculum*, 42 (1967), 1–31 (13); J. O. Prestwich, 'Richard Coeur de Lion: Rex Bellicosus', in *Ricardo Cuor di Leone* (above, n. 7), 1–15 (2).

[9] For a fuller account, see: J. Gillingham, *Richard the Lionheart* (London, 1978; 2nd edn. 1989), 170–84; H. E. Mayer, *The Crusades*, trans. J. Gillingham (Oxford, 1972), 142–4.

the hills outside the city, making retreat impossible. Though the Franks were able to keep the relieving army away, over the winter of 1190–1 they suffered acute food shortages, and by the time of the arrival of Philip and, slightly later, Richard in the summer of 1191, their position was desperate.

Ambroise presents Richard as a divinely sanctioned avenger of Christ's suffering people and the implacable enemy of the religion of the Saracens. His capture of Acre is an action of the grandest proportions.[10] The Middle English romance prepares us for a similarly heroic description of this feat by showing Richard successfully besieging Messina and capturing Cyprus from the ambitious governor and self-styled 'emperor' Isaac Comnenus on his way to the Holy Land. At Messina, Richard has been shown operating to great effect his six-storey siege tower named 'Mategryffoun', which had been assembled in England before the crusade embarked. The naming of towers occurs also in the romance of *Sir Ferrumbras*, where a siege tower called Brisour even has names for its three different stages (Mangunel, Laucepre, Hargefray).[11]

When he arrives near the harbour of Acre, Richard single-handedly demolishes the chain stretched across the harbour by the Saracens to prevent relief getting to the Frankish army. His arrival is heralded by trumpets and drums, and the terrified Saracens see Richard cast Greek fire into the sky and observe the weapons and provisions he has brought for the siege. On board Richard has mangonels 'off gret quentyse', crossbows (also known as arbalests), and what seems to be a mill for grinding corn, which the Saracens, fearing that Richard is 'the deuell of hell / That was come them to quell' (2677–8), perceive in the night as a machine grinding men's bones together (2643–80). Here, 'mill' could be interpreted as a siege engine, though the existence of a real mill on a ship would not be unusual. The scene gives us an idea of the difficulties of provisioning a besieging army in the Holy Land and the need to assemble and carry equipment over long distances. Richard is presented from the point of view of the enemy as a devilish figure with superhuman powers come to besiege them, an image which may owe something to the legends surrounding the ancestry of the Plantagenets, the 'devil's brood'.

---

[10] The description of the Siege of Acre occurs in Ambroise, ll. 2299–5542. His motives for the crusade are given as 'por lor lei desaengier / Et por cristienté vengier' ('that he might root up their religion, and that he might avenge Christendom', trans. Stone, 79).

[11] ll. 3255–74.

To expertise and enterprise is added the virtue of etiquette, as Richard is welcomed by the French king and other leaders of the Frankish army. The real Emperor Isaac Comnenus and the Archbishop of Pisa describe to him the story of the siege so far and the deprivations suffered by the Christians, and recount the famines and plagues which have devastated the army and the recent defeat by Saladin's relief force (2693–85). No mention is made of the limited successes which had been achieved by the French siege engines, and Richard, cast as the redeemer of the suffering crusaders, prays for Christ's help in the forthcoming siege against the heathen. Immediately he reassembles Mategryffoun and his other tower, named Robynet (also the name of a siege engine used by Edward I at Stirling Castle in 1304), from which Acre is bombarded with stones. Ambroise gives the siege engines the different names of 'Male Veisine', 'Maisen Acre', and 'Male Cosine' (4745–56).[12] Richard himself conducts operations from Mategryffoun: we see him releasing beehives into the city (a frequent feature of crusading sieges) and looking down over the walls at the troubled Saracen defenders. The poet places great emphasis on the might of these towers, making the episode in part a demonstration of crusading technical skill against a backward adversary. A similar focus is found in the account of a huge tower built on a ship in the description of the siege of Tyre in the al-literative *Wars of Alexander*, the author of this work, like the redactor of Lydgate considered previously, adds a detailed and dramatic account of the siege to his source. *Richard Coeur de Lion* makes some mention of other attackers, such as the French miners who work to bring down the tower known as 'Maudyt Colour' (2928), but, in contrast to Ambroise's account, there are no examples of the individual deeds of knights or foot-soldiers: Richard appears as a single source of energy and inspiration for the rest of the army.[13] Failures or setbacks are not mentioned, and the French contribution to the siege is given scant attention. A

[12] On naming of guns, see M. Vale, *War and Chivalry: Warfare and Aristocratic Culture in England, France and Burgundy at the End of the Middle Ages* (London, 1981), 145–6. The names of the engines at Stirling are recorded in *EHD* iii. 610.

[13] *Wars of Alexander*, 1508–71. The siege of Tyre appears in T. Turville-Petre (ed.), *Alliterative Poetry of the Later Middle Ages* (London, 1989), 191–3. The same book includes the illustration of the tower in Oxford, Bodleian Library, Bodley MS 264 on p.100. Ambroise's anecdotes include the following: a sergeant is struck in the breast by a crossbow bolt, but is saved by a piece of paper on which are written the names of God (3561–82); a knight is attacked while answering a call of nature in a trench, but manages to kill his assailant and steal his horse (3583–624); the dying wish of one woman, killed while filling the ditch with stones, is that her own body be thrown into the ditch as well (3625–60); a Welshman slays a Saracen in an exchange-of-blows agreement, by shooting his adversary while he is reloading (3731–70).

third, French tower existed as well as those constructed by Richard. All three had great initial success, and combustible defences against them did not work until an expert from Damascus changed the recipe for Greek fire and sent all three up in flames. Though the Maudyt Tower was eventually mined and breached, the earlier mining efforts by the French had nearly ended in disaster, as a section of the wall twisted and fell, almost crushing the miners.

Saladin's relief army, colourfully attired, appears on the hillside outside the town, but does not risk an attack on the Franks and crusaders (2967–3004). The author stresses the role of God in helping the besiegers: 'The Sarezynys hadden entryd negh, / But God almyghty thertoo segh' (3009–10). Instead they fill with hay the dyke which the besieging army has dug around itself as a defence, in an effort to bring reinforcements through to the beleaguered guardians of the city. They are, however, routed in a battle outside the dyke and flee. At this point, Richard falls ill, but the romance ingeniously turns this into a demonstration of his strength, as he gathers energy from a therapeutic cannibal supper of roasted Saracens.[14] Saladin sees the English king as a diabolical foe—'He sayde the deuyl was hem among' (3166) : using references to devilry such as this, the author presents the siege as a triumph of Richard's personal strength against the enemies of the faith, who come to perceive him as a superhuman agent of a higher destiny. As a hero depicted in these terms, Richard may seem at times to be of the devil's party: he is none the less clearly shown as a crusading hero with divine support, and the siege expresses his extraordinary energy and fervent piety. He represents a strength which his foes can only explain by attributing it to devilish forces: the English audience of the romance, seeing his pious affirmations elsewhere, know that he is undoubtedly a champion of Christianity, and the assault on Acre appears as a translation of strong faith into military terms. There may be a general undermining of chivalric ideals in the presentation of Richard as something akin to a wild man, but it is difficult to be sure about this, given the particular force of Richard's myth and the brutal conditions of crusading warfare. It is at least as likely that unsophisticated humour is intended, and that there is a risk of being too portentous in reading apparently popular romances.

Acre is eventually captured, after the defenders have been demoralized by the sight of Saladin's retreating army. The crusaders plant their

---

[14] See S. R. Hauer, 'Richard Coeur de Lion: Cavalier or Cannibal', *MFR* 14 (1980), 88–95.

flags on the towers, and there follows Richard's slaughter of 2,700 captives when Saladin is slow to pay their ransom (3230–756). This episode is one of the most notorious examples of the great cruelty towards the enemy which accompanied many medieval sieges. The English romance shows it to be divinely approved, however, as an angel appears to Richard to encourage him, crying 'Seynyours, tuez, tuese, / Spares hem nought, behedith these!' (3749–50). Ambroise thanks God for such a happy event (5542).

The description of the siege of Acre in this poem emphasizes the strength and energy of Richard, to the extent that it is seen as his personal victory over God's enemies. The most useful siege weapons are the engines and the miners who bring down the tower. In describing the siege, the author has compressed the time scheme of events, depicting it almost as one continuous battle without a pause, and omitted failures and reports of the heroism of others, which might detract from the glory of Richard himself. A jingoistic anti-French tone is maintained throughout, as in the comment that Richard achieved more in a single morning in the siege than the French would have been capable of in seven years (2956).

The danger of showing mercy to an enemy in a siege is a principal theme in the rest of the romance, which departs even further from historical accounts in pursuing the subject of siegecraft. After the spoils of Acre have been shared and the question of its new ruler is settled, the French and English armies separate and the English army is divided into three, the divisions commanded by Richard himself and the two English lords Multon and Doilly, neither of whom appear in the chronicles. Richard urges them to take the lives and seize the goods of anyone they defeat in a siege, unless their captives will be baptized (3965–70). There are then shorter descriptions of four sieges, illustrating various aspects of siegecraft and also the mistakes to which a commander may be prone. These sieges seem to be the invention of the author, and show the romance coming close to the detail and approach of the military manuals discussed earlier.

First we are given an example of the wrong way to deal with an enemy at a siege, demonstrated by Philip in his siege of Taburet (3866–910). As soon as the Saracen defenders 'manly gan hem to deffende' (3875) the French soldiers are paralysed by fear. Instead of pursuing the siege, Philip allows himself to be bought off with ransom: 'Ffor mede he sparede hys ffoon' (3901), observes the author disapprovingly, adding that to leave defeated defenders alive is only to ensure greater problems later (3925–6). Practitioners of the military arts of the time would not necessarily have been quite so condemning of Philip's behaviour: ransom was a common practice at sieges in the West and in the Holy Land. Both Richard and the author of the romance are interested in the display of national power at a siege through total destruction. Philip is condemned for adopting a more pragmatic approach, and for allowing himself to be tricked by his enemies, as happens in this instance.[15]

Richard besieges Sudan Turry, an instructive example of crusading siegecraft following Philip's craven and mercenary approach (3980–4068). As at the siege of Acre, Richard's presence at the siege has a great effect on the defenders, who are terrified when they see his banners. In the ensuing battle he kills seven defenders with a single bolt from his crossbow, similar to an incident in Abbo's poem on the siege of Paris when seven Danes are transfixed on a single bolt from a balista and sent by a jocular defender to the kitchen to be roasted.[16] Where Acre was successfully besieged by brute strength, Sudan Turry is an example of the way in which a place can be won by ingenuity. Richard lures the defenders to one side of the walls, and scales the undefended side with a small company which opens up the town to the rest of the army. Practising what he preaches, Richard proceeds to slaughter the defenders and takes especial care to see that statues of their religion are destroyed: 'They slowe euery Sarezyn,/ And tooke the temple of Appolyn,/ They ffelde it doun, and brende Mahoun' (4059–61). The siege is once again an illustration of the working of God's justice and of His anger with those who worship false gods.

Next we see the English general Sir Thomas Multon employing a similar strategy in his siege of the symbolically named Castle Orgylous (4069–302). Multon turns a Saracen spy sent against him to his advantage: learning that the Saracens intend to collapse the bridge over the moat as the army crosses it to attack the walls, he decides to use siege engines, capable of hurling missiles a great distance: this is probably a reference to the trebuchet, whose principal advantage over earlier artillery was its range, and which was used with great success on the Third Crusade.[17] Having no defence against this bombardment, Castle

---

[15] On the use of ransom, see M. H. Keen, *The Laws of War in the Late Middle Ages*, Studies in Political History (London and Toronto, 1965), 119–33.

[16] Abbo, *Le Siège de Paris*, ll. 108–10.

[17] See T. Wise, *The Wars of the Crusades 1096–1291* (London, 1978), 210. Relatively little attention is paid to siegecraft in the standard work by R. C. Smail, *Crusading Warfare 1097–1193* (Cambridge, 1956). For a full study, see R. Rogers, *Latin Siege Warfare in the Twelfth Century* (Oxford, 1992).

Orgylous is surrendered, and the keys are delivered to the victor, the usual emblem of defeat in siege warfare. The Bayeux tapestry shows the keys of besieged Dinan being shown to William the Conqueror, Edward III at Calais was brought the keys and a sword of peace, and keys were also yielded after the siege of Cordoba, and the siege of Pera in 1453.[18] The Saracens, most of whom have taken the option of baptism as an alternative to summary execution, attempt a counter-attack in the night but are foiled. There follows a general slaughter, a looting of the luxuriously stocked castle, and the mounting of Richard's arms from the tower: the last detail is a reminder that Multon is conducting the siege in the service of Richard and on his behalf. The victories of the two junior commanders add to the glory of the king.

Siegecraft continues with the last of the four examples given in this part of the romance, Sir Ffouke Doilly's siege of Ebedy (4303–620). His most effective weapon is also the mangonel, the artillery engine apparently unknown to the enemy:

> Sere Ffouke broughte goode engynes,
> Swylke knewe but fewe Sarezynes;
> In euery half he leet hem arere
> His enemyes a newe play to lere.
>
> (4323–6)

Missiles are cast with great accuracy, demolishing the guard tower over the main gate and the strongest tower over the battlements. The depiction of the Saracen defenders in a panic, wondering what force it is that is ranged against their fortress, has something in common with the description of the devils in the Harrowing of Hell dramas:

> 'Allas, Mahoun! What has he ment,
> This Ynglyssche dogge that hyghte Fouke?
> He is no man, he is a pouke
> That out off helle is jstole!
> An euyl deth moot he thole,
> Ffor vs he beseges ffaste.'
>
> (4352–7)

---

[18] Belgian burghers are shown surrendering the keys of a besieged city in a Flemish 15th-cent. manuscript, Oxford, Bodleian Library, MS Douce 208, fo.103. Other examples: Bradbury, 310.

The defenders use poisoned bolts, Doilly retreats and then decides on a
new tactic: the moat around Ebedy is filled with wood and Greek fire is
hurled over the walls to set light to houses inside. The Saracens risk
everything in a final battle outside the gates, but are defeated. When the
English march in, we are given an impression of the brutality of total
slaughter which often followed a siege in the Middle Ages. Not only the
warriors, but all the townspeople are put to the sword by Doilly's foot-
soldiers:

> The ffoote-men come behynde,
> And slow alle that they myghte ffynde.
> Man, wumman, al yede to swerde,
> Bothe in hous and eke in yerde.

> (4597–600)

No remorse is expressed for this carnage. Sir Ffouke Doilly instead
celebrates his action with a witticism: 'Al the fflok hoppyd hedeless; / In
this manere j made pes' (4673–4). He is congratulated on his pro-
fessionalism by Richard, while a chastened Philip vows to do better next
time. Taburet, which has risen in rebellion, is demolished by the English king. Two more castles —Alboury and Daroun—are besieged, and
Richard proceeds single-handedly to capture Gatris, whose inhabitants, convinced that he is an angel, promptly convert to Christianity
(6291–4).

These events in *Richard Coeur de Lion* illustrate many of the important features of sieges in the crusades in the Holy Land: we see the
difficulties of transportation, the use of Greek fire in attack and defence,
sophisticated siege towers with six levels from which the commander
can direct operations, and the effectiveness of a new siege engine, the
trebuchet. The beehives hurled at Acre, the spy at the siege of Castle
Orgylous, and Richard's strategy for the capture of Sudan Turry all illustrate the inventiveness which went with brute force in sieges throughout the Middle Ages and beyond. Also included in the narrative are
instances of the conventions governing this form of warfare, in the
killing of prisoners and inhabitants and the looting of towns, and the
symbolic gestures of surrender and victory. These were as much features
of siege warfare in the West as in the East. Indeed, the author may have
been influenced in his treatment by more local and contemporary conditions: there is very little description of desert landscape, and the cities
of the Holy Land, like Thebes in *The Prose Siege of Thebes*, are described
as castles rather than cities, suggesting that the author had in mind

the sieges of the Hundred Years War when depicting those of the crusades.

Dominating the various sieges of the poem is the figure of the warrior-king Richard, an indefatigable and zealous agent of God's will. By his enemies he is perceived as a superhuman, usually diabolical force. His demonstration of tactical superiority and ruthlessness in all forms of warfare (before arriving in Acre, he captures a supply ship heading for the harbour) is similar to the case studies given in military treatises of the period. One can only speculate on the relation of the romance to real sieges of the fourteenth century, but it is tempting to imagine English generals of the Hundred Years War listening attentively to the advice which Richard bestows on Multon and Doilly, and to picture the original audience of the poem being inspired as well as entertained by a heroic king's example. As a manic but canny warrior, indiscriminately destroying a common enemy, Richard has something in common with the violent popular heroes of modern cinema. Not unlike some films, the romance turns an ultimately failed campaign into a success story; the English win a moral victory, but are let down by their Continental allies.

TWO SCOTTISH SIEGES: CAERLAVEROK (1300) AND BERWICK (1319)

In *The Prose Siege of Thebes* we encountered a reference to the practice of heralds trying to keep a tally of the crests carried by the noblemen of a besieging army. The short Anglo-Norman poem known as *The Siege of Caerlaverok*, a contemporary account of Edward I's capture of Caerlaverok castle in County Dumfries in July 1300, is an example of a herald practising this craft. The poem features descriptions of the blazons of 106 coats of arms, including 87 bannerets, and is an important record of late thirteenth-century English heraldry. At the same time, the author recounts the events of the siege in language which combines some close report of strategy with the techniques of epic. His work has been called 'perhaps the last attempt by anyone in England to be a herald as well as a minstrel'; the poem may have been recited by the flemish minstrel Philip de Cambrai at the Feast of Swans in 1306.[19]

---

[19] See G. J. Brault, 'Heraldic Terminology and Legendary Material in the *Siege of Caerlaverok* (c.1300)', in U. T. Holmes (ed.), *Romance Studies in Memory of Edward Billings Ham*,

The poem presents what is in some ways a unique approach to the literary description of a siege, complementing heraldic expertise with an attempt to convey the events of the battle in a way which is at once realistic and heroic. But for the poem, little would be known of this siege, which is given only the briefest of mentions in chronicles of the time. The techniques of siegecraft frequently employed in the Scottish wars are vividly illustrated, and again a central feature of the account is the presence of a heroic leader and his nobles. Senior commanders accompanying the captain are especially notable in both texts. Just as *Richard Coeur de Lion* includes episodes illustrating the valour of two English nobles, Multon and Doilly, as well as King Richard, so *The Siege of Caerlaverok* praises not only Edward's direction of the siege but also the conduct of a nobleman in his army, Sir Robert Clifford, the Marshal of England, who is also given heroic stature. The poem indicates something of the development of siege technology in the thirteenth century, and testifies to the continuance of literary methods of presenting siege warfare, as developed in earlier epic literature, in later texts of English provenance. In its presentation of chivalry at a siege of contemporary history using techniques derived from epic literature, *The Siege of Caerlaverok* may be compared to the presentation of warfare by the Anglo-Norman chronicler Jordan Fantosme. Fantosme is similarly patriotic on the side of the English and also takes a particular interest in the qualities and skill displayed by commanders at sieges and in battle generally.[20]

Before the description of the siege itself, *The Siege of Caerlaverok* describes the raising of nobles for the expedition, and shows us the army, led by Prince Edward, filling the outlying countryside with the sound of their horses and the sight of their carriages carrying tents and provisions (1–27). The knights who are to accomplish the siege are described in the poem with frequent reference to heroes of epic and romance, preparing us for a story of an epic conflict. The comparison of living heroes with the worthies or other literary models is a common feature of other writings concerning the chivalric virtues of real figures: Ambroise is deeply influenced by the 'chansons de geste' and compares Richard and

---

California State College Publications, 2 (Hayward, Calif., 1967), 5–20. Quotation: N. Denholm-Young, 'The Song of Carlaverok and the Parliamentary Roll of Arms as found in Cott. MS Calig. A. XVIII in the British Museum', *PBA* 47 (1961), 251–62 (255).

[20] See e.g. Fantosme's account of a siege of Carlisle, ll. 645–764. His treatment of this episode is compared to the *Chanson de Roland* by S. Fleischman, 'On the Representation of History and Fiction in the Middle Ages', *History and Theory*, 22 (1983), 278–310, esp. 296–7.

his army to great warriors of the past. During the description of the siege of Carcassonne in the Provençal song of the Albigensian crusade, Charlemagne's own legendary seven-year siege of that town is alluded to, drawing an explicit parallel between the commanders of past and present.[21] The style of *The Siege of Caerlaverok* similarly suggests earlier epic ideas and models, and the poem throughout suggests a natural affinity between the English knights and the heroes of epic.

After the long heraldic description of the banners of the 'compaignons', the poet goes on to describe their camp, where the various siege engines which are to be the principal method of attack are prepared: 'Ainz i aura trait e lancié, / Engin levé e balancié, / Com nous vous en aviseroms' (589–91) ('Then there will be arrow and lance, engine arranged and fired, as we shall show you'). The castle itself is well defended by the sea to the north and west, and by woods and marshes to the south. It is thus only accessible from the east, and has the capacity to withstand a long siege, being well provisioned 'De gens, de engins e de vitaile' (599) ('with people, engines and food') and constructed like a shield with three points, each guarded by a strong tower and other defences including a ditch (598–609). The English prepare for a possible blockade, setting up tents which are described as houses built without carpenters or masons (645–9).

The English engines and further provisions arrive by ship and the siege begins, apparently without any opening parley (657–68). In the poet's careful account of the combat, the stages of the operation are clearly set out. First the foot-soldiers commence an assault close to the castle, throwing stones, arrows, and bolts; the defenders use the same weapons and there is much ensuing slaughter. The scene is vividly described, with close attention given to arms and the order of events:

> E lors descendirent nos genz
> A ki tantost si bien avint
> Ke la navie a tere vint
> O les engins e la vitaile
> E ja commençoit la pietaile
> Au devant du chastel aler.

---

[21] *The Siege of Caerlaverok* includes references to Guy of Warwick (185) and Arthur (532). Ambroise's work contains a passage in which the leaders of the crusading army are implicitly compared to Alexander, Arthur, Charlemagne, and other heroes (4180–94). *Chanson de la Croisade Albigeoise*, i. 64. See M. Keen, 'Chivalry, Heralds and History', in R. H. C. Davis and J. M. Wallace-Hadrill (eds.), *The Writing of History in the Middle Ages: Essays Presented to Richard William Southern* (Oxford, 1981), 393–414 (398).

> Si veïst on entre eus voler
> Pieres, sajettes, e quareaus.
> Mes tant chier changent lour meraus
> Cil de dedenz a ceus dehors
> Ke en petite houre plusours cors
> I ot e blesciez e navrez
> E ne sai quanz a mort livrez.
>
> (656–68)

Then our men went down, and happily the navy landed with the engines and provisions. And then the foot-soldiers began to advance to the castle. Then one saw stones, arrows, and bolts fly between them. But those within and those without exchange their blows so dearly that in a short time there were many wounded bodies, and I do not know how many slain.

The men-at-arms follow the foot-soldiers without speaking, such is their hurry despite the hail of great stones. Our attention is drawn to their arms and devices as they advance with 'meinte targe freschement / Peinte e guarnie richement, / Meinte heaume e meint chapeau burni' ('many shields freshly painted and richly decorated, many helmets and polished headpieces'). In this combination of violence and visual elegance, the lord of Kirkebride reaches the main eastern gate and strikes at it with a hammer; at the same time a mine is laid. The weapons used by the defenders include the same items of artillery used in defence in *The Prose Siege of Thebes*—crossbows (or arbalests), a springald or espringale, and other, unnamed throwing devices (804–49).

One of the attackers, 'Brother Robert', operates a stone-throwing machine referred to as 'robinet', possibly a small trebuchet: engines of the same name used by Richard at Acre (according to the romance) and by Edward I at Stirling have already been noted. It is finally the three great engines of the English which reduce the castle, being too powerful for the walls to withstand. Again the description is far from artless, bringing home the huge power of siege artillery against a fortress not designed to withstand such a battering:

> De autre part oncore i levoit
> Trois autres enginz mult plus granz.
> E il, penibles e engrans,
> Ke le chastel du tout confonde
> Tent e retent, met piere en fonde,
> Descoche e quanques ateit fent,
> A ses coups rien ne se deffent.
>
> (902–8)

On the other side were raised up three much bigger engines, painful and assidu-
ous, which entirely confound the castle, reaching it again and again and landing
stones deep inside, and as they hit it, nothing can be defended against their
blows.

The defenders show a pennon as a sign of surrender; King Edward
grants his captives their lives and, continuing the theme of wardrobe description, gives orders for them to be given new clothes (921–41). This
portrait of a commander at a siege showing mercy towards the defeated,
and even concern for their material and sartorial welfare, is unusual in
literature on siege warfare, and markedly different from Richard and his
apprentice commanders joking about decapitation in the desert. The
quality of compassion, despised by Richard, is here given respectful attention, perhaps under the influence of chivalric writing, and, of course,
perhaps because that is what really happened. Edward's banner is raised
above the captured castle together with those of Saints Edmund,
George, and Edward and three of his generals, including the chief
leader, Sir Robert Clifford, 'A ki li chasteaus fu donnez' (951) ('to whom
the castle was given'). As in the romance of Richard, the display of banners reinforces our sense of the siege as a victory for a larger group as
well as a personal one for the commander.

By the end of *The Siege of Caerlaverok* we are left in no doubt of
Edward's skill in capturing castles, which he had already established in
his earlier sieges at Northampton in 1264 and Kenilworth in 1266. The
presentation of the events of the siege allies the English nobles with the
heroes of romance; the treatment of the enemy by the poet is as beneficent as that shown by Edward himself. They are gently admonished
for their foolish pride in thinking they could resist the English king, but
otherwise they receive a complimentary portrayal as warriors fighting
with a desperate energy. The element of a moral victory, loudly pro-
claimed in the crusading sieges, is absent.

THE SIEGE OF BERWICK IN BARBOUR'S Bruce

The unsuccessful siege of Berwick in 1319 by the English under
Edward II is the subject of Book XVII of Barbour's *The Bruce* (1375).
This is one of the most detailed descriptions that exists of a siege in the
non-chronicle literature of the period, and, like *The Siege of Caerlaverok*,
it provides one of the less important conflicts of the Scottish wars with
a dramatized, heroic treatment. Both poems give a fuller account of the

siege they are concerned with than can be found in contemporary chronicles, and the present discussion will therefore be limited to Barbour's text.

Barbour celebrates the vigorous defence of Berwick and the cunning of Robert the Bruce in diverting the English army with a series of raids in Yorkshire. He does, however, also give detailed accounts of the preparations of the English attackers, and, though his sympathies are clearly with the Scots, the story of the siege is not entirely written from their point of view. More than the author of *The Siege of Caerlaverok*, Barbour shows an interest in the details of strategy and equipment as well as the qualities of the participants. His exact sources for the depiction of the siege are not known, though, as his most recent editors remark, 'it is impossible to read the remarkably detailed and well ordered account of the Scottish defence without assuming some written source, that of some Scots cleric and perhaps the lost chronicle of the herald Robert le Roy'. One could also easily imagine some oral source or sources in which the feats of the defenders might have been preserved; there remain some traces of a song sung by the Scottish after the relief at Berwick, perhaps a fragment of an extensive tradition of songs and ballads of battle.[22]

Book XVII begins with an account of the seizure of Berwick by the Scots through trickery, the counter-attack by the English, and the eventual Scottish capture of the town, after the castle has held out for a further five days (1–200). The governorship of the town, 'And the castell and the dongeoun' (224) is given by Robert the Bruce to Walter of Scotland, the hero of the siege. The reference to castle and dungeon, or keep, reminds us that the siege of a town only finally ended when the keep of the castle had been taken.[23] The central tower or fortress of a besieged town comes to have a particular importance in writings on sieges, as it was literally the place of last resort: in Troy, it is the palace-fortress Ilion which is held to symbolize the city and its culture, a reflection of medieval castle architecture.

Awaiting English attempts at recapture, Walter provides Berwick with enough provisions for a year, and a garrison including five hundred nobles 'that bar armys of awncestry' (238) to withstand a year's siege

---

[22] Comment in 'Barbour's history and its sources', in *The Bruce*, i, 38–45. See R. M. Wilson, 'More lost literature in Old and Middle English', *LSE* 5 (1936), 1–49 (43). See also J. A. W. Bennett, *Middle English Literature*, ed. and completed by D. Gray (Oxford, 1986), 101.

[23] P. Warner, *The Medieval Castle: Life in a Fortress in Peace and War* (London, 1971), 42–3.

(225–38). Walter also employs the services of John Crab, a Fleming and an expert in siegecraft, who immediately assembles an artillery of espringales, 'engynys', shot (stones for casting), Greek fire, and, more unusually, cranes (239–52). This text is the first in which we have encountered the figure of the master engineer, though Brother Robert in *The Siege of Caerlaverok* may play a similar role. Master engineers appear in medieval writing from at least the thirteenth century. One of the best known is Master Bertram, an architect employed as a royal engineer by Henry III and later in charge of the engines at some of Edward I's sieges in Wales.[24]

Barbour tells his readers that cannon were not used in Scotland at this time:

> Bot gynnys for crakys had he nane
> For in Scotland yeit than but wene
> The ws of thaim had nocht bene sene.
>
> (250–2)

A similar phrase, 'crakkis of war', is used in a text relating to Edward I's first campaign in Scotland, at Brechin, and is thought to be one of the earliest references to cannon.[25] The description of the siege of Berwick in this respect represents a turning point in the history of siege warfare: the defenders appear to be aware of the introduction of gunpowder in some form (possibly the tube used to fire bolts or arrows rather than shot, as illustrated in the Walter de Milemete manuscript) and are using older engines with all the sophistication and ingenuity they can.[26] Later Barbour mentions that the Scots first encountered cannon when they defeated the army of Edward II at Weardale in 1329 (XIX. 399).

Edward II is told of the loss of Berwick and sets out to recapture it with an army under the Earl of Lancaster (261–94). As in *The Siege of Caerlaverok*, attention is paid to the gathering of the army, the use of ships to transport ammunition, engines, and provisions, and to the sight of the camp of the besieging army, which, Barbour tells us, resembles a town: 'That thai a toune all sone maid thar / Mar than bath toun and castell war' (301–2). The harbour is filled with English ships. In contrast

---

[24] Bradbury, 254–5.

[25] See O. F. G. Hogg, *English Artillery, 1326–1716* (London, 1963), 196. Bradbury, 145.

[26] The cannon pictured in the Walter de Milemete manuscript (1326), presented to Edward III on his accession, is the earliest Western representation of this weapon: Oxford, Christ Church, MS 92, fo. 70v.

to the army at Caerlaverok, which is depicted as a small heroic band of 'compaignons' similar to Charlemagne and his peers, the force assembled outside Berwick is notable for its sheer size: the description of the great army lodged in pavilions reminds us of the army of Adrastus in *The Prose Siege of Thebes*. Barbour goes on to describe the preparations for assault: the English surround their camp with ditches, display their banners, and assemble

> With instrumentis of ser maneris
> As scaffaldis leddris & couering
> Pikkys howis & with staf-slyng.
>
> (342–4)

The 'covering' refers to the protective hide covering to be put over the scaling ladders and scaffolds in case of Greek fire and other combustibles being used in defence. As at the siege of Thebes, picks are prepared for mining, along with hoes. The 'staf-slyng' is probably a trebuchet, as this operates like a sling on a long beam or staff.

Having prepared their artillery and mining equipment, the English signal their assault with trumpets. Where the attackers of Caerlaverok were depicted rushing forward together in no apparent order to the castle walls without pausing to speak, here a highly organized strategy is shown: each soldier goes to his assigned place, and, under cover of archery fire, the dykes are filled to allow the scaling ladders to be brought to the walls (355–73). Barbour emphasizes the valour of the defenders, in knocking down the ladders and preventing the English from entering the town, pointing out twice in his narrative that the walls of Berwick were low and thus vulnerable to this form of assault (379, 729). A picture is created of a small and recklessly courageous group of defenders, surrounded by a vast and well-equipped army, and succeeding against overwhelming odds (389–96).

The English now try to attack from the harbour side, towing a ship to the wall with barges and attempting to lower a bridge from it to the town walls. The lack of a master strategist on the English side is felt here, as the Scots simply wait for the tide to go out and then rush out to the stranded vessel and set fire to it, in the process capturing an English 'engynour' whose skills they will employ later for their own purposes (398–437). Demoralized by the loss of the ship, and by the persistence of the defenders, the English sound a retreat and temporarily raise the siege following this failed first assault. During a lull of five days, we are given a glimpse of the long periods which would often elapse between assaults and battles in sieges: doctors are busy on either side, and watches are constantly kept. In keeping with common practice, a truce is agreed, during which neither side harms the other (438–90).

Robert the Bruce has meanwhile gathered a larger relief force, but decides against risking a battle against the English army. Instead, he sends the earls of Murray and Douglas on a campaign in the north of England, which eventually leads Edward to call off the siege. The English army, unaware that it has been outflanked in this manner, renews its attempts to capture Berwick. Barbour shows a great interest in the new engines which the English have constructed, such as the scaffolds which are taller than the town walls, and describes in some detail the 'sow' under which the miners will work:

> Off gret gestis a sow thai maid
> That stalwart heildyne abon it had
> With armyt men inew tharin
> And instrumentis for to myne,
> Syndry scaffaldis thai maid with-all
> That war weill heyar than the wall,
> And ordanyt als that be the se
> The toun suld weill assaillyt be.
>
> (597–604)

The 'heildyne' or covering would be made of hide over a rectangular timber frame, possibly reinforced with iron and steel. Sows could be large enough to provide cover for as many as four hundred soldiers, and clearly a large version is referred to here. The next hundred lines of the book are largely concerned with the various means attempted by the defenders to destroy the sow. First they prepare a variety of combustibles and heavy objects, including pitch, tar, lint (the inflammable refuse of flax), hards (the coarser part of flax), brimstone, timber, and a great quantity of faggots. When the sow approaches the wall, chains from the crane will hold it in position while this mixture is dropped on it:

> Thai fagaldis brynnand in a baill
> With thar cran thocht thai till awaill,
> And gyff the sow come to the wall
> To lat it brynnand on hyr fall
> And with stark chenyeis hald it thar
> Quhill all war brynt wp that thar war.
>
> (619–24)

Walter also has his artillery prepared, and, like Ethiocles preparing his defences in Thebes, ensures personally that each defender is in position (628–31).

When the English once again sound their trumpet for an assault, the attempts at scaling are repulsed, but the sow becomes threatening. The English engineer captured from the ship is threatened with death unless he finds a way to defeat the sow as it approaches the wall. He pulls the 'cleket' or trigger on a stone-throwing engine, and with the third cast manages to hit the sow, which is then set on fire by Crab with his fire-wielding crane. The episode has a strikingly dramatic and realistic tone, giving detailed information on the various casts with the engine and describing the rapid thoughts of the engineer, the cries of the soldiers in the sow in direct speech, and the jubilation of the defenders (658–710). The crane is an unusual element in the siege, as is the fortified platform on the mast of a ship, from which the English again attempt to mount an assault, only to be driven back by the engine (711–21). The fact that it was the engines that defeated Caerlaverok, while an English engineer is here using one against his own side with great effect, suggests that the English had a particular reputation for this aspect of siege warfare in the Scottish wars. Barbour praises the extraordinary courage of the Scots rather than their technical expertise, for which they depend on a Fleming and a captured Englishman. From this method of presentation, and the earlier comment on their not having gunpowder, one may infer that Scotland had remained peripheral to the important developments in siege warfare taking place in Europe: cannon artillery is not recorded as being in use in Scotland before 1384.[27] The siege of Berwick depicts doughty Scots continuing the older methods of siege defence while trained foreign engineers are given the task of using more advanced machines.

The English attempt to set fire to the 'barreris' (probably palisades) and the drawbridge, but, when this fails like the earlier mining and naval assaults, they return to hand-to-hand fighting by the walls before retreating at night, expressing astonishment at the vigorous defence. The element of the marvellous or miraculous, an important one in *Richard Coeur de Lion*, appears when Barbour recounts the extraordinary fact that women with children came up to the walls in the thick of the battle without any of them being killed or wounded, which he attributes to 'the myrakill of God almichty / And to noucht ellys it set can I' (825–6).

---

[27] P. Contamine, *War in the Middle Ages*, trans. M. Jones (Oxford, 1984), 140.

The siege is not renewed, as King Edward decides to raise it when news comes to him of the campaign in York. The book concludes with praise of the courage and cunning, or 'manheid' and 'sutelte', by which Berwick was saved, the subtlety referred to being Robert the Bruce's diversionary tactic (911). Walter Stewart is rewarded for his heroic defence of the town, especially for his part in the protection of the bridge, and Barbour comments that he would have been far more famous and ennobled had he not died shortly afterwards (912–46). Besides this, Barbour offers little commentary on the siege of Berwick, which was recaptured by Edward III in 1333.

THE SIEGE OF METZ IN THE ALLITERATIVE
Morte Arthure

The alliterative *Morte Arthure*, composed in the late fourteenth or early fifteenth century, has been described as 'primarily a poem of battles'.[28] It shows King Arthur fighting wars of foreign conquest, generally according to the military practice of the fourteenth century. The sieges of Metz, Como, and Milan give a dramatic impression of siege warfare in Europe in the later fourteenth century, though the picture is, as we shall see, slightly antiquated in some respects, like that in *The Prose Siege of Thebes*. Besides showing a detailed knowledge of the military tactics employed at a siege, the author of the *Morte Arthure* also includes detailed accounts of the diplomacy surrounding siegecraft and other forms of warfare.[29] In the scenes of the council of war held by Arthur and his knights, and their various parleys, the justification of war and the notion of chivalrous conduct by a commander emerge as important themes: in this respect the poem is similar to treatises on these subjects, such as Honoré Bonet or Bouvet's *Arbre des batailles* (*c.*1387) or Ramon Llull's book on the order of chivalry (*c.*1311), which Caxton translated from an intermediary French rendering. In his portrait of Arthur, the poet may have been drawing on recent chronicles and chivalric biographies such as the Chandos Herald's life of the Black Prince as well as older French and English romances. The depiction of warfare in the poem thus exhibits a combination of practical detail, chivalric and legal theory, and

[28] L. D. Benson (ed.), *King Arthur's Death: The Middle English 'Stanzaic Morte Arthure' and 'Alliterative Morte Arthure'* (Exeter, 1986), p. xv.
[29] See J. Wurster, 'The Audience', in K. H. Göller, (ed.), *The Alliterative Morte Arthure: A Reassessment of the Poem* (Cambridge, 1981), 44–56.

the concepts of chivalry and heroism as expressed in epic and popular verse.[30]

The siege of Metz illustrates all these aspects of the poem. Parallels have been suggested for the siege from the campaigns of Edward III in the Hundred Years War, but it is more likely that the poet is drawing on his evidently extensive knowledge of late fourteenth-century siegecraft as well as inherited literary conventions, without meaning to represent any one event in particular.[31] His interest in chivalry and in military conventions is shown in the description of Arthur's conduct of the campaign against the Roman emperor, and in the detailed account of the treatment of the defeated enemy. It is the legal justifications for the siege with which we will begin, however: more interest in this subject is shown in this text than in the others considered in this chapter, where the rightness of the cause is apparently assumed and it is always clear where the poet's sympathies lie. Here the grounds for the siege are explored in some detail, and the presentation of the siege itself is conditioned by the poet's attitude to its legal and ethical justification.[32]

Like Chaucer's knight, the Arthur depicted in this work has been regarded as a morally flawed figure, whose supposed heroism is tarnished by involvement in unjust and cruel sieges.[33] The siege of Metz represents a turning point in the alliterative *Morte Arthure*. Arthur had originally gone to war in defiance of demands for tribute from Lucius, the Roman emperor, to reclaim lost rights and territories, and to rescue the inhabitants of these territories from imperial oppression. These were regarded as legitimate causes of war in juridical writings of the time, but 'a just war could not be motivated by an unalloyed desire for conquest,

[30] On related chivalric texts, see J. Finlayson (ed.), *Morte Arthure*, York Medieval Texts (London, 1967), 12. On the Chandos Herald as a possible source, see J. Finlayson, '*Morte Arthure*: The Date and a Source for Contemporary References', *Speculum*, 42 (1967), 624–38.
[31] The siege of Hennebont (1342) is suggested as a parallel by G. Neilson:'*Morte Arthure* and the War of Brittany', *N&Q*, 9th ser. 10 (1902), 161–5.'The Baulked Coronation of Arthur in *Morte Arthure*', *N&Q*, 9th ser. 10 (1902), 381–3, 402–4. The siege of Calais (1346–7) is proposed as a model by W. Matthews, *The Tragedy of Arthur* (Berkeley and Los Angeles, 1960), 186. These arguments are convincingly challenged by G. R. Keiser,'Edward III and the Alliterative *Morte Arthure*', *Speculum*, 48 (1973), 37–51.
[32] See J. Vale, 'Law and Diplomacy in the Alliterative *Morte Arthure*', *NMS* 23 (1979), 31–46.
[33] See T. Jones, *Chaucer's Knight: Portrait of a Medieval Mercenary* (London, 1980). M. H. Keen,'Chaucer's Knight, the English Aristocracy and the Crusades', in V. J. Scattergood (ed.), *English Court Culture in the Later Middle Ages* (New York, 1983), 45–61. There is a useful consideration of the issues by E. Porter, 'Chaucer's Knight, the Alliterative *Morte Arthure*, and Medieval Laws of War: A Reconsideration', *NMS* 27 (1983), 56–78.

glory or wealth'.[34] It was recognized by Bouvet that just wars could be perverted into acts of illegal violence, pursued for greed rather than in self-defence.[35] This may be what is happening in this case: Arthur has defeated the Romans, but chooses to continue the war with campaigns in France and Italy, referred to as Lorraine and Lombardy. His motives seem to be mixed: he has a score to settle with the Lord of Lorraine, who has rebelled against him, but he goes on to claim that he will establish law in Lombardy, 'The tyrauntes of Tuskan tempest a little' (2408). The council ends with pious declarations by Arthur that God must not be offended in the battle and thus ministers and properties of the Church are not to be harmed (2412–15). Nowhere does he claim that the war is in any sense a restitution of his own rights, as were the wars against the Romans, which has led some readers to see the siege of Metz as the point at which Arthur's wars cease to be just and become 'wars of aggression and acquisition', equivalent to the earlier devastation of France by Lucius.[36] A siege campaign in Italy had, however, been one of Arthur's original aims in the war; he seems to forecast this in the first council of war in England. The passage reflects the dominance of this form of warfare in the Hundred Years War:

> I sall at Lammesse take leue,   to lenge at my large
> In Lorayne or Lumberdye,   whethire me leue thynkys;
> Merke vnto Meloyne   and myne doun the wallez
> Bathe of Petyrsande and of Pys   and of the Pounte Tremble;
> In the vale of Viterbe   vetaile my knyghttes,
> Suggourne there sex wokes   and solace my selfen,
> Send prekers to the price toun   and plaunte there my segge
> Bot if thay profre me the pece   be processe of tym.
>
> (349–56)[37]

Following the legally dubious decision to continue with this campaign, Arthur and a small company of knights then ride on to Metz, 'That es in Lorrayne alosed,   as London es here' (2418), and look for the positions for their siege engines. The defenders scowl at Arthur

---

[34] F. H. Russell, 'Love and Hate in Medieval Warfare: The Contribution of Saint Augustine', NMS 31 (1987), 108–24 (114). For wider discussion, see id., The Just War in the Middle Ages (Oxford, 1975).

[35] H. Bonet, L'Arbre des batailles, ch. 79. See N. A. R. Wright, 'The Tree of Battles of Honoré Bouvet and the Laws of War', in C. T. Allmand (ed.), War, Literature and Politics in the Late Middle Ages (Liverpool, 1976), 12–31 (15), which also explains the inconsistency over Bonet/Bouvet spellings (12 n. 2).

[36] Morte Arthure, ed. Finlayson, 81.   [37] References are to Hamel's edition.

('Bekers ... with bustous lates') and aim at him with crossbows (2420–7). Arthur is not wearing armour, and when he is rebuked by Sir Ferrer for this, he replies scornfully that a crowned king may never be killed by a 'harlotte' (2446). This behaviour strengthens any earlier suspicion that Arthur has become a belligerent warlord and is falling into the vice of 'surquidrie' or pride, against which he has been warned in a dream: the ensuing siege illustrates this change in his character.[38]

The rest of Arthur's army joins Arthur at Metz; the scouts, foragers, and infantry are mentioned together with the knights. Here the poet shares Barbour's interest in the organization of an army as a whole; other texts we have considered concentrate mainly on the nobles involved, and pay scant attention to support forces. There is the conventional description of the raising of banners at the camp and, without any opening parley, the siege begins (2448–63). The suburbs outside the city walls are searched carefully in case of ambush, and there is a skirmish with the 'shot-men' or archers, the shield-bearers and guards on the outer defences. Metz is, like the besieged towns in other texts so far discussed, depicted as a castle: a barbican, or outer gatehouse, guards the drawbridge to the main gate, or 'grete gates'. Arthur's knights are able to defeat the defenders at the barbican but are repulsed at the main gate, and have to return to camp to escape being crushed by the drawbridge being raised on them:

> Thane the price men prekes   and proues theire horsez,
> Satills to the cité   appon sere halfes,
> Enserches the subbarbes   sadly thareaftyre,
> Discoueris of schotte-men   and skyrmys a lyttill,
> Skayres thaire skottefers   and theire skowtte-waches,
> Brittenes theire barrers   with theire bryghte wapyns,
> Bett down a barbycan   and the brygge wynnys;
> Ne hade the garnyson bene gude   at the grete gates,
> Thay hade wonn that wone   by wyghtnesse of hondys.
> Than withdrawes oure men   and drisses them bettyre,
> For dred of the drawe-brigge   dasschede in sondre.

(2464–74)

After this first assault, which apparently takes the defenders by surprise, the English army pitch their silken tents, set watches, and arrange their siege engines. Arthur observes that the French are short of food,

---

[38] *Morte Arthure*, ed. Finlayson, 19. On Arthur's fall, see L. D. Benson, 'The Alliterative *Morte Arthure* and Medieval Tragedy', *TSL* 11 (1966), 75–87.

and sends a foraging party under Florent and Gawain to gather provisions for his own army from the neighbouring mountains and forests (2473–500). One literary source which has been suggested for this foray is the French romance *Le Fuerre de Gadres*, in which Alexander sends a party out during the siege of Tyre.[39] A contemporary audience recognizing the inspiration for this structure might also remember the presentation of Alexander in this part of the French poem as a rash and cruel commander, whose army suffers great deprivation; the echo could only add to a sense of discontent with Arthur's management of the siege.[40]

The poem follows the fortunes of the foraging party, and, continuing the parallels with the earlier romance on Alexander, the poet describes the battle between Gawain and Priamus. We return to the siege of Metz just as Arthur is mounting a full-scale assault with a siege tower ('somer-castel'), a sow, scaling ladders defended by shield-bearers ('skotifers'), and stone-throwing engines:

> The kynge than to assawte   he sembles his knyghtez,
> With somercastell and sowe   appon sere halfes;
> Skiftis his skotiferis   and skayles the wallis,
> And iche wache has his warde,   with wiese men of armes.
> Thane boldly thay buske   and bendes engynes,
> Payses in pylotes   and proues theire castes.

$$(3032–7)$$

The poet pays less attention than Barbour in *The Bruce* to the details of strategy or weaponry, mentioning instead a few details of the assault to give the reader a dramatic visual impression of the siege. The siegecraft itself is somewhat antiquated for the late fourteenth century. Once again, real cannon are excluded, though they may have been used in a real siege of Metz in 1324, were employed by Edward III at the siege of Calais (1346–7), and are recorded as being in use in France from 1338.[41] Treatises and chronicles roughly contemporary with the alliterative *Morte Arthure* include detailed descriptions of cannon, as we saw in the last chapter, and it is unlikely that a poet with such a strong interest in warfare could have been unaware of these developments. Other dated elements are the use of shields as protection by miners and scalers, which fell out of practice in the latter part of the fourteenth century.[42]

[39] *Morte Arthure*, ed. Finlayson, 32.
[40] See W. Matthews, *The Tragedy of Arthur* (Berkeley and Los Angeles, 1960), 44–7.
[41] Contamine, *War in the Middle Ages*, 139–40.
[42] See Vale, 'Law and Diplomacy in the Alliterative *Morte Arthure*', 31–46 (44).

Like *The Prose Siege of Thebes*, the alliterative *Morte Arthure* eschews describing a contemporary siege and depicts instead an earlier medieval
encounter, in which siege engines but not cannon are used. This may be
the result of adherence to an older literary tradition, and adds to the
impression that writers of the later Middle Ages felt that it would be
difficult to depict heroism or chivalry at a siege if guns were used. The
description of the siege represents a conflict felt between inherited ideals
and the experience of contemporary practice, a problem which taxed
other romance writers. Gunpowder and guns were criticized by several
writers as diabolical inventions, and this may have influenced the depiction of the subject in narrative literature where chivalry is an important
theme.[43]

The description of the siege of Metz continues with a picture of the
destruction and suffering within Metz itself under Arthur's bombardment, a subject which is given only the briefest attention in the treatments of other sieges previously discussed:

> Mynsteris and masondewes   they malle to the erthe,
> Chirches and chapells   chalke-whitte blawnchede—
> Stone stepells full styffe   in the strete ligges,
> Chawmbyrs with chymnés   and many cheefe inns—
> Paysede and pelid down   playsterede walles;
> The pyne of the pople   was peté for to here!
>
> (3038–43)

This has been described as 'a key passage, showing not only the tre-
mendous destructiveness of Arthur's engines but the corruption of his
purposes', since it emphasizes the destruction caused to religious build-
ings despite Arthur's earlier promise to 'spare the spirituell' (2414).[44]
The historical background to the scene is a complicated one and does
not facilitate easy conclusions as to whether the poet is being deliberately critical or presenting the facts of siege warfare as they were at the
time. It is important to remember the difference between pious intentions or a codified set of conventions and the messy and often anarchic
reality of battle. Churches and ministers were supposedly safe when a
town was stormed in sieges of the later Middle Ages, but the convention was not always observed. If an assault succeeded, the lives of all the

---

[43] On the presentation of combat, see M. A. Gist, *Love and War in the Middle English
Romances* (Philadelphia, 1947), ch. 8, 'Conduct on the Battlefield', 155–90. Criticism of gunpowder: Contamine, *War in the Middle Ages*, 138.

[44] Hamel's edition, 351.

defenders and their property were regarded as forfeit.[45] Consequently, close analogies to the assault on Metz from historical records are not difficult to find. The suffering depicted here and, later, at Como, where Arthur's army 'Stekes and stabbis thorowe   that them agayne-stondes' (3110) when they break into the town, is echoed in many late medieval sieges. John Gower admiringly describes the Black Prince as someone who 'attacked strongholds annihilating the people'; to the Burgher of Paris, writing in the early fifteenth century, general slaughter following an assault appears to be commonplace. Survivors of the English capture of Soissons in 1419 report that the English 'ont tué, navré tout ce qu'ils ont trouvé en leur voie' ('have killed and wounded all those they found in their path').[46] Froissart describes a comparable situation in the French siege of Breteuil, where the defenders, under constant heavy bombardment by engines, decided to sue for peace, knowing that 'if they were taken by assault, they would all be slaughtered without mercy'. After the capture of Poitou in 1346 by the Earl of Derby, his soldiers got out of control and 'put to the swerde, men, women and chyldren'. As at Metz, supposedly safe churches in Poitou are attacked, but the action of the Earl and Froissart's comment provide a context in which Arthur's action can be criticized: 'Dyvers churches were there distroyed and many yvell dedes done, and mo had ben done, and therle had not ben: for he commaunded on payne of dethe, no man to brenne no churche nor house, for he sayde he wolde tary there a ten or xii dayes, so that therby part of the yvell dedes were seased, but for all that there was roberyes ynough.'[47]

The defenders of Metz are thus in the same situation as numerous other beleaguered populaces of the fourteenth century, having no defence against constant bombardment by the English engines, and expecting only to be massacred once the English enter. While the destruction of church property might count as 'yvell dedes'—perhaps in a similar sense to a modern bomb landing on a civilian building—there was no surety in warfaring conventions for their own lives. Clemency would depend entirely on Arthur. In another frequent topic in siege

[45] See Keen, *The Laws of War in the Late Middle Ages*, 119–33, esp. 123–4. Bradbury, 317–24.

[46] John Gower, *Vox clamantis*, in *Complete Works*, iv. 257–8; trans. Stockton, 242. *Journal d'un bourgeois de Paris*, 144 (report of English brutality), 407 (French assault on Pontoise, where those in hiding are killed).

[47] Siege of Breteuil: J. Froissart, *Chronicles*, selections, trans. Brereton, 122. Siege of Poitou: Froissart, *Æuvres: Chroniques*, v. 112–16; trans. Berners, i, ch. 136, pp. 308–10.

descriptions, the ladies—here a duchess and the countess of Crasine inside the town—appeal to the siege commander to show mercy.

> We beseke yow, sir,   as soueraynge and lorde,
> That ye safe vs to-daye,   for sake of youre Criste:
> Send vs some socoure   and saughte with the pople,
> Or the ceté be sodaynly   with assawte wonnen!
>
> (3050–3)

Arthur here begins to appear in a more favourable light. He responds in chivalrous fashion, promising a 'charter of pees' to the noblewomen and their 'cheefe maydens' (3058), to the children and priests ('chaste men'), and to the knights, who in a real siege it would have been more usual to ransom. Similarly, after the capture of Como, Arthur forbids rape and indiscriminate killing by soldiers. The same instructions were given before the siege of Thebes by Adrastus, and differ markedly from the ruthlessness enjoined by the crusading champion Richard.

It is difficult to conclude whether the poet means us to see the siege of Metz as an illustration of brutal but necessary efficiency or as a stage in the moral degeneration of Arthur. In showing the waste of war, as he undoubtedly does, the author of *Morte Arthure* may be making a 'protest against the folly and unchristian cruelty of unjustified wars of the kind conducted by Alexander, Edward and Arthur of Britain'.[48] Such protest is tempered, however, by the depiction of Arthur avoiding further bloodshed by granting mercy to certain defenders and establishing order in his army. Against a background of indiscriminate slaughter at sieges and armies motivated by the prospect of looting and rape, Arthur's conduct of the siege, it has been suggested, 'should command admiration rather than horror, and his actions have a demonstrably legal basis'.[49] None the less, the emphasis on the destruction of churches and the suffering of the innocent hardly induces enthusiasm for Arthur's operation, and gives an ominous feel even to theoretically admirable behaviour. The siege is problematic, and a response which consists in unalloyed praise or criticism does not seem true to the difficult, and perhaps deliberate, ambivalence of the text.

Metz is surrendered unconditionally, and its duke is captured and sent to prison at Dover. The conventional emblem of possession, the banner, is raised on the battlements, and Arthur swiftly arranges for an ordered

---

[48] Matthews, *The Tragedy of Arthur*, 192.
[49] Vale, 'Law and Diplomacy in the Alliterative *Morte Arthure*', 39.

occupation of the town: the spoils are carefully divided among the knights, an estate is settled on the duchess, and wardens are appointed to keep law and order here and in other lands which Arthur has conquered. While the siege itself may have been dictated by mercenary motives, showing, together with the other details noted, some decline in Arthur's character, his command of the siege and his conduct in its aftermath have been both effective and, in a fourteenth-century context, lawful. Arthur's institution of a code of conduct among his soldiers to limit damage done after the siege is similar to the action taken by Edward III, who, on the first day of his invasion of Normandy in 1346, commanded that no one should harm any woman, child, or the elderly, rob a church or shrine, or burn any building. Edward's attempt at regulation, enforced, like Arthur's, by a system of constables and marshals, had only limited success, however.[50]

In the course of the battles and sieges in the rest of the *Morte Arthure* vivid images accumulate of the sufferings of ordinary people in Arthur's foreign wars: Arthur 'turmentez the pople . . . And all he wastys with werre thare he aweye rydez' (3153–6). It may fairly be read, 'at least in part, as a criticism of Edward's war policy', but in the description of the siege of Metz chivalric values are seen to persist and to be exemplified, if perhaps inconsistently, by Arthur himself.[51] By presenting the siege as one which might have taken place earlier in the fourteenth century but would have seemed old-fashioned at the time the poem was composed, the author evokes older values and practices alongside the details of modern fighting.

Besides the conduct of the siege itself, it is Arthur's justification for it and later his treatment of defenders which comes under scrutiny: in its interest in the issues of legal, diplomatic, and courteous conduct surrounding a siege, the *Morte Arthure* 'reflects a distinctly fourteenth-century chivalric ideal'.[52] In this respect it is similar to the short account of a siege as an exemplum of stoic princely conduct given by Antoine de la Sale in the first part of his *Le Reconfort de Madame de Fresne* (c. 1457). This brief piece presents a supposed siege of Brest by the Black Prince, and concentrates on the conventions of truce and hostages. The Black Prince holds as a captive the son of the defending commander, the

[50] J. Sumption, *The Hundred Years War: Trial by Battle* (London, 1990), 501.

[51] J. Barnie, *War in Medieval Society: Social Values and the Hundred Years War 1337–99* (London, 1974), Appendix D, '*Morte Arthure* and the Hundred Years War', 147–50 (147–8).

[52] G. R. Keiser, 'Narrative Structure in the Alliterative *Morte Arthure*, 26–720', *ChRev* 9 (1974–5), 130–44 (141).

Seigneur du Chastel, despite an earlier agreement that he would be released if supplies arrive. There is much legal argument among heralds,
and the piece presents an interesting example of a literary depiction of
the laws of war being observed at a siege. Eventually, the Seigneur has to
decide between the disgrace of surrender and the death of his son, and,
amid much weeping, he yields to the stoic counsel of Madame du
Chastel and sacrifices his son. There is some consolation in the fact that
the defenders in a sortie manage to capture four Englishmen, who are
maimed and executed, helping to persuade the Black Prince to raise the
siege, but one may doubt if Madame de Fresne, for whom the work was
written, was particularly cheered by this story. As in the *Morte Arthure*,
attention is focused on the conduct of the commander at a siege, the
deprivations suffered by the defenders, and the rituals surrounding
ceasefires and terms of surrender.

The depiction of siege warfare in the alliterative *Morte Arthure* thus
draws on sources in romance and possibly chivalric writing as well as
contemporary experience. It is perhaps this use of two separate sources
of imagery and ideas—the horrors of modern sieges and the more
idealized battles of literature—that results in the description of a siege
which suggests moral and legal issues without explicitly resolving them,
and evokes in an audience both dismay and admiration. The siege is an
episode in a biography of a prince, as in *Richard Coeur de Lion*, though
the examination of the hero's character is here more searching and
complex. General views of the poet's stance on warfare or the changes
in Arthur's character should not, however, deter us from seeing the siege
of Metz as being an example of a siege which is pursued efficiently and
settled, at least in the context of the brutal realities of the Hundred Years
War, with some degree of chivalry and justice.

In the texts considered in this chapter, the influence of the heroic
literary tradition is evident throughout, particularly perhaps in *The Siege
of Caerlaverok*. This sense of the formulations and topics appropriate
to the subject still allows for much variation by individual writers:
Barbour's close interest in particular events and strategies, for example,
is not shared to any great extent by the authors of the other pieces, who
prefer broader brushstrokes. The logistical background to sieges, from
the gathering and maintenance of an army to the relations between
leaders and the legal and moral justifications for war, also appear as a
major theme: writers appear to enjoy showing how things should be
done. There is a common interest in sieges of the past, and in the heroic
qualities of those who managed them, though these are also open to

examination and criticism, as in the *Morte Arthure*. Reliance on past models may itself imply an unease with present realities, and the romances, taken together, suggest some difficulty in coming to terms with the cruelties and mass destruction routinely inflicted by both sides in the brutal campaigns of the Hundred Years War. The depiction of sieges without guns is the most notable feature of this reluctance to update material, supporting a sense that the chivalric virtues which interest the authors were complicated by this development in siegecraft, and that the feeling of relation to older literary forms was at least as strong as any desire to record the contemporary practice of siege warfare. Commanders are perhaps heroic in so far as they are unrealistic in the context of late medieval warfare.

These commanders share basic qualities such as energy and expertise, but they are still interestingly varied. Richard is almost entirely destructive, while Edward I is an altogether more benevolent figure at Caerlaverok, his munificence towards defenders perhaps recalling an older type of prince, or the kind of courtesies which could be practised when the war is not of a religious or racist nature. At Berwick, Edward II is ineffective in attack, while Walter epitomizes the heroic defender, aware of his personal obligation to his lord, and, no doubt, of the disgrace which capitulation would entail. Finally there is Arthur, a commander much harder to categorize: he seems to represent an efficient type of leader with a sense of justice and compassion at the siege of Metz, even if his aims in war and subsequent practice of it invite criticism. In three of the four poems discussed, a depiction of victorious assault is couched in terms derived from the heroic tradition, and the same sense of past heroism is equally strong in the description of valiant defence in *The Bruce*. This last type of heroism should be explored further: at its highest level, the valour and suffering of the beleaguered brings them close to the presence of God.

3

Sieges and Salvation: Heroic Defences
at Rhodes and Belgrade and
The Sege of Melayne

HEROISM in defence became a particularly important concern in the fifteenth century, with various Turkish incursions in the Mediterranean and the East, principally the capture of Constantinople in 1453, evoking widespread fear across Europe. Writers of romances responded with accounts of sieges at which piety and courage are seen effecting miraculous salvations from larger and better-equipped Turkish forces. Romances in various Western countries reflect the anxiety felt at a time of Turkish expansion in Europe, and the need for popular chivalric heroes to defend the citadel of Christendom from the invaders.

The texts to be considered here describe the sieges of Rhodes in 1444 and 1480, of Belgrade in 1456, and the siege of Milan in the late English romance *The Sege of Melayne*: the last work does not appear to be closely based on historical reality, but it echoes several of the contemporary concerns apparent from the other pieces. The siege of Rhodes in 1444 is described in two Catalan texts: it is the subject of a poem by an eyewitness to the events, the merchant Francesc Ferrer, and is an episode in the long chivalric prose romance written mainly by Joanot Martorell, *Tirant lo Blanc* (1460–8, published 1490). Consideration of poems and romances written outside England shows the general interest in sieges taken by writers across Europe in the later Middle Ages, while comparison of the two accounts further illustrates some of the different approaches to the literary treatment of sieges taken by romancers. The confrontation of 1480 is recorded in a chronicle by William Caoursin, Vice-Chancellor of the Order of the Knights of St John who defended the island; the translation of this chronicle by the Englishman John Kaye shows how literary conventions of sieges influenced the way in which real ones were represented. Finally, the relief of Belgrade by Janós Hunyadi and Friar John Capistrano, as depicted in the late English romance *Capystranus*, and *The Sege of Melayne*, both metrical romances of similar content, provides further examples of the relationship in literature between the realities of war and the concepts of chivalry, as well as of the changes in siegecraft in the fifteenth century.

THE SIEGE OF RHODES, 1444: TWO CATALAN TEXTS

The island of Rhodes was occupied by the crusading order the Knights Hospitallers, or Knights of St John, early in the fourteenth century. As an outpost of Christendom with the capacity to exploit trading opportunities in the Mediterranean and to disturb Muslim shipping coming from Asia Minor, it was always a likely target for siege and blockade and defended itself accordingly, with a great castle overlooking the harbour and surrounded by the walls of the city.

As well as being an important base for the knights, the island was inhabited by Greek settlers and experienced a constant traffic of traders, particularly from Genoa, which financed the original occupation; merchants also came from Catalonia, Valencia, and Aragon, supported by King Alfonso the Magnanimous of Aragon. Fierce rivalry between Genoese and Catalans led the former to ally themselves with the Sultan of Egypt, Abusaïd Djakmak, who sent a navy to besiege the island in August 1444. An earlier expedition in 1440 had been called off when seventeen of the Egyptian vessels were lost.

The ensuing siege, which lasted for forty days, from 10 August to 18 September, is recorded in Western writings in the history of the Order of St John by Bosio, and in vernacular chronicles including that of Jean de Waurin.[1] One of the most detailed accounts of the siege is the 240-line poem *Romans de la armada del Soldà contra Rodes*, written by a merchant from Barcelona, Francesc Ferrer, who is also the author of a number of other poems on various subjects.[2] This piece, probably written shortly after the event it relates, is similar in some respects to earlier writings such as Abbo's account of the siege of Paris by the Danes: it seeks to give an informative historical account of events, paying attention to military strategy and to the conduct of the defending commander, the Master of the Order, Jean de Lastic. Like Abbo, Ferrer

---

[1] J. Bosio, *Dell'istoria della sacra religione et illustrissima militia di San Giovanni Gierosolimitano*, vol. i, part 2.

[2] References are to Auferil's edition. The earlier edition by d'Olwer contains a useful commentary.

emphasizes the piety of the defenders and the miraculous salvation which this brings about. Unlike Abbo, Ferrer is not a churchman. Nor is he a knight of the Order or one of the dignitaries of Rhodes, and his account reads as that of a passing merchant, caught up in the siege while probably not being directly involved in the fighting, strongly sympathetic to the defenders but far enough away from the principal conflicts and the actions of the townspeople to give a general view.

Ferrer's poem gives a straightforward narrative account of the siege, from the time of the arrival of the Turkish fleet to the day of their departure. He emphasizes the magnitude of the event, which only a witness could describe, and throughout the poem Ferrer attempts to convey the awesome drama and the emotions of the defenders, as well as giving a factual account. His poem is in part an example of Christian piety having spectacular consequences at a siege, and it also presents us with another picture of a heroic leader in the figure of Jean de Lastic.

Close attention is paid in the *Romans* to factual detail; the term 'romanç' itself seems to mean here 'historical account in verse', which would imply some attempt at verisimilitude.[3] Ferrer certainly has an eye for data: he distinguishes the various vessels of the Turkish fleet and counts eighty-five of them. He gives the exact date of their arrival—the tenth of August, St Laurence's day, 1444—and names their general, Aynal Gecut. The first battle is preceded by a description of the appearance of the 500 Mameluke cavalry and infantry. Other details include the names of the various churches in Rhodes where the defenders pray for help and the two principal scenes of battle, the towers of St Anthony and St Nicholas.

Ferrer includes the details of siegecraft in his account, although he seems more interested in the faith and courage of the knights and their leader than in their proficiency as soldiers. The battles he describes most vividly are the hand-to-hand combats beneath the towers and walls, with both sides fighting furiously and crying for aid to Mahomet, or St John or St George, the latter the patron saint of Catalonia, and one with particular crusading connections.[4] On the attacking side, we see the use of mining and bombardment with trebuchets, balistas, and conventional archery from behind a palisade, or fence, constructed close to the weakest part of the wall as cover for an attack. The Turkish engines cause several breaches, but despite renewed assaults on the gates and towers,

[3] On the meaning of 'Romans', see Auferil, 95–6.
[4] In the French version of *Octavian* there is an apparition of St George (ll. 4705–16), again indicating his significance in war.

the besiegers do not effect an entry. The defenders also use engines, which cause damage both to the besieging army and to their navy in the harbour.[5]

Gunpowder also makes an appearance in the reference to the 'colobrines' or culverins used by the defenders of Rhodes. These were early hand-guns, mentioned from about 1410 and in use at sieges in the earlier part of the fifteenth century alongside older forms of artillery: Don Pedro, brother of the King of Castile, was decapitated by gunshot at the siege of the castle of Capuana in Naples in 1438.[6] Ferrer writes, 'Los desparam ab colobrines prou' ('We fired at them, with culverins enough', 38). In contrast to the romances discussed earlier, guns are here part of the artillery of an exemplary Christian force at a siege, despite the sinister associations they had for writers such as John Mirfield, who referred in 1390 to 'Instrumento illo bellico sive diabolico quod vulgariter dicitur gonne' ('this warlike or diabolical instrument commonly called a gun').[7] Developments in artillery are here incorporated into a literary account which emphasizes the traditional heroic values of faith and valour. Ferrer does not refer extensively to the culverins, though: the relative absence of guns and technical detail from his account might indicate lack of comprehension of military detail by a merchant, or a familiar desire to present the conflict as an open and heroic battle in an older epic mould, uncomplicated by new inventions and technicalities.[8]

The chief weapon of the defenders is their faith. Ferrer devotes a considerable part of the poem to illustrating the piety of the knights and townspeople, even listing the various priests of the Greek and Latin churches who urge them in their devotions.[9] When the enemy fleet arrives, the fear of the people is assuaged by Jean de Lastic, who displays the ring of the Order and proclaims, 'Ecce Agnus Dei qui tollit peccata mundi' (24). Phrases from the Bible are repeated regularly in the course of the poem as the conclusion to each verse, portraying the siege as a battle between those with faith and God's enemies. The defenders reassure themselves by declaring that 'Qui babtitzatus fuerit salvus erit; qui vero non, condempnabitur' ('He who has been baptized shall be

[5]   Mining and artillery: ll. 97–104. Engines of defenders: ll. 105–8, 121–6.

[6]   M. Vale, *War and Chivalry: Warfare and Aristocratic Culture in England, France and Burgundy at the End of the Middle Ages* (London, 1981), 136–7.

[7]   BL, MS Harl. 3261, fo. 69r. Vale, *War and Chivalry*, 137. P. Contamine, *War in the Middle Ages*, trans. M. Jones (Oxford, 1984), 138.

[8]   A list of other weapons appears at ll. 135–7.

[9]   This is the main subject of verse 4, ll. 73–96.

saved, and he who has not shall be condemned', 72) and pray, 'A gente pagana libera nos, Domine' ('Free us from a pagan people, Lord', 96), as they walk through the streets. Awaiting a final assault which they have little hope of repulsing, the defenders prepare themselves for death, making their confession and forgetting old enmities. Together, they pray to the Virgin, and, miraculously, she is heard to intercede with Christ on their behalf. On the next day, during a battle beneath the tower of St Nicholas, the besieging army is turned back by the image of the Virgin on the battlements (verses 8–9).

The siege is thus depicted as a struggle by believers against a pagan army. There is an emphasis on the defenders as a whole, and on the piety which is born from their tribulation. As well as praising the valour of the knights, Ferrer's poem demonstrates the effect of being under siege on ordinary people: the townspeople become one univocal mass, thinking and praying alike. There is scarcely any suggestion that the people of Rhodes and the knights of the Order were of different countries, and were entrusted according to their nationality and language with the defence of specific parts of the city walls. In the siege, they are simply presented as Christians whose loyalty is to their fortress-town which has come to symbolize Christendom itself. Neither does Ferrer describe the rivalry between the Genoese and Catalans and Valencians in the Order, though there is a hint of politics in the remark that Jean de Lastic's plan to pursue the Egyptians by sea is not put into effect because of discord among the knights (225–9). Otherwise he prefers to describe the siege as an example of a beleaguered Christian populace redeemed from heathen invasion by the bravery of crusading knights through a miracle achieved by the power of prayer. The poem reads as an exemplary tale with universal implications for Christians, as well as a contemporary account of a historical siege. Just as the loss of towns in the Holy Land was often attributed to the sins of the Christians by poets and commentators, so the miraculous rescue of the besieged place suggests the salvation of the faithful soul, rewarded for its continued faith at a time of crisis.[10]

Ferrer's account of the siege is thus instructive and edifying: it records facts and gives the struggle a spiritual significance by emphasizing the religious belief of the defenders and the miracle of their salvation. The

[10] Ambroise states that Christians in the Eastern kingdom have been punished for their folly and that the fall of cities is retributive (*L'Estoire de la Guerre Sainte*, ll. 1–34). Similarly, the defeats of the Third Crusade are explained as the effect of sinning by Christians in *The Crusade and Death of Richard I*, ch. 2.

siege is essentially a crusading conflict between Christ's soldiers, who are here on the defensive side, and His enemies. A strikingly different approach to the same siege is taken by the Valencian writer Joanot Martorell, who uses it as the setting for an adventure by the eponymous hero of his long prose romance *Tirant lo Blanc*. Martorell's description presents the historical facts of the siege, of which the author could easily have been aware, selected and shaped to become part of a longer prose work describing the chivalric exploits of Tirant. Where Ferrer emphasizes the heroic virtues of unshakeable faith and bravery, Martorell is more concerned with using the siege of Rhodes to illuminate the chivalric qualities of loyalty, courtesy and etiquette, generosity, skill in warfare, and graceful eloquence, as exemplified by Tirant himself.

Warfare of various sorts forms a major part of *Tirant lo Blanc*, in which the hero fights the Turk throughout the Mediterranean and eventually saves Constantinople from assault: the long prose romance is an example of chivalric literature rewriting contemporary history and reflecting the ideal aspirations of readers at a time when reality seemed far less attractive. Expertise in siege warfare is illustrated in several other episodes of the book: in the earlier part, devoted to the exploits of Guy of Warwick, Guy saves the King of England from a siege by the King of Canary using caltrops, or metal balls with spikes, to disrupt the besiegers' advance (ch. 24). Later Tirant is seen supervising operations at a siege in North Africa, ordering a countermine to be filled with brass bowls which would rattle at the blows of the miners' pickaxes. In these details, Martorell seems to have been using a copy of the military treatise of Francesc Eiximenis, *Dotzè del Chrestià*, published in 1484. Like the redactor of Lydgate's book on Thebes, Martorell was clearly familiar with weapons and stratagems, as recorded in treatises and chronicles, and as experienced by his contemporaries.[11]

The depiction of the siege of Rhodes of 1444 in *Tirant lo Blanc* is based on close knowledge of the events, though these are freely altered or omitted to fit the purpose of the narrative, which is to show in Tirant how an ideal Christian knight would behave at a siege. The description of the siege in this work also provides an unusually detailed picture of the day-to-day existence of a threatened population and of the diplomacy of the commanders and nobles. Close interest is shown in

---

[11] See M. de Riquer, *Aproximació al Tirant lo Blanc*, Quaderns Crema, Assaig, 8 (Barcelona, 1990), 213–18.

ceremonies and rituals which are only cursorily described elsewhere. Martorell's account also illustrates the rise of the professional soldier. While Tirant is credited with relieving the island, strategy is left to veterans, whose specialist role recalls the skilled engineer hired by the Scots at Berwick. Advances in technology have produced the professional practitioner whose skill may exceed the conventional attributes of the chivalric nobleman: *Tirant lo Blanc* illustrates particularly clearly such changing patterns.

Martorell himself was in Valencia in 1444 and was thus not an eyewitness like Ferrer, but he could easily have heard first-hand accounts of the siege from the many Valencian merchants who were present. It is possible that he met Ferrer or read his poem, although there are no verbal parallels between the two works. From 1447 he would have been able to hear of the siege from his friend Jaume de Vilaragut, a Valencian privateer who participated in the defence of the island, and who was taken prisoner by the Sultan, escaping after only two days.[12] Another possible source of information, and a probable model for Tirant at Rhodes, was the Burgundian knight Geoffrey de Thoisy: even during his lifetime de Thoisy was a famous knight, who had served in numerous sieges for Philip the Good in France, and whose exploits at Rhodes resemble those of Tirant. Like Tirant, Geoffrey combined pious observance with soldiering, and made pilgrimages to the Holy Land between battles; his career reminds us that chivalric conduct at a siege in the fifteenth century does not belong only to the world of literature.[13]

Whatever his sources, Martorell takes a strong interest in the siege and, unlike Ferrer in the *Romans*, is equally fascinated by the political events surrounding it: in his account, the Genoese are at least as wicked as the Egyptians, if not worse. The episode of the siege is introduced when the Duke of Brittany and Tirant in Nantes are told of a failed Genoese attempt to capture the island, which has been followed by an Egyptian naval blockade. Jean de Lastic's plea for help to the Emperor and Christian princes, including the King of France, has met with little response. Tirant displays the chivalric virtue of loyalty to fellow Christians and of constant service to his lord. He wishes to sail to the relief of Rhodes at once:

Com Tirant sabé que tanta morisma estava sobre Rodes e que negú no els socorria, parlà ab molts mariners demanant-los de consell si seria possible que

[12] Ibid. 127–30.
[13] For a full discussion of sources, see C. Marinesco, 'Du nouveau sur *Tirant lo Blanch*', *ER* 4 (1953–4), 137–203, esp. 148–9 on de Thoisy.

ell los pogués socórrer. E digueren-li que si ell hi anava, així com deia, ell los
poria bé socórrer e poria entrar dins lo castell de Rodes, no envers la part del
moll, mas a l'altra part. (ch. 99, p. 167)

When Tirant learned that so many Saracens were threatening Rhodes and no
one would help, he spoke with many sailors, asking their advice if it would be
possible for him to help them. And they told him that if he went there, just as
he said, he would be able to help them and could enter the castle of Rhodes,
not through the harbour, but on the other side.

Tirant then follows a mainly land route to Rhodes, fighting at Gib-
raltar and along the African coast as far as Tunis. The attention given to
Tirant's chivalry and to the constant threat of Turkish invasion implies
a particular significance for Rhodes, which represents both assailed
Christendom and the virtues of the knights of St John: these appear to
be threatened with extinction, as they have clearly become a rare com-
modity in Western Europe.

Tirant's involvement in the action of the siege begins with the entry
of his 'grossa nau', a great ship large enough for four hundred soldiers,
into the harbour, blockaded by Genoese vessels. The spectacular entry
of a relieving commander recalls the arrival of the hero in *Richard Coeur
de Lion*, which gave rise to a separate legend of a miraculous leap on his
horse from ship to land.[14] The Genoese at first mistake Tirant's vessel
for one of their own supply ships and allow it to pass through, only identifying it as an intruder when it is too late and Tirant has sped through
to the shore. Throughout the episode, Martorell is more interested in
Tirant's model appearance and behaviour than in his warfaring exploits.
He enters the city finely dressed, accompanied by his men and admired
from the windows by women and maidens: Tirant is constantly associated with splendour and plenitude, and is warmly welcomed as a
bringer of provisions into the city in an exchange of formal speeches
with the Master of the Order.

Where Ferrer describes the terror of the people of Rhodes, Martorell
emphasizes their physical needs. In a scene similar to the one in *Richard
Coeur de Lion* where Richard is apprised by the Archbishop of Pisa of the
sufferings of the Franks, Tirant is told by Jean de Lastic of the problems
caused by the blockade: the people have been driven to eating horses
and cats, pregnant women have had abortions, and children are dying of
hunger. Tirant responds by having the many provisions on his ship

---

[14] The story is an example of strength of faith in the collection of edifying tales by Don
Juan Manuel, *El Conde Lucanor*: Exemplo Tercero, 'Del Salto que Fizo el Rey Richalte de
Inglaterra en la Mar contra los Moros' (pp. 67–72).

brought into the city square and carefully distributed among the towns-
folk; flour is provided for the long-disused mills. This again reminds us
of the romance of Richard the Lionheart and the mysterious mill-
engine which he brings to Acre.

In Ferrer's *Romans* there is much description of fierce fighting at the
siege. Martorell's version has little actual combat before the Egyptians
are eventually driven away, but concentrates instead on the discussions
between the principal defenders and the minor events taking place between battles. On the night of Tirant's arrival, his presence is celebrated
with bonfires and music, which causes some Egyptians to assume that
the island has been captured. Egyptians are regarded as contemptibly
ignorant; the craftier Genoans are said to be the real enemy. On the suggestion of a senior knight, food is sent to the Sultan to show him that the
town is well provisioned. The Sultan responds to this psychological
tactic by gravely thanking the Master for his generosity.

Tirant accompanies the Master on a tour of the defences. Meanwhile
a sailor in his company, promised a large reward if he fulfils a promise
made earlier to burn the ship of the Genoese captain, devises a plan.
Swimming undetected beneath the ships in the harbour, the sailor
manages to draw a rope through an iron ring below the rudder of the
captain's vessel so that a burning ship can be drawn alongside it. The
process is described in great detail, and the ensuing chaos is vividly presented:

los de la nau no pensaren altra cosa sinó de fugir ab les barques; altres se
llançaven en la mar per passar en les altres naus, per bé que no pogueren excusar
que molts n'hi moriren cremats per no haver temps de poder eixir, e a molts que
lo foc aconseguí dormint.

Los qui feien la guaita alt en lo castell anaren prestament a dir al Mestre . . .
(ch. 106, p. 187)

Those on the ship did not think of doing anything but fleeing with the boats;
others threw themselves in the sea to reach the other ships, though there were
many who burned as they did not have time to escape, and the fire reached
many while they were asleep.

Those on guard high in the castle went quickly to tell the Master . . .

Tirant rewards his sailor with 3,000 ducats, a robe, and a brocade
doublet. Yet it is Tirant who is later credited with raising the siege,
which is effectively accomplished by this one action. The episode illustrates a particular system of loyalty and reward, whereby the deed of the
sailor in Tirant's company reflects well on his master, Tirant, and
Tirant's contribution to the defence is in turn to the glory of his lord,

the Duke of Brittany. The code of chivalry appears to dictate that ordinary soldiers can be given material rewards, while the prize of lasting renown is reserved for noblemen.

The havoc in the harbour precipitates a retreat by the Sultan, during which many Egyptians are killed in ambushes led by Tirant. The account of the siege ends with the Master's formal speech of thanks, in which he begs Tirant to accept a reward and describes him as the epitome of chivalry. Here the extent to which the victory is presented as a personal feat of Tirant becomes clear, as the hero is depicted as a saintly or even a Christ-like figure:

Tu est estat consolació e vera salut de tots nosaltres, car gran temps havem estat ab molta fam e set e altres dolors e misèries que pernostres pecats comportades havem, e per tu sol havem obtesa via de salvació e llibertat, car tota la nostra esperança era ja perduda, que si tu no fosses vengut en aquell beneït dia, fóra desolada la nostra ciutat e tota la Religió. (ch. 107, p. 191)

You have been the consolation and the true health of us all, for during a long time we have suffered great hunger and thirst and other griefs and miseries which we have brought on ourselves by our sins, and by you alone we have gained the way of salvation and liberty, for all our hope was quite lost, so that if you had not come on that blessed day, our city and order would have perished.

Also evident in this passage is the idea, already commented on, of the siege as a punishment and a purgatorial experience for the beleaguered, at the end of which they are cleansed and possibly saved. In reply, Tirant continues the idea of the hero as God's agent, linking military escape with spiritual salvation: 'In the same way I, with God's permission, hurried here with strong faith and firm resolve to help your Reverend Lordship and his order.' Before leaving, he gives a further demonstration of exemplary Christian conduct: he offers thanks that he was able to rescue the island from the infidel, relieves the town of its debt to him, and asks for a daily mass to be said for his soul. When this business is completed, he departs with two Venetian galleys bound for Jerusalem.

The two Catalan writers, Ferrer and Martorell, thus differ interestingly in their literary treatments of the same historical siege. Ferrer communicates what facts he remembers of the event, showing the courage of the knights under Jean de Lastic, and the salvation of the despairing townspeople through faith. Martorell uses the situation of the siege as a stage upon which his hero exhibits the qualities of the chivalric Christian knight—piety, courage, generosity towards the people he has come to save, courtesy, and honesty in the treatment of his sailor. Ferrer alludes briefly to the political context of the siege and the

Catalan–Genoese rivalry, while Martorell explores it more fully, showing us the conflicting attitudes of powerful lords in Europe. The *Romans* pays little attention to the personalities involved, besides portraying Jean de Lastic as a significant figure at the beginning; instead it concentrates on the general characteristics shared by the people, their fear, religious reverence, and deep courage. Martorell, by contrast, creates a narrative involving distinct characters: as well as the dominating presence of Tirant, we see the ingenuity of a veteran mariner, the gracious eloquence of the Master of the Order, and the captains of the Sultan's fleet who angrily turn against their leader. Both writers emphasize the symbolic significance of the siege as a model of Christendom defending itself against heathens, and draw on military knowledge, Martorell in particular showing a detailed knowledge of the subject of tactics at land and sea.

THE SIEGE OF RHODES, 1480: KAYE'S TRANSLATION OF CAOURSIN'S CHRONICLE

Rhodes was again besieged in 1480, this time by a Turkish force under the Greek Grand Vizier Misach Palaeologus Pasha. An attempt at an assault the previous year had been defeated. The Grand Master of the Order leading the defence on this occasion was the Frenchman Peter d'Aubusson, who had served under Charles VII against the Swiss, and came to Rhodes at the age of 21. Under him he had 600 knights and about 1,500 mercenaries and other troops; the town was this time adequately provisioned for two years. The Turkish force sent was even greater than the Egyptian one of 1444, equipped with sixteen large guns and twenty-two engines. This time the defenders also used guns, and the siege illustrates the steady growth in the use of gunpowder at sieges in the fifteenth century, with the consequences of this for artistic treatment.[15]

The siege of 1480 lasted for two months, when the Turks withdrew after an attack on the tower of St Nicholas—the key point in the defences—on 27 July was held off and answered with a counter-attack. According to the Italian eyewitness Giacomo de Curti, the guns used made the ground tremble; despite the victory of the Christians on this

---

[15] See E. Brockman, *The Two Sieges of Rhodes, 1480–1522* (London, 1969). E. Bradford, *The Shield and the Sword: The Knights of Malta* (London, 1972), ch. 13, pp. 93–102. Bradbury, 228–35.

occasion, Giacomo declared it impossible to recount the tale of beleaguered Rhodes without weeping: 'Chi potra frenare le lacrime, o
narrare ad occhi asciuti i casi di questa città?'[16]

An eyewitness record of the events of the siege was made in Latin by
William Caoursin, the Vice-Chancellor of the Order; his account was
soon printed and made available to readers in Europe in translation.[17]
An English translation was made by the 'laureate' John Kaye for King
Edward IV in 1482 and published: the work is 'unusual among fifteenth
century printed books in being concerned directly with contemporary
history, with one of the greatest threats which faced Western Christendom in the later fifteenth century—the seemingly irresistible progress
of the Ottoman Turks'.[18] It reflects a strong interest in the siege by the
princes of Europe and a general interest and anxiety in face of the
Turkish threat, following the fall of Constantinople in 1453, the occupation of the Peloponnese completed in 1460, the capture of the Venetian port of Negropont in 1470, and the battle for possession of Otranto
in 1480. Against such a background of breaches in the defences of
Europe, the need for an inspiring account of a heroic Christian defence
must have been strongly felt.

John Kaye's translation also provides another example of a description
of a siege in which literary considerations influence the way in which
factual material is presented. Like the Catalan writers discussed in the
previous section, Kaye is clearly aware of literary models of sieges and
chivalry from romances, and also appears to have extra sources of information about the technology of siegecraft. Kaye makes various
changes to his source, and reshapes the chronicle to present the siege as
a narrative with a distinct moral purpose, with heroic or villainous
characters in the tradition of romance writings. *The Dylectable Newesse*
shows chivalric and heroic actions in the context of a siege, especially in
the central character of Peter d'Aubusson.[19] Not only the sieges of antiquity, but also those of contemporary history, it is implied, can provide
examples of exemplary knightly conduct. At the same time, as in the

[16] E. F. Mizzi (ed. and trans.), *Le Guerre di Rodi: Relazioni di diversi autori sui due grandi assedi
di Rodi (1480–1522)* (Turin, 1934), 68–87 (68).
[17] References to Caoursin's Latin text (first pub. Venice, 1480) are to a facsimile of the
Snel 1482 print, edited by Isager. J. Kaye, *The Dylectable Newesse and Tithynges of the Glorious
Victorye of the Rhodyans agayenst the Turkes* (London, 1482). References are to the facsimile edition in the English Experience series.
[18] Facsimile edn. (1975), 1. On the textual history of Kaye's translation, see R. H. Robbins,
'Good Gossips Reunited', *BMQ* 27 (1964), 12–15.
[19] See K. M. Setton, *The Papacy and the Levant (1204–1571)* (Philadelphia, 1978), ii. 346–63:
'Pierre d'Aubusson and the first siege of Rhodes (1480)'.

two accounts of the siege of 1444, the defence of Rhodes in 1480 illustrates the strength provided by Christian faith.

Kaye introduces his translation as a kind of gospel, bringing 'the dylectable newesse and tithynges' of the defence of Rhodes to the English people 'wherof they redyng shal have joye & consolacyon & shal alwey deuoutely knowe by dayly miracles & goddes werkes the inestimable power and certente of our crysten fayth' (1r). The siege itself is an instructive illustration of this inestimable power and certainty in action. Caoursin's chronicle, in its printed form, contains thirty-two brief chapters giving the details of various episodes. Kaye abolishes chapter divisions to create a narrative of the siege which moves forward quickly, in the spirit of a romance, and is governed by the main objective of showing the power of Christianity in a beleaguered city. He adds a moral and dramatic dimension to events at various points: Caoursin's description of Mahomet as 'turcorum tyrannum mahumetum potissime', for example, is expanded by Kaye to 'the cruell tyraunt Mahumete grete Turke and insacyable enemye to oure crysten fayth' (2r). The besieging captain in the translation has more symbolic status as representative of the enemies of Christ, and is similar to the many cruel tyrants of romance. Similarly, the deserters from Rhodes are in Caoursin's version simply those 'qui . . . ad turcos defecerant', while Kaye describes them as 'the traytours of crystes fayth' (2v–3r). Kaye reminds us throughout that it is not only Rhodes but the Christian faith which is under attack.

Another feature of Kaye's translation is his interest in the figure of the commander Peter d'Aubusson and his brother Anthony. Caoursin gives a good deal of information on the feats of these two captains, but Kaye adds to it imaginatively, drawing on literary conventions. Perhaps the portrait of the defender of the faith and of the people is intended in part as a model for Edward, in the tradition of books of advice to princes:

recellentissimus princeps noster rhodiorum magister his conspectis diuino quodam ingenio agendis incumbens. nil preter mittere decreuit quod saluti urbis conducere videat. (9r)

Then the Lorde mayster of Rhodes consyderyng and seeyng openly the grete hardynesse of the turkes: and also the grete daunger that the cytee of Rhodes stode in/ he as a noble Prynce louyng and defendyng hys sayde cytee and lordshyppe and hys people . . . (14v)

The figure of the ideal prince is joined with that of the skilled practictioner of the military arts, using his knowledge in a crusade against

God's enemies. One of Kaye's most substantial additions to his source is the depiction of Anthony d'Aubusson, Peter's brother and second-in-command. Philippe de Mézières, warning Charles VI against admiring King Arthur too much, enjoined him instead to 'read often the fair and true history of the valour of Duke Godfrey of Bouillon, and of his noble and holy chivalry'.[20] With such a model of a crusading hero in his mind, Kaye presents Edward with a portrait of a Christian warrior for whom the defence of Rhodes against Turkish siege presents a spiritual calling. The resulting character is similar to that of Tirant lo Blanc: the fifteenth-century defender of the faith at a siege clearly owes something to portrayals of earlier heroes such as Godfrey, as well as to actual figures such as Geoffrey de Thoisy.

sancti sepulchri visitandi gran cupiens summopere tam glorioso certamini interesse transfretarat Is eum a fratre patrum decreto ob fidei integritatem. agendorum experienciam artisque militaris disciplinam. commilitonum dux et urbis capitanem designatum. (9r)

And hys entente and purpos was: to vysyte devoutely the blessyd and holy sepulchre of oure Saueur Jhesu cryste in Jerusalem. But whenne he understode and perceyued: that the grete Turke sholde come and laye sege to Rhodes: he pourposed to helpe and defende the cytee of rhodes wyth juberte of hys lyfe and all hys companye. for he thoughte: that in noo maner place: nor in noo maner wyse he myghte spende hys bloode better: and more for the welfare of hys soule: thenne there: where he shulde fyghte for the precyous name of oure lord Jhesu cryste: and for the ryghtfull quarell of all crysten fayth: and to kepe from captyuyte of the turkes the noble cytee of Rhodes. and be cause that hys holynesse and hys herty loue whiche he hadde to the fayth of Jhesu cryste: and also that hys grete manhode was well knowen to all the knyghtes of Rhodes: the Lord Mayster his brother and all the counseyle of Rhodes. elected and chesed hym capetayn and gouernour of all the men of werre. (14v–15r)

As well as adding exemplary meaning and character portraits influenced by chivalric literature to the chronicle, Kaye also takes a close interest in the weapons and strategies of siegecraft. In this area, too, he sometimes supplements Caoursin. Kaye seems well-informed on siegecraft, and evidently wants the reader to see he is familiar with his subject: perhaps, like Martorell, he referred to a military treatise during his composition. The following passage, describing the Turkish preparations for the siege, not only illustrates this aspect of Kaye's treatment of the action,

[20] Philippe de Mézières, *Le Songe du vieil pèlerin*, ii. 222. See M. Keen, 'Chivalry, Heralds, and History', in R. H. C. Davis and J. M. Wallace-Hadrill (eds.), *The Writing of History in the Middle Ages: Essays Presented to Richard William Southern* (Oxford, 1981), 393–414 (395).

but also introduces us to the various types of gun which have joined the
culverin, which was the only one mentioned in the texts on the 1444
siege:

Quare si cum celeritate et diligencia exercitus maritimus atque terrestris com-
paretur. urbem haud dubio expugnatum iri putant Accersiuntur ad hanc con-
sultacionem consultacione diffiniendam machinarum viri periti. (2r–v)

Therfore hyt was fynally and in alle haste concluded in the foresayd parlement
and counseyle. That bothe by lande: and by see they shold make them redy for
to goo to the siege of the sayd cytee of Rhodes. And forthermore were there
called many connynge men in makyng of instrumens of werre/ that is to saye
Bombardes/ gownes/ culverynes/ serpentines & such other. (4r–v)

The bombards and guns referred to are cannons. Besides the culverin,
the serpentine appears: this is the earliest form of gun-lock, with a two-
shaped lever pivoting on the side of the stock. The guns, equipped to
fire leadshot, would probably have been fitted with lugs on to the side
of parapets; smaller infantry hand-guns were not in common use until
the middle of the sixteenth century.[21] Kaye also elaborates slightly on
the defensive measures made in Rhodes in the expectation of the siege:

Disponuntur ea parte murorum urbis bombardes et tormenta que triremes et
turcorum nauigia expugnent: perfrigantque. Prope quoque cautes eius arcis
cimbe combustibilibus opplete stacionem habent: que in oppugnacione in-
cendantur. et hostium classi incendium afferant. (5r)

for in that part were ordeyned bombardes & other grete instrumentes castyng
grete stones for to breke the galeyes of the turkes. and also under the tour that
the Lorde mayster kepte were lytill shippes fylled with gonne pouder and
brymme stone and other suche thynges: the whiche when the galeyes of the
turkes came ner: shulde be putte in fyre to the destructyon of the galeyes of the
turkes. (8v)

Ferrer describes in his poem on the 1444 siege the effect it had on
bringing the defenders together. Both Caoursin and Kaye stress that
everyone in Rhodes joins in the defences, Kaye going further to imply
that their strength for this comes from their piety:

Interdiu noctuque operi intenditur. Non magister. non baiuliui non priores
non milites non ciues non negociatores non matrone non nupte non virgines
opere vacant. (5v)

---

[21] See A. V. B. Norman, and D. Pottinger, *English Weapons and Warfare 449–1660* (London,
1979), 142–3.

and therfore they made day and nyghte grete werkes/ as walles of tymbre and many other thynges defensybles/ to the whiche labour euery creature in rhodes of alle maner of aage bothe men and women of alle maner states putted and aplyed theym selfe and theyre goodes wyth grete wylle and grete deuocyon for Jhesus sake. (9r)

In his description of the various battles outside the walls, Kaye, frequently embellishing the source text of Caoursin, provides vivid details: heads are cut from the corpses of warriors, there are agreed times for burial and mourning, and both sides seek to give the impression that their spirits are high; Turks dance with tabours in the ditches, singing 'songes of myrthe', and the defenders reply in kind from behind a breached wall 'wyth trompettes and claryons' (18v). God is frequently seen to be intervening on the side of the besieged, 'so that by the myracles of god & prayers of crysten people fewe men or bestes of the cyte were hurted' (10v). The besieging force is depicted as cruel and ignorant, demonstrating 'hardynesse' but without the spiritual guidance which the faithful defenders of Rhodes enjoy. Although attention is given to the ingenious defensive devices employed, there is still perhaps an implication that in their dependence on advanced technology the Turks are being devious and unchivalrous: 'But the more that the Rhodyans wythstode the turkes wyth myghte and wysedom: the more waxed the turkes furyous agaynes Rhodes. And anon after thys wyth grete bombardes/ gonnes/ engynes and all other suche instrumentes of werre: they vexed and greved the Rhodyans' (18r).

Kaye often touches up the rather dry record presented by Caoursin to create something more akin to romance. Where in the Latin chronicle it is stated that the head of a dead Knight of the Order is severed from the body by a Turkish foraging party, Kaye gives us the gruesome picture: 'and thenne they toke hys heede and putte yt on a spere and ranne with grete myrth and joye to theire companye and oste' (6v). Caoursin records that the Turks offered to treat with the knights but were dismissed by Peter d'Aubusson. Kaye brings the scene, with the heroic besieged commander shaming his enemies, before us:

Quo dictu turci vultu demisso extemplo discedunt. (11r)

After the whyche answere/ the turkes wyth loe chiere and halfe shamely contenaunce/ departed from theyme and tourned agayne to their oste and to theyre capeteyne. (18r)

Kaye also shapes and colours his narrative by the use of comparison with heroes of literature, as in his allusion to the siege of Troy in the description of the defence of the tower of St Nicholas, 'Where afterward the knyghtes/ bothe of latyn tonge and grekys tonge dyd worshipfully as euer dyd Achylles or Hector' (13r). The detail, also in Caoursin, of Latin and Greek knights fighting together, suggests a unifying of divided Christendom in the face of a common enemy.

Kaye's greatest addition to his chronicle source is in his treatment of the miraculous salvation of the city and the accompanying moral commentary. In the midst of the final great assault on 27 July, the defenders of Rhodes mount images of Christ, the Virgin, and St John, the patron of the Order, on the battlements. Ferrer records the effect of the image of the Virgin on the walls on the Egyptians in 1444, suggesting that this was common practice in sieges, at least in Rhodes. The advancing enemy is stunned by the images and sees 'in the myddest of the clene and bryght eyer/ a cross all of shynyng gold' (21v). The Turkish army is prevented by this from continuing the assault; many Turks are converted, and the fleet departs. Caoursin follows the scene by noting, 'Agamus igitur gracias de tanto beneficio ei. qui nos ab imporium manibus preseruauit' (13v). Kaye adds his own exposition of the deliverance. For him the historical events of the siege are a revelation of even greater truths:

By the crosse of golde we may justely understande: oure saueour Jhesu cryste. And by the vyrgyne we may understande/ oure lady the blessed marie. And by the man pouerly clothed we may understande the holy seynte Johan baptyste Patron and auowre of the ordre of Rhodes: whiche was acompanyed with seyntes & angeles of God for to helpe the Rhodyans ... Thees myracles in so moche more are in confirmacyon and deuocyon to our crysten fayth be cause that the firste knowleche of theyme came by the vysyon and syghte of the turkes enemyes to oure crysten fayth. (22r)

Finally, Kaye adopts a homiletic tone, and explains the 'sens' or real significance of the whole siege:

But who letted theym then to come down fro the walles to the cytee: afore that the Rhodyans clymed with ladders to feght with theim & dryue them fro the walles: Certainly hit was none other but god. Who was he/ that blynded their witte/ so that anon after the firste assaute/ they ordeyned not an other agaynes our crysten men: whiche by the first assaute had ben pyteously hurte & wonded & were all wery of fyghtyng. Hit was non other but god. Who was cause of the deth of so many of theym in the space of two owres in the grete & last assaute: but god & his angels that were seen in the bright eyer. (22v)

The rhetorical procedure of extended anthypophora employed here is strikingly reminiscent of Chaucer's *Man of Law's Tale*: 'Who fedde the

Egipcien Marie in the cave, / Or in desert? No wight but Crist, sanz faille' (ii. 500–1).

Kaye's translation of Caoursin's chronicle of the siege of Rhodes of 1480 is an example of a translation where 'the translator has a specific intention in making the translation [and] that intention may differ from the original author's'.[22] Kaye's intention seems to be to represent the siege as an example of the protection God provides to His believers in their time of trouble, while also creating a vivid and brisk narrative, similar in several respects to such popular works as the Charlemagne romances or crusading epics. Other influences may include chivalric biography, books of advice to princes, and military treatises. From such diverse materials, Kaye creates a piece with ambitions to inspire and enlighten as well as to inform and to entertain the reader.

THE SIEGE OF BELGRADE, 1456: *CAPYSTRANUS* AND *THE SEGE OF MELAYNE*

In the texts so far considered on the sieges of Rhodes, writers make use of inherited literary conventions when treating contemporary siege warfare: the adopted codes of chivalry and heroism are seen in action against a contemporary background, where historical and technological changes are noticeable. Crusading literature of the fifteenth century provides a context for the treatment of sieges in these writings, which present examples of ancient heroism in the conduct of embattled Christians abroad. The adoption of militant crusading and religious rhetoric in narrative treatment of sieges is also evident in the late English romances *Capystranus* and *The Sege of Melayne*.[23]

Capystranus is more removed in time from the event it describes—the defence of Belgrade in 1456—than the writings on Rhodes previously discussed. It is preserved in a print of 1515 and two later prints of 1527 and 1530, though it is possible that the original composition preceded publication and that the poem may have been known in some form

---

[22] D. Kelly, 'Translatio studii: Translation, Adaptation, and Allegory in Medieval French Literature', *PQ* 57 (1978), 287–310 (292).

[23] See commentary by I. Petrovics, and G. Szónyi, '*Capystranus*, a Late Medieval English Romance on the 1456 Siege of Belgrade', *NHQ* 27/104 (1986), 141–6. References are to the more accessible edition of the part of the poem dealing with the siege in D. Gray (ed.), *The Oxford Book of Late Medieval Verse and Prose* (Oxford, 1985), 199–203, 459. References to *The Sege of Melayne* are to the edition by Mills.

towards the end of the fifteenth century.[24] The print, and early reprints, reflect the immediate interest of the theme of salvation from
the Turk in the early sixteenth century: Belgrade fell to Soliman the
Magnificent in 1521, Rhodes was finally overcome in 1522, and the
Hungarians were defeated in the battle of Mohács in 1526. These disasters inspired several literary treatments, and are referred to in other
writings: in *The Knight of Curtesy* and *The Squire of Low Degree*, for example, heroes go to the defence of Rhodes, answering the call of
Alexander Barclay in the *Ship of Folys* (1509), who says of Rhodes, 'O
noble place! thou moste the payne abyde / Though thou assayld be on
every syde'. Thomas More's *A Dialogue of Comfort Against Tribulation*
takes place the night before the battle of Mohács. *Capystranus*, at least in
its printed form, provides, as comfort and inspiration, a story of heroism
and miraculous preservation against God's enemies, at a time of continuing Turkish advance. It may have been composed specifically for
this purpose.

The event recalled by *Capystranus* is the defence of Belgrade against
a besieging Turkish army in 1456.[25] At this time Hungary was the principal obstacle to further Turkish expansion, Constantinople having
fallen in 1453; earlier victories by the Turks at Varna in 1444 and
Kosovo-Polje in 1448 indicated likely future attacks on Hungary. Because of political and religious differences within the Balkans and the
Holy Roman Empire, only the Papacy could provide support against
the Turk for the Governor of Hungary and chief defender, János
Hunyadi. Consequently, Pope Calixtus III acted to raise funds and a
crusading army, sending Cardinal Carjaval to Hungary in 1455. It was
Carjaval who enlisted the support of the Franciscan friar John
Capistrano, who raised a force of 20,000 Hungarians. Hunyadi himself
raised a force of 10,000 mercenaries, while there were 6,000 defenders
inside Belgrade itself. This army managed to resist the siege of the Turks
and finally to defeat the Turkish army in July 1456.

The victory of Hunyadi was soon known and celebrated across
Europe: there were formal acts of thanksgiving in various capitals, and
the actions of Hunyadi and Capistrano in the siege soon became the
subject of popular legend. Reports of the defence, including a letter

---

[24] In addition to the apparatus of editions, see E. Rona, 'Hungary in a Medieval Poem:
"Capystranus", a Metrical Romance', in M. Brahmer *et al.* (eds.), *Studies in Language and
Literature in Honour of Margaret Schlauch* (Warsaw, 1966), 343–52.

[25] See R. N. Bain, 'The Siege of Belgrade by Muhammed II, July 1–23, 1456', *EHR* 7
(1892), 235–42.

purportedly written by a Dominican, brought to England by an ostensible priest from Hungary, and copied into the register of St Alban's
Abbey, share with the romance some vivid description and strong anti-
Turkish sentiment. Hunyadi may even be the source for Tirant's appellation 'lo Blanc'.[26] It is in these legends that *Capystranus* has its origin,
particularly, as the title suggests, in the stories associated with the miracle worked at the siege by the friar Capistrano, who is credited in the
romance both with instigating the crusade and with conducting the defence of Belgrade. The author shows some interest in the historical and
military detail of the siege, but the focus is clearly on the personal
charisma of the Friar, represented as the defending commander, and the
lifting of the siege is seen as an act of miraculous salvation rather than as
a purely tactical triumph.

Capystranus begins with a reminder of the notorious cruelty of the
Turks at the siege of Constantinople. At the siege of Belgrade itself, we
are first reminded of the great artillery with which Constantinople had
been won; the skilled engineers on the Turkish side who appeared in
the accounts of the siege of Rhodes in 1480 suggested a sense of Turkish superiority in the use of guns at sieges. In *Capystranus* the guns are
described in action. When Soliman sees the relief army led by Hunyadi
and Capistrano approaching, 'Fyve .c. gonnes he lete shote at ones, /
Brake doune the walles with stones; / The wyldefyre lemed lyght'
(10–12). An accumulation of details emphasizes the material superiority of the Turks. While the besieging army is 'Clean clad in plate and
mail', the Christians wear only the chain-mail hauberk. They 'had no
myght' against the cannon, and their horses are easily borne down by
the Turkish dromedaries.[27]

The detailed description of arms and armour at the siege in *Capystranus* does not appear to be in the service of historical accuracy. Rather,
the author is emphasizing how the Christian defenders cannot match
the weapons or numbers of their assailants, and are in immediate peril of
suffering the slaughter seen at Constantinople. Technological inferiority

---

[26] Letter: *Registrum Abbatiae Johannis Whethamstede*, i. 268–79. See C. Tyerman, *England
and the Crusades 1095–1588* (Chicago, 1988), 320–1. Hunyadi and Tirant: Hunyadi was from
Walachia, and hence named 'Valachus' or 'Balachus' (the Walachian) in some contemporary
texts. In its Western form, the word becomes 'Blach', by popular corruption Blanc, Bianco,
Bianchum, etc. Hunyadi was referred to as 'the white knight' in a French chronicle account of
the battle of Belgrade. The victory was publicly celebrated in Valencia and Barcelona: thus it
is probable that the appellation 'lo Blanch' was known by Martorell, and may have been applied to the fictional hero to associate him with the historical one. See de Riquer,
Aproximació al Tirant lo Blanc, 169–70.

[27] Armour: ll. 3, 71; 'had no myght': l. 9; cavalry: ll. 73–83.

on the part of the Christians is stressed in order to show their reliance on spiritual strength. The heathen enemy has changed from the ignorant cowards depicted in *Richard Coeur de Lion*, who attribute their enemy's powers to the devil and are defenceless against his engines, to the highly skilled practitioners of sieges depicted here and in Kaye's piece. In the English romance on Richard the superior strength and arms of the Christians and their moral superiority seem to go together. *Capystranus*, by contrast, draws on older traditions of heroic poetry and shows traditional fighting methods winning against the better-equipped Turkish forces: the siege is a model of older virtues proving their worth against technical advances which are not supported by Christian faith.

In common with several chroniclers, the author of *Capystranus* reduces the number of battles to one, fought after a long and continued bombardment. No interest is shown in details of strategy. Instead, the besieged army is seen relying on the strength of the spirit, going into battle behind Capistrano, who holds the banner of Christ aloft. As in *Richard Coeur de Lion*, two English captains—here the mercenaries Richard Morpath and Sir John Black, a naturalized Turk—are shown performing valiantly in the army, alongside crusading clerics, who chant while administering fatal blows: 'Our preestes *Te Deum* songe; / The hethen fast downe they donge' (60–1). The besieged and besieging armies are further distinguished in battle by the level of physical detail accorded to the description of the injuries they inflict: the buffets of the Christians burst the occasional brain, but there is little mention of blood or anguish suffered by their victims. By contrast, there are frequent references to the wounds of the defenders, and to the slaughter of the women and children by the Turks, as the retreating army is followed into the besieged city in the first assault. The injuries of the defenders, who 'Had woundes many one, / That blody were and wyde' (89–90), loosely suggest the Passion of Christ, and the massacre of children inevitably conjures up images of the Holy Innocents. Allusion takes a more explicit form in the cry of Capistrano from the tower in the midst of the city, where he sets the banner and brandishes a crucifix: 'O my lord, Cryste Jesus, / Why hast thou forgoten us? / Now helpe of the we crave' (109–11).

Capistrano calls on God and the Virgin Mary to help His people, and reminds them of his service, asking the due reward in return: 'For all my servyse I have done the, / I aske no more to my fee, / But helpe thy men today' (124–6). He threatens never to say Matins for Mary again, unless she intercedes to Christ for the beleaguered citizens of Belgrade. In answer to this prayer, with its strong overtones of feudal contract, the drama of suffering and death is completed with a mass resurrection, as twenty thousand slain defenders rise again and rout the Turkish army. Their fury as they 'hew on other with ire' (537) recalls the extraordinary energy of Richard in *Richard Coeur de Lion*. Having started with a graphic description of the atrocities inflicted by the Turks on the people of Constantinople, *Capystranus* ends with the depiction of Christians as an irresistible and superhuman force routing the heathen. Like the texts on the sieges of Rhodes, *Capystranus* describes a dramatic reversal of fortunes, expressive of the miraculous regenerative powers of the Christian soul and body in the face of the forces of darkness: through phrases, imagery, and structure, the siege is related to Christ's Passion, as a story of suffering followed by resurrection and salvation.

The Sege of Melayne survives only in an incomplete version, which breaks off just as the siege appears to be on the point of starting. It describes the capture of Milan by Saracens, and the appeal of the lord of the city, Alantyne, to Charles for help. The first Christian relief force is heavily defeated by the Saracens, though the Sultan is killed and various Saracens are miraculously blinded. Charles himself is initially reluctant to go, although he has been shown a sword by an angel in a vision as a sign that it is his Christian duty to defend the faith. He is excommunicated by a furious Archbishop Turpin, who threatens to besiege Paris with his own army of clerics. Charles repents and complies, and Turpin leads the French army to the rescue of Milan. Reinforcements for the besieging army arrive, and there the fragment ends.

Though an earlier poem, probably written in about 1400, *The Sege of Melayne* has much in common with *Capystranus*: the later piece seems to be echoing some of the motifs of the earlier one, perhaps drawing on a continued tradition of popular ideas and the rhetoric of crusading propaganda. Both poems show a crusading Christian army led by a charismatic priest, include miraculous episodes, and make various references to the Passion. The heroic and crusading nature of *The Sege of Melayne* is shared by the other romances in the Thornton manuscript in which it appears, *The Siege of Jerusalem* and *Otuel and Roland*. The common theme to these pieces is the recovery of the Holy Land and the defence of Christendom against the Saracen, described with an energetic crusading rhetoric.[28] Central to this type of romance is a heroic figure

---

[28] See J. J. Thompson, *Robert Thornton and the London Thornton Manuscript*, Manuscript Studies, 2 (Cambridge, 1987). H. Hudson, 'Middle English Popular Romances: The Manuscript Evidence', *Manuscripta*, 28 (1984), 67–78, esp. 72.

who shows extraordinary powers of endurance and inspiration: just as Richard in *Richard Coeur de Lion* recovers from illness to besiege Acre successfully, so Vespasian in *The Siege of Jerusalem* besieges Jerusalem after being miraculously cured of a cancer, while Turpin in *The Sege of Melayne* 'sustains wounds that would fell other heroes'.[29]

Turpin, like Capystranus, is the main figure of the narrative and the chief agent of God's will. He overcomes human weakness in vowing not to be treated for his wounds until the city of Milan is won, and achieves a divine miracle when bread and wine for the Mass are sent down from heaven. The injuries of the defenders in *Capystranus* have an analogy in the wound Turpin receives in his side (1301–2), which is explicitly compared to the wounds of Christ. *The Sege of Melayne* shows an interest in Christian iconography, in recording the destruction in Milan of 'The emagery that ther solde bee, / Bothe the rode and the Marie free' (25–6). This 'emagery', here meaning sculpture, is followed by further references to Christian images, such as the blood mixed with water which the Christian soldiers drink (1206). As a belligerent cleric, Archbishop Turpin is similar not only to Capistrano but to other priests who are recorded as playing an important combative role in real sieges. In Abbo's poem on the Danish siege of Paris, for example, Abbot Ebolus is shown attacking the enemy single-handed and is rather confusingly described as the favourite abbot of Mars in tribute to his prowess. Ambroise describes the Archbishop of Beauvais furiously heading an assault with a battering-ram at the siege of Acre, while in the Latin chronicle of the siege of Lisbon a siege tower is blessed by an archbishop and serves as a temporary pulpit for a priest (possibly the author of the chronicle) who urges the crusaders to fight and vows not to leave the engine himself while he is alive. Real and legendary priests serve as a sign of Christ's presence with an army; Turpin appears also as an embodiment of divine strength and anger who, in some mysterious way, takes the Passion upon himself. One also suspects that his excesses of anger and energy may have had a more frankly comic appeal.[30]

The figure of the fighting churchman thus links the two poems both with each other and with historical record. Also common to both poems is an 'angry complaint to God for his apparent failure to keep his part of the implicit "feudal" contract' which includes anti-Marian invective on

[29] D. Childress, 'Between Romance and Legend: "Secular Hagiography" in Middle English Literature', *PQ* 57 (1978), 311–22 (316).

[30] Abbo, ll. 244, 601–20. Ambroise: Archbishop of Beauvais, ll. 3819–96. *De expugnatione Lyxbonensi: The Conquest of Lisbon*: sermon in siege tower, pp. 146–58.

the part of the clerical hero.[31] The siege is regarded as in some sense a re-enactment of Christ's suffering and salvation and as a model of the human and divine patterns of duties and loyalties which form the ideological fortress of Christendom and Christianity. In order to emphasize the moral and feudal codes shown at work in a siege, mechanical aspects are given less attention: as in *Capystranus*, the Christians in *The Sege of Melayne* are shown as being less equipped technically than their adversaries, armed only with simple weapons and 'bowes of devyce' against the springalds and other engines of the Saracens (1283–90). Crusading siege warfare in these poems shows the strength of the spirit overwhelming the machinations and material advantages of the heathen.

The various texts discussed in this chapter indicate some of the prevailing sentiments of Western Europe in the later fifteenth century. In the face of the Turkish advance, a siege mentality is articulated, in which writers turn to traditional codes of chivalry, epic heroism, and crusading propaganda to portray the strengths of Christianity against a technically mightier adversary. The siege itself becomes a model of Christendom defending both its secular and spiritual identity against invasion by heathendom. Looking over the battlements at the enemy, the defenders of the faith also look into the foundations of their own culture: chivalric and crusading rhetoric is used not only to provide inspiration but to provide a positive image of the citadel of the Christian people. The unity of the besieged is an important theme in these texts, perhaps suggesting a need for such an image by an audience painfully aware of divisions between leaders and states.

As well as addressing immediate political concerns, the texts discussed here also offer patterns of conduct on an individual and communal level: the Passion is invoked to remind Christians of the importance of enduring and suffering, and as consolation. This in turn suggests a sense of history as a pattern of suffering and salvation, an idea which is taken further in romances on Troy and Jerusalem, in which the siege appears not only as an event in history but as the model for history itself.

---

[31] S. H. A. Shepherd, '"This grete journee": *The Sege of Melayne*', in M. Mills *et al.* (eds.), *Romance in Medieval England* (Cambridge, 1991), 113–31 (124).

4

Troy: Treason and Tragedy

MEDIEVAL treatments of the fall of Troy tend not to include much detail on siegecraft: battles are usually fought outside the city walls, and in the various accounts Troy is won through treachery or guile, not by assault. Consequently there is little, beyond the basic elements of a blockade and pitched battles in the open field, which relates directly to medieval siege warfare. It is evident from romances and other writings, however, that the story of Troy was regarded as in some sense a model or metaphor for the overall pattern of history. The significance of Troy lies in the fact that it is a great city, physically invincible, which is besieged and falls. Explanations of the disaster which befell the Trojans had important ramifications for medieval perceptions of later history. Related to this theme are the subjects of the identity of royal houses who traced their foundation back to Trojan exiles, the use of Troy as a reference point in commentaries and other works, the portrayal of a besieged king, and the ways in which Troy itself was imagined.

Troy might usefully be considered together with Thebes: both great cities of antiquity ended in siege and represented both the glories and the disasters of the ancient world. Certainly the evidence of manuscript compilations would suggest that the sieges of the two cities were regarded as being closely related: *The Prose Siege of Thebes*, discussed in Chapter 1, is collected together with a prose redaction of the siege of Troy; the same juxtaposition of the two stories is to be found in some French manuscripts.[1] Lydgate—the main source for the English prose epitomes—writes of both Thebes and Troy; Chaucer's *Troilus and Criseyde*, while set in Troy, makes extensive use of source writings on Thebes and uses the siege of Thebes suggestively, in the scene in which Criseyde and her ladies read a romance of Thebes together (ii. 99–108). The sieges of these ancient cities clearly often went together in the medieval consciousness, evoking complementary images of beauty and

---

[1] Oxford, Bodleian Library, MS Rawlinson D. 82 (*Prose Siege of Thebes*, fos. 1–11r; *Prose Siege of Troy*, fos. 11v–25v). Oxford, Bodleian Library, MS Douce 353 contains French prose treatments of the sieges of Thebes and Troy.

barbarism. Both provide examples of the fall of great houses, of the warfaring and chivalry of the classical past, and of cities which fall victim to
the movement of Fortune. To a large extent, ideas surrounding Troy are
echoed in writing on Thebes, in terms of what it was held to represent
of the past and the significance attached to its destruction.

As an example of the siege as a model for history, the fate of Troy
contrasts with the Roman defeat of Jerusalem:

> Note the crucial distinction: the fall of Jericho or Jerusalem is merely just,
> whereas the fall of Troy is the first great metaphor of tragedy. Where a city is
> destroyed because it has defied God, its destruction is a passing instant in the
> rational design of God's purpose. Its walls shall rise again, on earth or in the
> kingdom of heaven, when the souls of men are restored to grace. The burning
> of Troy is final because it is brought about by the fierce sport of human hatreds
> and the wanton, mysterious choice of destiny.[2]

These remarks, taken from the context of a discussion of the founda-
tions of Western tragedy, are intended to elucidate the main differences
between Hellenic and Hebraic conceptions of history. They also serve
as valid distinctions with regard to later medieval treatments of the fall
of Jerusalem and Troy. In the next chapter we shall examine more fully
the significances of the divinely ordained destruction of Jerusalem, as it
is universally regarded in medieval treatments. The siege of Troy will
here be examined as a 'metaphor of tragedy' and as an example of the
workings of a destiny which could not be absorbed into the Christian
pattern of events.

The sieges of Troy and Jerusalem exemplify, respectively, what have
been called the Boethian and Augustinian views of history, 'the two
principal medieval genres of history-writing'.[3] The Boethian doctrine,
as expounded in the *Consolation of Philosophy* rather than in Boethius'
theological writings, provides an image of secular history, presided over
by the figure of Fortune, which includes political and military events
and the rise and fall of dynasties and empires. History, according to this
view, is cyclical and dynastic, characterized chiefly by a sequence of falls:
this model dominates almost all medieval narrative outside universal
histories, biblical stories, or hagiographies. The sieges of Thebes and
Troy are not presented in medieval treatments primarily as the fulfilment of God's purpose—despite some adverse references to the pagan
deities in Trojan temples—but as examples of the inevitable collapse of

---

[2] G. Steiner, *The Death of Tragedy* (London, 1961), 5.
[3] F. P. Pickering, *Literature and Art in the Middle Ages* (London, 1970), 168–97 (173).

great cities, kingdoms, and royal houses. They mark a revolution in the wheel of Fortune that is to be repeated at different moments in history. The story of Troy is part of a wider literature on the fall of princes: the continued fascination with this subject is illustrated by the success of *The Fall of Princes*, Lydgate's translation of Boccaccio's *De casibus virorum illustrium*, which was printed in the sixteenth century, and by the popularity of *A Myrroure for Magistrates*, 'wherein may be seen by examples of other, with howe grevous plages vices are punished', which went through three editions in the second half of the sixteenth century.[4] Troy's fate exemplifies both the collapse of wealth and power and the nemesis for human weakness. Fortune determines the rise and fall of cities and deities; Providence, to which Fortune according to the Boethian scheme is subordinate, is outside the scope of the treatments of the Troy story.

While the Boethian model provides a pattern for secular history, dominated by swift and tragic descents, the Augustinian scheme treats of Church history, those events which reveal something of the intentions of God, who has decreed all events. Hence it is a pattern of meaningful history, in which martyrs, saints, and heresies, in addition to biblical episodes, have a place while the destinies of secular powers are ultimately irrelevant. Human dynasties and kingdoms, in the Augustinian scheme, may have a destined role as the furtherers or opponents of the City of God, but they have no interest in themselves. The destruction of Jerusalem by the Romans reveals something of God's intentions for man. The siege of Troy may invite Augustinian commentary in so far as it helps explain why Rome fell to the forces of darkness; ultimately, however, it is not included among the events which the Church chooses to remember and which are interpreted as instances of God's guidance of history. The similar fates of Troy and Rome, as centres of civilization which fell to invasion from without and corruption from within, did however have a special interest for St Augustine: his reflections on Troy in the *City of God* will be considered later.

The Boethian pattern, based on the ascents and tragic reversals of Fortune, is exemplified by the narrative of Troy. Before examining further the essential elements of secular history which the siege of Troy illustrates, it is worth emphasizing that the siege was regarded as history

---

4 Lydgate's translation was variously titled, e.g. *A treatise shewing in maner of tragedye, the falles of sondry princes and princesses* (London, 1554) and *The tragedies . . . of all such princes as fell from theyr estates throughe the mutability of fortune* (London, 1558). *A Myrroure for Magistrates* (London, 1559), was reprinted in 1563, 1571, and 1587.

rather than legend or myth in the Middle Ages. Indeed, it was held to be more authentically historical than other cycles of classical legend:

In fact, the Trojan War is the only major classical tale that was available during the Middle Ages in the form of history . . . In the late Middle Ages a reader could find a classical epic on each of the cities (the *Aeneid* and *Thebaid*) and also a French romance on each (the *Roman de Troie* and *Roman de Thebes*), but only Troy had a *Historia Destructionis*.[5]

While 'the distinction between history and fiction cannot, in its modern clarity, be applied to medieval books or the spirit in which they were read', one of the most attractive features of the Troy legend in medieval literature seems to have been its claim to historical authenticity, if not on the level of particular detail, at least with regard to the main events.[6] The siege of Troy provided both an image of the pattern of dynastic history, and illustrious—if fatally flawed—predecessors for the ruling houses of Christendom. These and other aspects of the siege are illustrated by the tradition of writings on Troy, and references to the fall of Troy in commentaries and other related writings, which provide a useful context for the Middle English romances.

THE TRADITION OF TROY

Interest in the siege of Troy expressed in Latin writings after Virgil precedes substantial narrative treatments of the subject. For St Augustine, the explanation of the fall of Rome was partly to be found in the destruction of the city built by Rome's founders, the Trojans. In the *City of God*, St Augustine devotes eight chapters to Troy, in an attempt to answer what is for him a crucially important question:

Primum ipsa Troia vel Ilium, unde origo est populi Romani, neque enim praetereundum aut dissimulandum est, quod in primo libro attigi, eosdem habens deos et colens, cur a Graecis uictum, capyum atque deletum est?

Why was Troy (or Ilium), the source of the Roman people, conquered, captured and destroyed by the Greeks, when it possessed and worshipped the same gods as the Greeks?[7]

The conventional answer, that Troy was deserted by its gods as a punishment for Laomedon's refusal to pay Apollo and Neptune for the

---

[5] C. D. Benson, *The History of Troy in Middle English Literature* (Woodbridge, 1980), 5.

[6] C. S. Lewis, *The Discarded Image: An Introduction to Medieval and Renaissance Literature* (Cambridge, 1964), 179.

[7] St Augustine, *De civitate dei*, III. 2; *CCSL* 47, p. 66; trans. Bettenson, 90.

building of the city, is dismissed: this would imply belief in the powers of those gods, and would fail to explain why the perjuring Romans were not similarly punished. Similarly, Augustine contends that the fall of Troy could not have been a punishment for the adultery of Paris, since Rome would then have been destroyed as a result of the fratricide committed by Romulus. The close identification made between the two cities, which assumes that their destinies must follow the same logical pattern of cause and effect, continues throughout the tradition of medieval writings about them. Augustine sees Troy as a model for Rome, constructed and finally deceived and abandoned by the same false deities who flatter the fortunate and desert the afflicted:

Non est, ut arbitror, quod dicatur quid mali Troia meruerit, ut eam dii desererent, quo posset exstingui, et quid boni Roma, ut eam dii inhabitarent, quo posset augeri; nisi quod uicti inde fugerunt, ad se ad istos, quos pariter deciperent, contulerunt.

There is, in my judgement, no way of showing why Troy deserved so ill that the gods abandoned her to destruction or why Rome deserved so well that the gods dwelt in her to promote her increase—unless perhaps the conquered gods escaped from Troy and took refuge with the Romans, to delude them in the same way?[8]

The fate of Troy, like that of Rome, illustrates for St Augustine the destruction caused by a belief in false gods and the fallibility of all great human institutions. The sack or siege of a city is taken as a sign of the inherent weaknesses in the system of beliefs and code of conduct of its people.

The belief in the destruction of Troy as a historical event as real as the fall of Rome, and the emphasis on the similarities and continuities between the two cities, inform secular treatments of the siege as much as spiritual commentaries. Thus two of the most striking aspects of the story of the siege of Troy, as treated in medieval texts, are its strong relation to Rome and its supposed historicity. The tradition of Western medieval narrative writings on the subject begins with the brief prose texts attributed to the Cretan Dictys and the Trojan Dares. Links identified by St Augustine between Troy and Rome are here repeated on the level of textual inheritance, as the Latin accounts written by Dictys and Dares purportedly had their origin in writings made during the siege itself. These works were believed to be first-hand accounts of the event written by participants on either side of the conflict. Though said to be

---

[8] Ibid. III. 6: *CCSL* 47, p. 69; trans. Bettenson, 94.

based on Greek originals, the chronicles of Dictys and Dares survive only in Latin texts of the fourth and sixth centuries respectively, written in a style regarded by most Latinists as wretched. To later medieval writers, these pieces provided an indubitably historical foundation to later works on the siege of Troy, while also leaving scope for imaginative and romantic re-creations of classical chivalry and courtly conduct.[9]

Together with a Latin paraphrase of Homer, the *Ylias Latina*, possibly composed in the first century AD, Dictys and Dares gave the siege its historical credentials, and introduced the subject into the Latin literary tradition, shorn of some of the Homeric elements which might have discredited it.[10] A later Latin account of the siege, the *Excidium Troiae*, probably written in the ninth century and independent of Dares and Dictys, incorporates related classical legends and seems to have been used as a teaching aid in classical studies.[11] Troy was thus seen as a repository for classical, and in particular Roman, cultural values, and the siege was resonant with reminders of the fall of the Roman empire. The chivalry exhibited in the chronicles and romances on Troy is essentially Roman rather than Greek, and the fall of the city, with which Virgil's epic begins, was always of interest as a stage in the history of the foundation and fall of Rome and consequently as the basis of Western history and culture. Rome was frequently referred to as 'Troia renascens', a new beginning following the fall of the city that was its cultural progenitor.[12]

In addition to being a pattern of rise and fall which would repeat itself in the cities and dynasties of the medieval West, the history of the siege of Troy also provided a means by which the royal houses could legitimize their rule and the aristocracy in general could establish its own identity. Trojan founders were discovered for the emerging states of Western Europe, normally on etymological grounds. Theodoric claimed descent from the Trojans, Priam was claimed as the first Frankish

[9] See N. E. Griffin, *Dares and Dictys: An Introduction to the Study of Mediaeval Versions of the Story of Troy* (Baltimore, 1907). R. M. Lumiansky, 'Dares' *Historia* and Dictys' *Ephemeris*: A Critical Comment', in E. B. Atwood and A. A. Hill (eds.), *Studies in Language, Literature and Culture of the Middle Ages and Later*, (Austin, Tex., 1969), 200–9.

[10] See N. E. Griffin, 'Un-Homeric Elements in the Medieval Story of Troy', *JEGP* 7 (1907), 32–52. P. Venini, *Ditti Cretese e Omero* (Milan, 1981). A. Grillo, *Tra filologia e narratologia: Dai poemi omerici ad Apollonio Rodio, Ilias Latina, Ditti-Settimo, Darete Frigio, Draconzio*, Bibliotheca Athena, NS 4 (Rome, 1988).

[11] E. B. Atwood, 'The *Excidium Troiae* and Medieval Troy Literature', *MP* 35 (1937–8), 115–28.

[12] See E. Panofsky, *Renaissance and Renascences in Western Art* (London, 1965), 43.

king in the seventh century, Antenor was the supposed founder of the Normans, and Brutus was cited as the founder of Britain, a lineage given great popularity by Geoffrey of Monmouth.[13]

Together with the identification of nations and rulers with the Trojans, Troy itself was claimed as a forebear not only of Rome but of the other cities founded by the Trojan exiles. Geoffrey of Monmouth describes the foundation by Brutus of 'Troynovant', later renamed London, and it has been argued that the association was so immediate that the depiction of Troy in *Troilus and Criseyde* would have been understood by a contemporary audience as a commentary on events in late fourteenth-century London.[14] The link between Troy, Rome, and London implied inherited vice as well as glory, however: the Trojans bequeathed a form of original sin to their descendants in the West, which always carried the threat of another fall. The idea of the siege as punishment, an equivalent of exile from paradise, which concerned St Augustine, was an important part of the popular mythology of Troy. As late as the sixteenth century the Tudors were identified with the Trojans, and the fate of Troy was still regarded as a prefiguring or premonition of the catastrophe which would attend modern ills. The tragedy of *Gorboduc* (1561–2) includes a speech in which 'Gorboduc acknowledges that the disaster now overtaking Britain is a continuance of the same curse that doomed Troy itself; no citizen of New Troy, or Troynovant (alias London), could fail to spot the significance of this association, still less the sovereign who was herself the last of the line'.[15]

The notion of European culture rising phoenix-like from the ashes of Troy thus had several implications for prevailing views of secular history. For the ruling houses of Europe it provided a suitably splendid ancestry, linking the achievements of the classical past with the conduct of those presently in power and suggesting an unbroken line of succession which was a particularly useful official version of events in countries such as England, whose past had been especially fragmented. Royal and

[13] See A. M. Young, *Troy and her Legend* (Pittsburgh, 1948), 57. J. Seznec, *La Survivance des dieux antiques: Essai sur le rôle de la tradition mythologique dans l'humanisme et dans l'art de la Renaissance*, Studies of the Warburg Institute, 11 (London, 1940), 27–8. Brutus and Britain: G. Gordon, 'The Trojans in Britain', *E&S* 9 (1923), 9–30; T. Silverstein, '*Sir Gawain*, Dear Brutus and Britain's Fortunate Founding: A Study in Comedy and Convention', *MP* 62 (1965), 189–206.

[14] D. W. Robertson, 'The Concept of Courtly Love as an Impediment to the Understanding of Medieval Texts', in F. X. Newman (ed.), *The Meaning of Courtly Love* (New York, 1968), 1–19.

[15] G. Wickham, *Early English Stages 1300 to 1660*, 3 vols. (London, 1981), iii. 244.

courtly culture is the central theme of twelfth-century works on the
siege of Troy, such as Joseph of Exeter's *De bello Troiano* (*c.*1188) and
Benoît de Saint-Maure's long romance, the *Roman de Troie*, written for
Henry II. Aristocratic interest in Troy is evident in works of art such as
the tapestries executed on the theme of Troy for the Duke of Orléans
before 1400, and in the beautifully illuminated late fifteenth-century
manuscripts of Raoul Lefèvre's *Recueil des histoires de Troie* (1464, written
at the suggestion of Philip the Good, Duke of Burgundy) and other
French prose accounts of the sieges of Thebes and Troy.[16] Theatrical
representations include one given in Paris in 1389 before Charles VI of
France, apparently similar in structure and spectacle to a 1378 drama of
the siege of Jerusalem by Godfrey of Bouillon, a *Jeu du siège de Troie* performed at Avignon in 1400, and Jacques Milet's *L'Istoire de la destruction
de Troye la grant* (1450–2) in which the author finds in a flowery meadow
a tree surrounded by shields, where he digs and finds ancient Trojan
weapons.[17] In the remnants of one royal house, European aristocracy
excavated and announced its own roots. When Troy has fallen, subsequent dynastic flowerings, heroic enterprises or acts such as the founding of cities, come to be regarded as repetitions of the Trojan story,
chapters of re-creation and rediscovery linking the present to a splendid
past.

The legend of Trojan ancestry, thus appropriated by the royalty and
aristocracy, provided modern rulers with a supposed legitimacy and allowed them to enjoy the reflected glory of the founders of Rome, and
hence of Rome itself. Trojan precedents were taken seriously enough
to be used to reinforce legal and political claims at least into the Tudor
period.[18] As well as offering a flattering mirror to the modern aristocracy, the city of Troy also served as a more general image of cultural
identity across Christendom with some pleasingly positive features.

---

[16] Tapestries: A. M. Young, *Troy and Her Legend*, 120. Lefèvre: Paris, BN, MS fr. 22552.
Oxford, Bodleian Library, MS Douce 353 was presented by the King of Spain to the King of
France: inscribed on fo. 30v. See also A. Bayot, *La Légende de Troie à la cour de Bourgogne*
(Bruges, 1908). M. R. Scherer, *The Legends of Troy in Art and Literature* (New York and London,
1963).

[17] See L. H. Loomis, 'Secular Dramatics in the Royal Palace, Paris, 1378, 1389, and
Chaucer's "Tregetoures"', *Speculum*, 33 (1958), 242–55; repr. in J. Taylor and A. H. Nelson
(eds.), *Medieval English Drama: Essays Critical and Contextual* (Chicago, 1972), 98–115. G.
Cohen, *Études d'histoire du théâtre en France au Moyen Age et à la Renaissance* (Paris, 1956),
164–6.

[18] For further discussion see L. Patterson, *Negotiating the Past: The Historical Understanding
of Medieval Literature* (Madison, Wis. and London, 1987), 197–230. A. E. Parsons, 'The Trojan
Legend in England: Some Instances of its Application to the Politics of the Times', *MLR* 24
(1929), 253–64.

The stress on the founding of nations and the rebuilding of cities as an image of history, starting with the fall of Troy, suggested a history in the West of growth, endeavour, and achievement from within rather than invasion from without. Ironically, the siege and fall of Troy was used to emphasize the continuity and survival of classical culture in the Christian West and to reinforce a sense of common identity between some rulers, omitting the history of barbarian invasion and upheaval. A story ending in destruction becomes an emblem of cultural creation.

The fall of Troy thus appears in medieval writings to be the means whereby the foundation not only of the great cities of Christendom but of the imagined fortress of the West could be achieved. Culture was identified not only with aristocratic interests but in the institution of the city: the movement of history is illustrated by the rise and fall of great cities, which stand as testaments to the successes, failures, and spiritual identity of a people. The centre of culture also moves gradually westward according to the tradition of 'translatio imperii': Troy leads to the founding of Rome, which is itself 'rebuilt' in Paris or London. The ending of a great city marks a decisive moment, and the genesis of Western history is to be found in the calamity of Troy: chroniclers such as Sir Thomas Gray in his *Scalacronica* begin their histories with brief accounts of the siege of Troy, a secular equivalent to the Fall leading to an expulsion, enforced wandering, and the founding of cities, tribes, and dynasties.

Because of its importance as a beginning and an image of history, and as the point at which the prehistory of myth is transformed into the story of modern states, the siege of Troy was described in explicitly historical texts as well as romances. The most important of these as a source for Middle English and other writings is Guido de Columnis' *Historia destructionis Troiae* (completed 1287). Though Guido claims to be using the most respected sources, Dares and Dictys, his work is in fact a recension of Benoît's long poem, excising the lengthy descriptive passages dealing with courtly luxury and retelling the story of the siege as serious and sober history in contrast to Benoît's colourful romance. The *Historia* was quickly and extensively disseminated and was for a long time popular with the aristocracy: one manuscript copy bears the signatures of Richard III, James I, Charles I, and Oliver Cromwell.[19]

---

[19] See Meek's translation of Guido, p. xi. O. Golubeva, 'The Saltykov-Schedrin Library, Leningrad', *The Book Collector*, 4 (1955), 99–109. See also W. B. Wigginton, 'The Nature and Significance of the Medieval Troy Story: A Study of Guido delle Colonne's *Historia destructionis Troiae*' (dissertation, Rutgers University, 1964).

Guido's work was also the most important source for many later vernacular verse treatments of the siege of Troy. Of the Middle English
romances on the subject, only the earliest, *The Seege or Batayle of Troye*,
composed in the first quarter of the fourteenth century, makes no use of
Guido, being based largely on Benoît, Dares, and the *Excidium Troiae*.
The *Laud Troy Book*, written at the end of the fourteenth or in the early
fifteenth century, draws on Guido and a variety of other sources to present the siege of Troy as a series of battles, vigorously described, and in
part as a biography of Hector, the hero of the poem. The alliterative
Destruction of Troy, roughly contemporary with the *Laud Troy Book*, is an
embellished translation of Guido's history, adding colour and drama
while retaining the detailed, informative texture of the Latin.[20] In his
Troy Book, Lydgate makes use of Guido and other sources, and Guido's
work is also the ultimate source of the so-called *Scottish Troy Fragments*,
fifteenth-century texts closely related to Lydgate, and formerly attributed to Barbour. All of these romances emphasize the battles and ad-
venturous aspects of the material, at the same time as keeping the love
stories first added by Benoît. While appealing to an audience with an
interest in the depiction of combat by ancient heroes, the romances also
point out the historical authenticity of the matter of Troy with frequent
references to their sources. Hence they combine the popular appeal of
romance narrative with the gravity proper to a historical event of great
importance.[21]

REFERENCES TO THE SIEGE OF TROY IN OTHER WRITINGS

While poets, artists, and their patrons were inspired by the achievements
of their Trojan forebears and their subsequent resurrection in the Latin
West, commentators, following St Augustine, worried over the causes
of the destruction of the great city. Troy has a paradoxical meaning in
medieval tradition: it is frequently depicted as the seat of the arts and
sophistication, but it is also an example of treachery and human fallibility. As much as the creation of Troy was glorified, its siege and destruction was moralized. Gerald of Wales, for example, had some peculiar

---

[20] See D. A. Lawton, '*The Destruction of Troy* as Translation from Latin Prose: Aspects of
Form and Style', *SN* 52 (1980), 259–70.

[21] See C. D. Benson, *The History of Troy in Middle English Literature* (Woodbridge, 1980).
P. Strohm, 'Storie, Spelle, Geste, Romaunce, Tragedie: Generic Distinctions in the Middle
English Troy Narratives', *Speculum*, 46 (1971), 348–59.

views on the matter. In the *Description of Wales* he cites the Trojans in an excursus on prophets, saying they were too proud to give credence to Cassandra. Later he gives an idiosyncratic explanation of the fall of Troy, which once again reminds us of the strong sense of identity felt between the Trojan kingdom and medieval Christendom:

Praeterea, peccatis urgentibus, et praecipue detestabili illo et nefando Sodo-mitico, divina ultione tam olim Trojam quam postea Britanniam amiserunt. Legitur enim, quia Constantis imperator, occidentali imperio beato Silvestro et successoribus suis cum urbe relicto, Trojam reaedificare proponens, ibique ori-entalis imperii caput erigere volens, audivit hanc vocem, 'Vadis reaedificare Sodomam'; et statim mutato consilio versus Bizantium vela pariter et vexilla convertit; ibique imperii sui caput constituens, urbem eandem felici suo nomine decoravit.

It was because of their sins, and more particularly the wicked and detestable vice of homosexuality, that the Welsh were punished by God and so lost first Troy and then Britain. We read that when the Emperor Constantine handed over the Western Empire and the city of Rome to Pope Silvester and his suc-cessors, he had in mind to rebuild Troy and to establish there the capital of the Eastern Empire; but he heard a voice which said: 'It is Sodom that you are going to rebuild.' Thereupon he immediately changed his plans, and turned his sails and war-pennants towards Byzantium, making that city the capital of his empire and giving to it his own propitious name.[22]

Commentary also occurs in romances and other literary texts, in which there is a remarkable consistency in the subjects associated with the siege, its causes, and its consequences. The vice most commonly attributed to the Trojans, and by extension to their supposed descend-ants in the West, was that of treachery. Since no external means on earth could bring down the city, its fall must illustrate the consequences of human weakness. Consequently it was felt that duplicity as well as glory was the legacy from Troy: Antenor, the founder of the Normans, was a traitor, and Brutus himself was a parricide. The idea that failings as well as virtues were passed down is reflected in the Arthurian legends: Vortigern's tower collapses to reveal two fighting dragons in the founda-tions, and the Arthurian empire itself is finally lost in internecine civil warfare, a part of which is illustrated in the siege of Benwick. The faults which led to the destruction of Troy threaten to bring down the cities and great families which originate there: the siege marks the natural end

[22] Giraldus Cambrensis, *Descriptio Kambriae*, II. 7, ed. J. F. Dimock, Rolls Series, 21f (London, 1868), 215; *The Journey through Wales and the Description of Wales*, trans. L. Thorpe, 264.

of a city and dynasty which, despite its capacity to resurrect itself, contains the seeds of its own destruction. In Gower's *Confessio amantis*,
Genius interprets the fall of Troy as a warning against hypocrisy and
treachery (i. 1072–226), and Barbour's *Bruce* also cites it at the beginning of his speech on that subject:

> Bot off all thing wa worth tresoun,
> For thar is noyer duk ne baroun
> Na Erle na prynce na kyng off mycht,
> Thocht he be neuer sa wys na wycht,
> For wyt worschip price na renoun,
> That euer may wauch hym with tresoune
> Wes nocht all Troy with tresoune tane
> Quhen [ten] yeris off the wer wes gane
> Then slayn wes mony thowsand
> Off thaim with-owt throw strenth of hand,
> As Dares in his buk he wrate,
> And Dytis, that knew all thar state.
> Thai mycht nocht haiff beyn tane throw mycht,
> Bot tresoun tuk thaim throw hyr slycht.

> (vol. ii, bk. 1, ll. 515–28)

The next victim of treason mentioned in this speech is Alexander, who
in the Middle English romance *King Alisaunder* is shown pictures of
Troy by Queen Candace shortly before his death, perhaps as a veiled
warning that the curse of Trojan duplicity is about to touch him:

> Scheo ladde him to an halle of nobleys
> There he dude of his harneys
> Of Troye was ther sen the storye
> How Gregeys hadde theo victorye.

> (L MS, 6375–8)

A similar image is seen by Chaucer in the Temple of Venus in *The House
of Fame*, in a passage reminding us both of the popularity of Troy as a
subject in the visual arts and of its association with calamity:

> First sawgh I the destruction
> Of Troye thurgh the Grek Synon,
> [That] with his false forswerynge,
> And his chere and his lesynge,
> Made the hors broght into Troye,
> Thorgh which Troyens loste al her joye.
> And aftir this was grave, allas,

How Ilyon assayled was
And wonne, and kyng Priam yslayn
And Polytes his sone, certayn,
Dispitously, of daun Pirrus.

(i. 151–61)

Several features of this brief description recur in other texts on the siege
of Troy: the status of Troy as the 'first' event in the historical sequence,
the emphasis on treason and an individual traitor, and the particular interest in the royal family and their palace at Ilion, as well as the sense of
the great tragedy of the siege, are typical of various medieval references
to, or representations of, the subject. Some of these themes had been
touched upon by Chaucer earlier in *The Book of the Duchess*, in which
the story of Troy is mentioned three times: in a digression on hardiness
including a reference to Hector and Achilles (1065–9); as an illustration
of sorrow, typified by Cassandra 'that soo / Bewayled the destruccioun /
Of Troye and of Ilyoun' (1246–8); and, in a list similar to that of the
Bruce, as an example of treachery, in which Antenor is named alongside
Achitophel and Ganelon (1117–23). It is hardly surprising that
Chaucer's most substantial enquiry into betrayal in private and public
affairs should be set during the siege of Troy, where the plight of the city
is set against a siege of love.[23]

Chaucer is typical of several poets in his interest in the siege of Troy,
and in the aspects of it to which he chooses to allude. The author of
Wynnere and Wastoure begins his poem with a reminder of the Trojan
founding of Britain, the siege as a beginning of history, and the fall of
Troy as a result of treachery:

> Sythen that Bretayne was bigged   and Bruyttus it aughte
> Thurgh the takynge of Troye   with tresone withinn
> There hathe selcouthes bene sene   in seere kynges tymes
> Bot neuer so many as nowe   by the nyne dele.

Sir Gawain and the Green Knight also starts with a reference to the siege
and destruction of Troy, citing it both as the origin of later history and
as an example of treason in the 'truest' of nobles:

> Sithen the sege and the assaut watz sesed at Troye,
> The borgh brittened and brent to brondez and askez,
> The tulk that the trammes of tresoun ther wroght

---

[23] See A. Sprung, 'The "Townes Wal": A Frame for "Fre Chois" in Chaucer's *Troilus and
Criseyde*,' *Medievalia*, 14 (1988), 127–42.

Watz tried for his tricherie, the trewest on erthe:
Hit watz Ennias the athel, and his highe kynde,
That sithen depreced prouinces, and patrounes bicome
Welneghe of al the wele in the west iles.

Such passages suggest that the matter of Troy had a particular importance for writers of romances and other poems even on apparently unrelated subjects. The use of an opening reference to the fall of Troy in
several texts suggests that the siege would have had an established range
of meanings which a contemporary audience would have understood
without an authorial gloss. In *Sir Gawain and the Green Knight*, it not
only creates an arresting beginning to the story—perhaps consciously
echoing Virgil—but also suggests a thematic link between the siege and
the events of the romance. The contrasting terms of truth and treason
are examined at some length as elements in the chivalric and feudal
code in the poem, the end of which is to turn on treason of a more do-
mestic kind.[24] The opening lines stress both the theme of treason and
that of the founding of the kingdoms of the West by the descendants of
a race or 'kynde' famous for treachery: if this vice is to be found in the
truest and greatest of rulers, Arthur's court is suspect even before it appears. That Troy was generally associated with truth undermined by
treason is suggested by the romances dealing directly with the siege, as
in this passage from *The Seege of Troy*, spoken by King Priam:

> Thoru treson arn we alle for-loren.
> Hade treowthe beon amongis vs alle;
> Troye hadde neuer this chaunse by-falle.
> Trow the wolde, with ryghte and lawe,
> That traytours scholde beo to-drawe.
> Trowthe, certes, is leyd doun to-day
> And treson vp resed, welaway.
>
> (1985–91)

The alliteration of 'Troy', 'truth', 'treason', and 'traitor' indicates the key
concepts involved; in the last two lines, the fall of a city becomes a metaphor for the destruction of truth and the ascendance of treachery.
Alluding to the siege of Troy in this way also facilitates criticism of contemporary ills, given the likely association of old and new Troy in the
minds of an audience.

---

[24] See W. R. J. Barron, *'Trawthe' and Treason: The Sin of Gawain Reconsidered* (Manchester,
1980).

The opening lines of *Sir Gawain* also suggest ways in which the siege of Troy functioned more broadly in the romances as well as other writings as a metaphor for secular history and as a reminder of that history's ultimate source and origin. Troy's status as a foundation and model for later events is also illustrated by one of the manuscript books in which the romance *The Seege of Troy* appears, where the romance occupies the first eight leaves of the book, apparently serving as an introduction to a prose translation of Geoffrey of Monmouth's history, which immediately follows, leading directly from the story of a fall to one of foundation.[25] This status of origin equates the siege of Troy in some sense with the Fall, and the reconstruction of Troy in later cities with the foundation stories of the Old Testament. The phrasing of the first lines of *Sir Gawain* and *Wynnere and Wastoure*, setting a particular story in a vast historical frame, is echoed by that of *St Erkenwald*—another poem with several references to Troy and 'New Troie' or London—which begins 'At London in Englond noght full long sythen / Sythen Crist suffrid on crosse and Cristendome stablyd'. Both secular and sacred stories begin by mentioning an appropriate event of immense significance, which stands as the beginning of a new era.

Besides the combination of glory and disaster through treason, the matter of Troy contains other contrasting themes: to truth and treachery may be added 'wrake and wonder' and 'blysse and blunder', pairs established in the opening of *Sir Gawain*. By starting in this manner, the Gawain poet sets his story within a scheme of history and 'establishes a contrastive pattern, which envisages civilization as alternating between "bliss" and "blunder"'.[26] The siege and destruction of the greatest of cities, a seat of richness and civilization, provides a powerful image of the transience of earthly glory and a reminder to later dynasties and empires not only of the antiquity of their supposed parentage but of the certainty of their own mortality before fortune. The siege of Troy is an expressive image of the kind of disaster which was to haunt the medieval West concerned for its own survival. The toppling of the topless towers of Ilion in the siege makes it a lesson against vanity, and a warning of the humiliation which can follow pride.

The humbling of majesty is effectively shown in the description of King Priam. As the head of the royal house from which Western monarchs claimed descent, he is given particular attention in the romances.

---

[25] London, College of Arms, MS Arundel XXII, fos. 1–8.
[26] M. Andrew, 'The Fall of Troy in *Sir Gawain and the Green Knight* and *Troilus and Criseyde*', in P. Boitani, (ed.), *The European Tragedy of Troilus* (Oxford, 1989), 75–93 (79).

The agony and final impotence of Troy are mirrored in its monarch. The various medieval accounts of the siege of Troy tend to depict King Priam as an important and sympathetic figure, somewhat removed from the personal rivalries and intrigues indulged in by the other leading figures on either side. While previous sieges considered have served in part as opportunities for a poet to portray qualities or vices of a commander, King Priam is unusual in being for the most part a helpless onlooker, increasingly unable to organize any important military action. Indeed, human agents on both sides can seem strangely ineffective: in medieval versions the war of Troy appears to be out of the control of the Greek and Trojan chiefs, while the behaviour of the gods is ambiguous. Thus the chief importance of King Priam is not as a military captain, but as a leader who experiences and articulates the dismay of the beleaguered city. Throughout he appears as a medieval monarch, a tragic figure who gradually loses the power to fulfil his military and political responsibilities.

King Priam is first mentioned in most accounts as being absent when Troy is first destroyed by a small force, as he is himself laying siege to a castle held by rebels against his father, Laomedon, a credible situation to a medieval audience. His mourning for Troy links family bereavement with a sense of the loss suffered by the state. The scene is dramatically portrayed by the poet–translator of *The Destruction of Troy*:

> Now as this kyng vmbe the Castell lay closit abute,
> With his folke all in fere & his fyn childur,
> He was enformyt of the fare & of his fader dethe;
> How his towne was takon and tirnyt to grounde;
> His Suster sesyd and soght into syde londis;
> His knightes downe kylde vnto colde vrthe.
> Soche sikyng and sorow sanke in his hert,
> With pyté and complaint pyne for to here,
> He toke vp his tentes & the towne leuyt,
> Teght hom vnto Troy with tene that he hade,
> Segh the buyldynges brent & beton to ground.

(1506–16)

On seeing Troy, Priam is physically incapacitated by grief, and mourns for three days before commencing the reconstruction of the city. During the course of the siege, Priam's feelings mirror the fortunes of the city and of the Trojan people. Besieged king and beleaguered city are closely identified, both following the same tragic course from grandeur and power to defeat and destruction. Priam embodies the emotions and apprehensions of the besieged Trojans—or at least the noble warriors in whom the romancers are mainly interested—and his palace is the chief expression of their culture. The identification of Priam and Troy is made clear early in *The Seege of Troy*, in which the siege is described as a battle personally directed against the king himself:

> Thrytty wynter, with-oute faile,
> Men of grece heolden gret bataile
> With the kyng of troye stout and grym
> And at theo laste they ouercome him.
>
> (11–14)

Later in the same work, in a defiant speech given to Greek ambassadors before the third assault, Priam is personally possessive of Troy, whose richness expresses the power of the forces he has at his disposal:

> Y haue here, y do you vnderstonde,
> Al the power of my londe
> ffor to defende vp and doun
> Troye my riche toun.
>
> (1050–3)

To begin with, King Priam is decisive and practical. He rebuilds Troy and its defences. Sitting with the Trojan council or gathering the inhabitants of the outlying areas into the city in anticipation of a siege, Priam's practical concerns for his people are similar to those shown by Ethiocles in *The Prose Siege of Thebes*, and would have suggested real and modern sieges to a contemporary audience:

> The kyng of troye was in gret drede,
> ffor his folk weore brought to dede;
> And made feorme his dyches vp and doun
> And sette good warde ouer al the toun
> And comandede his bailyfs feor and wyde
> To fache more folk on vche a side.
>
> (1642–7)

The author goes on to describe the engines brought to the walls of the city by the Greeks under a 'grete' engineer and the springalds and arbalests used by the defenders. As we saw in *The Prose Siege of Thebes*, there is a clear instinct to modernize the scene, which is described in contemporary terms. *The Seege of Troye* also contains elsewhere detailed descriptions of armour and weapons and their effectiveness, and the copier of one manuscript appears to have kept the account up to date by interpolating references to more sophisticated siege machinery.[27]

While King Priam is shown at intervals directing operations during the siege, he is depicted more often as the grief-stricken voice of Troy; as he becomes older and more frail, so Troy crumbles away around him. Both city and king are examples of the transience of earthly glory, brought low by inexorable forces. The story of King Priam echoes that of the siege on an individual level, as the fall of the greatest of cities and its empire is set alongside the fall of a man into the weakness and final indignities of old age. Treason or 'untruth' has finally broken into the citadel of Priam's certainties and rendered them mortal:

> 'This no wende y neuer to seo
> That myn enemy myn eyr scholde beo.'
> Theo kyng weopte for theo mukil vntrewthe;
> To seo olde men weope hit is gret rewthe.

> (1998–2001)

THE MAKING OF TROY

Several reasons for the great medieval interest in the siege of Troy are suggested by the description of the interior of the city, which is the subject of lengthy passages in Benoît, Guido, and the English romances. The cumulative effect of these is to create an image of Troy as the foundation of Western culture, parallel to its status as the beginning of history, a city which is glorious but impermanent because it lacks the true Christian faith. Fascination in the siege and destruction of Troy implies a keen sense of exactly what it was that had been destroyed. Although unrelated to the process of siegecraft itself, the subject of the making of Troy helps us to understand the importance attached in medieval literature not only to Troy but also to other cities of antiquity and of more recent history which came to a violent end. Troy was the masterpiece of human craft, art, and skill; the fall of this impregnable city demonstrated the ultimate vanity of earthly ambition.

The sense that the siege of Troy is a parable of human pride meeting its nemesis is strengthened by a consideration of the way medieval writers imagined the city. In the descriptions of its reconstruction by Priam, pride is symbolized by the aesthetic magnificence of the city, in

[27] London, British Library, MS Harley 525, fos. 1–34.

particular of the royal palace of Ilion. Employing motifs which also occur in the *Roman de Thèbes* and the *Roman d'Eneas*, Benoît conjures up an image of the palace as a work of art.[28] Royal wealth and supposed permanence are evoked by the great marble towers, richly carved and painted (lines 3009–14). The themes of beauty and strength are combined in various descriptions of Ilion and the rest of Troy. Benoît describes the windows of the palace set in golden frames, and the exquisite stone and metalwork of the columns and pillars (3075–8). The palace has ten floors, is surrounded by crenellated battlements 'ovré a cisel', and its walls are decorated with images in gold (3079–88). The images on the walls of the palace and the city are of beasts and forests: such scenes perhaps represent the apparent triumph of human artifice over natural forces, and constitute an artistic imitation of the original divine Creation. The author of the *Laud Troy fBook* pays particularly close attention to this aspect of Troy:

> On here chambres and on here halles,
> Ther was wroght alle maner best,
> That was walkynge In any forest,
> Were koruen on the walles enviroun.
>
> (1808–11)

The parallel with the biblical Genesis is pointed out: 'Sithen god made first the werld, / Off suche on haue ye not herd' (1815–16). Just as the one paradise was lost, it may be implied, so this futile human attempt to repeat the act of creation will end in tragedy, ruin, and exile, especially since it is built in the name of false gods who will desert the Trojans. The topics of art and strength are closely combined in *The Destruction of Troy*:

> With gret toures vmb-tilde & torettis aboute,
> Well wroght for the werre, wacches O lofte.
> Ymagry ouer all amyt there was,
> Of beste and babery breme to beholde,
> Bost out of the best the byg toures vmbe.
> The wallis in werre wikked to assaile
> With depe dikes and derke doubull of water.
>
> (1560–6)

---

[28] On the correspondences, see: E. Langlois, 'Chronologie des romans de *Thèbes*, d'*Eneas* et de *Troie*', *BEC* 66 (1905), 107–20. E. Faral, *Recherches sur les sources latines des contes et roman courtois au Moyen Age* (Paris, 1913), 169–87. P. Riché, 'Les Représentations du palais dans les textes littéraires du Haut Moyen Age', *Francia*, 4 (1976), 161–71.

The ensuing siege is the result of human vanity in constructing this
alternative paradise: if Troy can be humbled, the implicit message might
be, then no city, dynasty, or work of man is safe.

It is not only the magnificent art and beauty of Troy which inspire
reverent description: its institutions and technical construction also ex-
cite great interest in medieval writers, particularly Guido. Troy was regarded not only as the fount or exemplar for later art, but as the origin
of the technical achievements of the West, an earlier and grander version of Rome. Perhaps wishing to stress Troy's similarity with later
cities, Guido spends less time on the fantastic and marvellous aspects of
Troy than Benoît and concentrates instead on its technical features. He
gives precise measurements of houses and walls, includes a long list of
tradesmen and craftsmen, and, presumably with Rome in mind, credits
Troy with an advanced sewer system and a river running through its
centre (chapters 45–8). Benoît, while writing with less attempt at scient-
ific precision and with more effusiveness, also presents Troy as a marvel
of military architecture which should withstand any siege. Walls and
towers are furnished with the most sophisticated defences and look over
a formidable moat (3015–18). Set on a mountain, Ilion, 'le maistre donjon' or central keep of the castle-city, disappears into the clouds. It is a
juncture between earth and heaven, the symbol of human skill rivalling
divine power, and so resistant to the weapons of a human siege:

> Onques Deus cel engin ne fist
> Qui i poüst estre menez
> Par nul home qui onc fust nez.

> (3060–2)

God never made that engine which could be brought there by any man born.

The accounts of artistic beauty, architectural strength, and technical skill
in the descriptions of Troy add further meaning to the siege. The story
of destruction is a counterpoint to the creative endeavour which the
city, the image of civilization, represents. Troy reminds us of Babel,
standing as a monument to man's ingenuity and man's vanity: the
treachery which brings down Troy is not only that of Antenor and his
compatriots who allow the Greeks into the city, but man's betrayal of his
own nature in thinking that his works will equal those of Creation and
stand against the assailing forces of natural adversity.

One of the many striking claims made by Guido is that in Troy were
founded both the tragic and comic creative arts. This idea helps us to
understand the fascination which the legendary city had for medieval

readers and romance writers. While Troy is a metaphor for tragedy of the greatest kind—a calamitous fall from unprecedented greatness to misery—it is also a story of essentially comic re-creation. Troy will be reborn and reappear in the form of Rome, and its spirit will inhabit the great empires and dynasties of the West. The siege is not a final end, but a turn of Fortune's wheel, a lesson in how the city of man falls by its own inherent corruption, and history moves on.

5

The Siege of Jerusalem

THE siege of Jerusalem by the Romans in 70 AD was a popular subject in medieval romance. The material provided a combination of legend, miracle, history, and Roman chivalry, as well as opportunities for vivid description of siege warfare in the East; the triumph of Western Christendom in the form of the Roman army must have provided a pleasing contrast to the present situation in the Holy Land at a time when the recapture of Jerusalem was still the dream of monarchs. While the combination of the religious and the chivalric, crusading elements in the story of the siege and the events leading up to it contributed to its popularity, the matter of Jerusalem also contains deeper resonances concerning the pattern of history. The romances, like those on Troy, tend to concentrate on action rather than reflection, but the ways in which the historical event is re-created bear traces of a wider context of ideas concerning destiny and salvation which give the episode a special significance.[1]

As an image of history, the siege of Jerusalem contrasts with that of Troy. Where the fall of Troy illustrates a Boethian model of history as a cycle of rise and fall of power and fortune, the destruction of Jerusalem by the Roman emperors Titus and Vespasian illustrates the separate, Augustinian conception of history as a succession of great events which reveal part of the divine scheme of things. The siege of Troy is a warning against human vanity and folly, while that of Jerusalem reveals the will and power of God. Where Troy is a tragic fall of power and pride, Jerusalem even in its tribulations is seen as a sign of the triumphal march of destiny.

In their treatments of the siege of Jerusalem, medieval writers emphasize its significance as an example of divine judgement on the Jews, who rejected and executed Christ, and amplify the story of the siege with much legendary and apocryphal religious material. They

---

[1] For a modern historical account, see R. Furneaux, *The Roman Siege of Jerusalem* (London, 1973). Desire to recover Jerusalem: J. Huizinga, *The Waning of the Middle Ages*, trans. F. Hopman (London, 1924), 92–3.

differ in their depiction of the war, however, and close consideration of
the Middle English writings illustrates the range of approaches which
could be taken to the same event. The romances belong to a much
larger literary tradition of treatments of the subject, ranging from
chronicle to epic and hagiography. As with many of the texts which
mention Troy, several of these pay little attention to the siege itself.
However, a summary of the tradition of writings on the subject shows
the different strands—historical, religious, and heroic—which are combined in the various later narrative treatments, and which are important to an understanding of the significance of the siege to later medieval
readers. The sieges of Troy and Jerusalem are both important for the
narratives which surround them and for the themes associated with
them: both serve as the culmination or central element of a large
number of other stories. Dramatically, the siege works as a catastrophe
in which these distinct narrative strands and themes are brought together.

THE LITERARY TRADITION

An important element of the sieges of Troy and Jerusalem was their historical veracity, better attested for Jerusalem but none the less claimed
for Troy as well. While medieval treatments of the siege of Troy ultimately derived for the most part from the pseudo-historical accounts of
Dares and Dictys, the siege of Jerusalem has more substantial founda-
tions in real historical writings, later to be embellished by romance
writers. Poets could draw upon and adapt the lengthy account in
Josephus' history of the Jewish wars, also known through the translation
by Hegesippus. As well as being real and momentous events, both sieges
were held to illuminate some kind of historical inevitability: the fall of
Troy shows how the rise of a city leads ineluctably to its fall, while any
event in Church or Augustinian history, such as the destruction of Jerusalem, must be an inevitable part of the divine plan. Medieval writers
consequently stress the inevitability of the siege of Jerusalem, for example by describing the portents of the destruction of the city before
the siege rather than after it, as Josephus does.[2]

---

[2] A more detailed survey of the literary tradition is provided in the Introduction to P. Moe
(ed.), *The ME Prose Translation of Roger d'Argenteuil's Bible en françois*, Middle English Texts, 6
(Heidelberg, 1977).

To the historical details of the siege were added legendary and religious materials. The most important of these was the legend that Titus
and Vespasian were cured of terrible illness by the veil of St Veronica,
which bore a miraculous impression of the face of Christ, and that they
were subsequently converted to Christianity. The Romans vow to
avenge Christ for His death at the hands of the Jews and to make war in
His name in the Holy Land. By replacing the political background to
the siege with the story of the miraculous cure and the conversion,
writers gave an aggressive campaign a spiritual motive and satisfied a
popular interest in pious legends and chivalric crusading matter.[3] The
legend of St Veronica appears in Eusebius' *Ecclesiastical History*, and is
combined with the life of Pilate—an important figure in medieval
treatments of the siege—in the fourth-century text known as the *Acta
Pilati*. By the seventh century, the Veronica legend had been combined
with the subject of the Jewish wars, in the *Cura sanitatis Tiberii* (*c*.600), a
text in which Veronica heals Tiberius and Pilate is punished for refus-
ing to pay tribute. The implications of a moral basis to the siege of
Jerusalem are taken further in the *Vindicta Salvatoris* (*c*.700), where Titus
is healed of cancer and the siege is explicitly portrayed as vengeance for
the torture and execution of Christ: the sale of Jews at thirty for a penny
after the siege, for example, is presented as a reminder of Judas's thirty
pieces of silver. In the eleventh century, a prose piece known as *De
Pylato* has Vespasian as the cured Roman who undertakes to avenge
Christ by besieging Jerusalem. Through the transmission of such texts,
with their emphasis on the miraculous and their forthright moral commentary, the siege of Jerusalem is changed from a historical episode to a
profoundly meaningful event linked to the divine history of saints and
miracles, effectively linking violence and reverence.

The subject of a Roman campaign in the Holy Land, culminating in
a great siege against God's enemies, appealed to audiences at the time of
the crusades, for whom the Romans—as the popularity of Vegetius
attests—were the exemplars of chivalry. The essentially religious and
historical material was transformed into epic in the twelfth-century
'chanson de geste', the *Venjance Nostre Seigneur*. This work stresses both
the historical authenticity of the subject and its unquestionable moral
justification: Josephus is frequently cited as the authority for the account,

---

[3] For further discussion of the legend of St Veronica and its incorporation into treatments
of the siege of Jerusalem, see E. Dobschütz, *Christusbilder: Untersuchungen zur christlichen
Legende*, in O. Gebhardt and A. Harnack (eds.), *Texts und Untersuchungen zur Geschichte der
altchristen Literatur*, Neue Folge, vol. iii (Leipzig, 1899).

and the destruction of the city is insistently presented as the culmination of a predestined series of events. The siege is depicted as an act of
divine vengeance on an impious city, put into execution by a force
newly awakened to divine truth. The Pope, St Clement, baptizes not
only Vespasian but the entire Roman army, which descends on Jerusalem just as the forty years of grace granted to the Jews for conversion
and repentance expires. Sanctioned by God in its endeavours, the besieging Roman army appears as a model of nobility and expertise in
war, epitomizing the military skills and disciplines expounded by
Vegetius and admired by his medieval readers. The epic treatment of the
siege was the source for numerous prose versions in the fourteenth century, in which Roman chivalry is again presented as a marriage of religion and ruthlessness. Several fifteenth-century manuscripts of the prose
redactions and an English translation, *The Dystruccyon of Iherusalem by
Vespazian and Tytus*, published by Wynkyn de Worde in 1507, show the
subject's continuing popularity.[4]

The Roman subjugation of Jerusalem also features as an important
episode in other works. The *Legenda aurea* (1246–55) includes details of
the portents of the fall of the city in chapter 67 on St James the Less,
three manuscripts of the *Estoire del Saint Graal* contain accounts of the
siege drawn from the French prose *Joseph d'Arimathie*, and a separate
treatment also appears in the *Joseph d'Arimathie* of Robert de Boron.[5]
Such contexts indicate the importance the event was felt to have in
divine history, as a matter worthy to be placed alongside miracles and
revelations. Its popular and edifying content made it the subject of
numerous dramatic presentations, which combine religious instruction
with the rhetoric of crusading propaganda. A late example of the religious and political usefulness of the story is a seventeenth-century
drama performed in Mexico in the indigenous Indian language, depicting Titus and Vespasian as righteous Christians fighting against a comically foolish enemy. Representations of the siege in the visual arts are

---

[4] On French treatments, see: W. Suchier, 'Über das altfranzösische Gedicht von der
Zerstörung Jerusalems (La Venjance Nostre Seigneur)', ZRP 24 (1900), 161–98; 25 (1901), 94–109,
256; A. Micha (ed.), 'Une rédaction de la *Vengeance de Notre Seigneur*', in *Mélanges offerts à Rita
Lejeune*, 2 vols. (Gembloux, 1969), ii. 1291–8. P. Moe, 'On Professor Micha's *Vengeance de Notre
Seigneur*, Version II', *Romania*, 95 (1974), 555–60. An example of a 15th-cent. MS is London,
British Museum, MS Add. 32090 (dated 1445). On de Worde's edition, see: A. Esdaile, *A List
of English Tales and Prose Romances Printed before 1740* (London, 1912), 81.

[5] Grail manuscripts: Paris, BN, MS fr. 770; Le Mans 354; Leningrad F. F v. xv. 5. See W. A.
Roach, 'The Modena Text of the Prose *Joseph d'Arimathie*', *RPh* 9 (1955–6), 313–42. W. A.
Nitze (ed.), *Le Roman de l'Estoire dou Graal*, CFMA 37 (Paris, 1927).

equally numerous, from miniatures in world histories to the tapestries depicting the destruction of Jerusalem held in Windsor Castle by
Henry VIII.[6]

Middle English treatments of the siege illustrate its different levels of
significance and the various reasons for its appeal. The longest, *Titus and
Vespasian*, was written in rhyming octosyllabic couplets in the middle of
the fourteenth century. This is primarily a work of religious instruction, containing passages on such subjects as the healing of the Roman
leaders and the life of Pilate; throughout, the idea of divine punishment
of the Jews is stressed. The poem exists in numerous manuscript books,
all of which contain mainly religious material.[7] The author is more
interested in the religious and didactic aspects of the subject than in the
scope it provides for colourful crusading epic: the principal sources are
Josephus and a prose redaction of the *Venjance Nostre Seigneur*, with additions from other works including the *Legenda aurea* and the apocryphal
Gospel of Nicodemus.

In the second half of the fifteenth century, a prose redaction of the
essential parts of *Titus and Vespasian* was made, known as *The Prose Siege
of Jerusalem*: this concentrates on the events immediately concerning the
attack on the Holy City, excising much of the surrounding legendary
material. This work exists in only one manuscript copy, a miscellany
with a slight preponderance of religious material, suggesting at least that
the story had attractions besides those afforded by miraculous legend.[8]

A different approach is taken by the author of the alliterative romance
The Siege of Jerusalem, written in the last decade of the fourteenth century. Here there is greater emphasis on the presentation of warfare, in
particular on the siege itself, with long and vivid set-piece descriptions
of the battle revealing an imaginative re-creation of Roman chivalry
and of siege warfare in the East. Of the eight manuscripts in which it

---

[6] Theatrical representations: S. K. Wright, *The Vengeance of Our Lord: Medieval
Dramatizations of the Destruction of Jerusalem*, Pontifical Institute of Mediaeval Studies, Studies
and Texts, 89 (Toronto, 1989). Mexican version: *Destrucción de Jerusalén*. The tapestry is mentioned in an inventory of Henry VIII's possessions: London, British Library, MS Harley 1419,
fo. 298.

[7] See e.g. London, British Library, MS Add. 36523, in which *Titus and Vespasian* is the first
item (fos. 1–71) in a book containing the *Seven Penitential Psalms* and the *Lay Folks Mass Book*.
The poem is also the first work in London, British Library, MS Add. 10036 on fos. 2–61b,
which contains *The Assumption of Our Lady* and an English prose rendering of the *Visio Sancti
Pauli*, a meditation of the divine city possibly placed here as a balance to the fall of Jerusalem.
For details of other manuscripts, see *Titus and Vespasian*, pp. xxiv–xxviii.

[8] A. Kurvinen, 'MS Porkington 10: Description with Extracts', *Neu.Mitt.* 54 (1953),
33–67.

appears, only two consist of gatherings of religious writings. Elsewhere it appears in the company of other romances, particularly those with a crusading theme or dealing with a siege: one manuscript, for example, contains a text of Guido's *Historia destructionis Troiae* and the Latin source for *The Wars of Alexander*. *The Siege of Jerusalem* also appears immediately before *The Sege of Melayne* in the London Thornton manuscript.[9] Such manuscript contexts suggest not only an interest in crusading and siege warfare as a theme but different intentions on the part of the authors of the two English verse treatments of the siege of Jerusalem: 'Whereas in the manuscripts, *Titus and Vespasian* is clearly considered a religious poem, the *Siege of Jerusalem* remains in the border area between romance, legend and historiography.'[10]

A fourth treatment of the siege in English exists in the fifteenth-century translation of a French prose work by Roger d'Argenteuil known as the *Bible en françois*. This piece, which was used as a source for *The Siege of Jerusalem*, is a collection of diverse religious material drawn from the Gospels and the apocryphal gospels, and ending with a detailed description of the Roman conquest of the Holy City.[11] The English rendering of the *Bible en françois*, which we shall refer to as the *English Bible*, contains the most detailed and the most brutal description of the siege of all the Middle English accounts, emphasizing the violence of the Romans while also insisting on the ethical legitimacy of their actions; its detailed use of terms of siegecraft also makes it a vivid picture of a late medieval siege.

THE DEPICTION OF THE SIEGE

Different aspects of the siege are emphasized in the various Middle English writings, from its religious symbolism and significance to the

---

[9] Religious miscellanies: Oxford, Bodleian Library, MS Laud misc. 656. San Marino, Huntingdon Library, MS HM 128. MS with Guido and Alexander: Cambridge, University Library, MS Mm. V. 14. Thornton MS: London, British Library, MS Add. 31042, fos. 50r–66r. *The Sege of Melayne* follows on fos. 66v–79v. See H. Hudson, 'Middle English Popular Romances: The Manuscript Evidence', *Manuscripta*, 28 (1984), 67–78. I. Doyle, 'The Manuscripts', in D. Lawton (ed.), *Middle English Alliterative Poetry and its Literary Background*, (Cambridge, 1982), 88–100.

[10] G. Guddat-Figge, *Catalogue of Manuscripts Containing Middle English Romances* (Munich, 1976), 41.

[11] See P. Moe, 'The French Source of the Alliterative Siege of Jerusalem', *MÆ* 39 (1970), 147–54.

spectacle and vicissitudes of crusading campaigns. In discussing the
topics associated with the siege of Jerusalem we shall also be returning
to themes discussed earlier, such as the portrayal of attacking and defending commanders and the use of technical military terms in a narrative account.

The author of *Titus and Vespasian* is chiefly interested in incorporating religious material into a long account of the events leading up to the
siege and the siege itself: the poem seems to have grown with numerous
accretions, and may not be entirely the work of one author: one manuscript copy is so heavily interpolated with apocryphal and exegetical
material 'as to make it practically another work'.[12] The Romans do not
depart for Judaea with an army for nearly three thousand lines, in which
time there has been a brief life of Christ, an account of legends concerning Nicodemus and Joseph of Arimathea, and a long description of
the cure of Velosian by Veronica's veil and the consequent conversion
of the Romans. This loose narrative framework sets the scene for the
siege as an event comparable to the miracles of the saints and the life of
Christ, not simply a local encounter but an occurrence of universal
significance. The siege ends a story which begins with the life and Passion of Christ: it is presented as the consequence of the death of Christ,
and as His act of vengeance: 'Lete we now the Jewes dwelle. / Here
gynneth her wrech for to telle' (1163–4). The siege also forms a part of
the redemption of man for the fall of Adam, a purgatorial experience by
which he is violently cleansed of vice (1585–630). Human malice and
foolishness is personified in the figure of Pilate, and the siege is depicted
as his personal castigation for failing to save Christ from the Jews. The
paradox that the Jews are being punished for something they were destined to do in any case is not apparently sensed in the poem, nor indeed
in any of the Middle English accounts.

The long account of the background to the siege involves both
human history, in the political relations between Rome and Jerusalem,
and divine history in the interlaced stories of saints and martyrs. The
siege thus appears as an event in both human and divine time: on the
one level it marks a decisive moment in the spreading of the Christian
faith and the defeat of God's enemies, while on the higher plane it is part
of a series of revelatory expressions of God's purpose. In addition, the
siege of Jerusalem, like that of Troy, is the culmination of numerous

---

[12] Oxford, Bodleian Library, MS Douce 78, fos. 19–75b. Herbert's comment, *Titus and
Vespasian*, p. xxxvii.

personal destinies: great attention is paid to the agonies of Pilate and to the increasingly intense devotion to the siege by Titus and Vespasian.

One manuscript of *Titus and Vespasian* separates the story of the siege from the rest of the poem, suggesting that it may have been regarded as a distinct work in its own right in some copyings and performances. Another divides the poem into passages, perhaps designed for reading aloud or meditation.[13] The siege is depicted in such a way as to stimulate pious reflection in the course of events; the long speeches of the participants and the numerous emotional dialogues between them articulate important ideas, and are similar to dramatic representations, which may have influenced the author. Details of the siege are also included in the account, which serve to balance the wider theological themes with realistic touches. The story is both a human one, involving boldly characterized chief protagonists and the soldiers and citizens under them, and a more abstract drama of ideas concerning divine justice and vengeance. The siege is a meeting point of the human and the divine, as it is in the miraculous episodes in the accounts of the sieges of Rhodes and Belgrade previously discussed.

Before the attack on Jerusalem, other conquests are briefly mentioned. The illustration of different ways of winning a town or fortress is reminiscent of the campaign described in *Richard Coeur de Lion*. Acre surrenders without resistance to Vespasian, who leaves it in the charge of his warden and ravages the surrounding area (2743–56). Jaffa is besieged and assailed by stormy winter weather which is attributed to God. The inhabitants of Jaffa refuse to surrender and Vespasian vows not to leave until the town is his; the defenders prefer death at each other's hands to the shame of surrender (2757–808). This action has its equivalents in history, as when in 1190 the Jews of York fled to Clifford's tower pursued by a crowd and chose suicide rather than surrender to the Christian mob. Perhaps more than a pitched battle, a siege allows for the expression of a single will on the part of a mass of people: the coherence achieved by a heterogeneous populace under siege was an important theme in the description of the sieges of Rhodes, in which factional animosities were forgotten. Here it allows writers to emphasize the similarity of an enemy perceived as the enemy of Christ. At the same time, practical details are not forgotten. Like Arthur at Metz, Vespasian makes arrangements for the protection and government of the

---

[13] The Douce MS mentioned above divides the poem into sections. London, British Library, MS Add. 36523, fos. 1–71, separates the campaign and siege from the rest of the poem under the heading 'Here bygynneth the passage of Vaspasian and Titus' (fo. 38r).

conquered town. These passages take us away from a specifically Eastern setting: throughout, the re-creation of siege conditions in the Holy
Land is only intermittent, and the poet often seems to be imagining a
Western landscape: 'He lefte at Jaffe kepers gode / To kepe the cite,
feelde and wode' (2807–8).

The Roman army moves on to the Holy City and surrounds it. We
are reminded of the spiritual symbolism of the siege, in lines which
compare the beleaguered city to the soul of a sinner awaiting the day of
judgement:

> The Jewes were trappede and holden inne,
> For thei were combrede all with synne.
> There nys noo gode dede unyolde
> Ny no wickede be ne shulde.

> (2825–8)

The metaphor of the Jews bound in by their own sin is similar to the
image of the fortress of the wicked soul used in several sermons of the
period:

This world mai wel be likenyd to a castel; for rith as a castel is a stronge hoold
maad of stones ioyned with lym to kepe oute men with-oute forth, so wickede
men confederid togidir with falce love and evele wille ben strengthid in her
malice and kepeth evere goddes word oute of hir soules and hateth the true
prechoures therof.[14]

Before the assault begins, there is a description of the actions taken by
Pilate, who sends out spies to assess the strength of the besieging army
and appeals for allies. It is important to the poet's intentions that Jerusalem is seen to be defended by a coward: Pilate quickly becomes desperate, and has to be reassured by his chief ally, Archelaus, the king of
Galilee, that Jerusalem is well provisioned and defended. By depicting
Pilate as an inadequate commander, the poet reinforces the impression
that the siege is in part his personal punishment. As Pilate becomes
increasingly fearful, Vespasian consolidates his own strength, laying
waste to the surrounding area, raising his banners around Jerusalem,
and organizing preparations.[15] There are occasional practical details

[14] Cited by G. R. Owst, *Literature and Pulpit in Medieval England* (Cambridge, 1933; revised
2nd edn. Oxford, 1961), 79. See also the sermon by Master Rypon: London, British Library,
MS Harley 4894, fo. 1v.

[15] Pilate's gathering of allies: 2829–44; wasting of territory: 2845–52; use of spies: 2853–6,
2872–5; Archelaus' speech: 2876–902.

throughout the description of the siege which suggest, again, conditions in the West:

> Than the Emperour sende is sonde
> For dikers thurghout that londe,
> And bade yeve everiche to his pay
> Foure pens upon the day;
> Every maister twey shelynges had.

(3335–9)

The description continues to combine moral commentary, the contrasting portrayals of the commanders as a pious and skilled attacker against a dithering, feeble defender, and realistic individual details. The siege starts, symbolically, on Easter Day, thirty-four years after the crucifixion of Christ. Thus it represents the suffering meted out to the Jewish people on the same day as Christ rose from the dead, and after a length of time which was traditionally that of the life of the Saviour. Both the Passion and the siege are part of the fulfilment of destiny, linked by the logic of a divine scheme: the numerical symbolism is extended in a prophecy that the siege will last seven years, so that Jerusalem falls after its forty years of grace have expired (2961–76). The poem moves on from these calculations to give us another arresting glimpse of siege combat as the Romans bombard the suburbs of Jerusalem:

> And ofte to the toun thei caste
> And shete with bowes and alblaste,
> With tarbarelx and with wildefyre,
> With stafslynges and with othur atyre.

(2934–7)

Following this, we see rope and leather ladders, 'spryngals' and other engines supervised by master engineers, and 'berffreys' or towers erected to see into the town (2948–56). Besides such instances of the realities of medieval siege warfare, there are also occasional references to the conditions of campaigning in the desert, drawn largely from Josephus: an example is the ingenious supply of water to the Roman army, created by filling the arid vale of Jordan with water carried in wineskins (2977–3024). For the most part, however, there is little detailed description of warfare, either outside the city or at its walls. Scarcely any attempt is made to place the siege in a specific landscape: it is presented rather as an archetype, the city being defined as a castle and the area around it as a vaguely suggested battlefield. Possibly this depiction owes something to the sense of Latin 'castellum', which could extend from 'fortress' to 'fortified town'. The significance of the siege does not depend on our imagining it as a realistic encounter in the Holy Land. Images of it are built up through the contrast of perspectives as we look into and out of besieged Jerusalem. These passages also highlight the personal conflict between Vespasian and Pilate:

> And as thei stode and out byhelde,
> Vaspasian stode there in the felde.
> He sogh hem on the walles goon
> Up and doun full gode woon.
>
> (3049–53)

As the Romans mount their blockade, much space is devoted to an account of the defections from within Jerusalem and the advisers serving the commanders: Jacob leaves Jerusalem to become Vespasian's personal counsellor, and we see an alarmed and defeatist Pilate being advised to make night sorties by Archelaus, Barrabas, and Josephus as the defenders' situation becomes more desperate. Various anecdotes illustrate the results of a blockade: the defenders, recognizing that they are being punished by the Messiah, beg to be allowed to make a last attack on the besiegers; eleven thousand Jews kill each other as they expect to be conquered; a woman eats her own child; the people are ordered by Pilate to swallow their own treasure, while many die from the stench of putrescent corpses left in the street.[16]

The same themes of desperation, shame, and physical degradation are evident in the description of the Jewish defenders at the final defeat of Jerusalem. Determination and lack of compassion are the most noticeable attributes of the Roman generals, whose characters are similar to that of Richard the Lionheart on crusade, though perhaps without his edge of manic ferocity. After seven years of beleaguerment, the townspeople surrender, but Vespasian is intent on carrying out the vengeance of Christ on His persecutors: when he enters the town, only the genuine Christians identified by Josephus are freed and the remaining citizens are massacred. Jews are sold for thirty a penny, in memory of the betrayal of Christ, and then tortured and killed. The city is demolished entirely, with the exception of the Temple and the Tower of David. Archelaus commits suicide and Pilate is captured; much of the

---

[16] Defection of Jacob: 3221–56; council of leaders: 3257–390; events during blockade: 3391–546.

remainder of the poem is devoted to an account of the last days of
Pilate.[17] In this respect, the narrative is similar to some of the Troy -
romances, such as the *Laud Troy Book*, which also incorporate lengthy
biographies of protagonists into their account. Responsibility for the
violence perpetrated at the ending of the siege is attributed to God.
Little detracts from the general exultation at the Christian victory,
though a passage in which Titus declares that the Romans are not
motivated by cruelty, but are simply the instruments of God's terrible
justice, might suggest some residual doubts as to the morality of the torture and massacre of the defenders:

> Lorde, foryeve my fader and me,
> For thurgh us lye thei not deed,
> But for her owne feble reed.
> Hadde thei erst hem yolden to us,
> Ne shulde thei noght have leyn thus.

> (3536–40)

Titus and Vespasian is essentially a religious work, presenting the siege
as the workings of God through his agents on earth. The siege of Jerusalem in the poem resembles an illustration of the siege of Jerusalem in
the first Crusade in a manuscript of the chronicle of William of Tyre, in
which the crusading soldiers are shown scaling the walls with various
weapons, while being inspired by a vision of Christ's Passion within the
city. Parallels drawn between the action of a siege and the life of Christ
also occur in epic poetry, as when Ambroise compares the storming of
the walls of Acre by the crusaders to the Ascension. Under siege, the
Holy City brings man into contact with God, who is perceived as a
beneficent healer to His followers the Romans and as a terrible de-
stroyer to those who reject Him.[18]

The Siege of Jerusalem shares the basic premisses of *Titus and Vespasian*
in its treatment of the story, which is again shown as the carrying out of
God's vengeance and hence a morally just crusade; the description of
the siege itself, however, is more closely imagined in its use of realistic
detail and its evocation of siege warfare in the East. The Passion of
Christ and the miracles of St Veronica, which motivate Titus and Vespasian to undertake their expedition, are treated within the first three

---

[17] Surrender of city: 3829–49; massacre and destruction: 4149–288; life of Pilate:
4289–486.
[18] The illustration is reproduced in M. Billings, *The Cross and the Crescent* (London, 1987),
68. Ambroise, *L'Estoire de la Guerre Sainte*, ll. 3395–400.

hundred lines. The greater part of the poem is devoted to a dramatic narrative account of the military action, in which the excitement of a crusading siege is the focus of attention rather than its moral or theological implications. Technical detail is allied to themes and images which have much in common with early heroic poetry, to give an impression of the siege which emphasizes the heroism of the Romans and the exotic strangeness of the defenders.

The practical images of siegecraft in *The Siege of Jerusalem* include elaborate descriptions of the Roman camp, and tactics such as the damming and pollution of streams running into the city with dead bodies. Titus and Vespasian exemplify military expertise as well as piety. Though their status as Romans serves to heighten their chivalric lustre, the poet takes little interest in any uniquely Roman qualities. Rather, in describing the siege, he adapts the material to themes derived from heroic crusading literature and portrays the generals as modern nobles at war, as J. A. W. Bennett points out:

Vespasian is an earlier Coeur de Lion. The battle scenes suggest both the zeal and the cruelty of the Crusaders. The account of the siege itself is modernized, or rather made topical, so that it resembles a crusading enterprise rather than a Roman; it is also a chivalric 'layk' (sport): when off duty the knights go hunting and hawking by day, and dance by night. The appeal would be to audiences who knew at first or second hand of the siege of foreign towns, including those in France that Froissart was describing at this very time. Titus's soldiers solemnly swear allegiance to a feudal lord (1005–6). Their tents, like those of the Crusaders, are 'stoked ful of storiis [paintings] . . . kerneld [crenellated] alofte' (330–1). They make a siege engine called a sow, as the English had done at the siege of Berwick.[19]

These observations also illuminate the similarities in poetic descriptions of sieges from different historical periods and different parts of the world: poets employ realistic detail, chivalric and aristocratic motifs in their depiction of siege commanders, and draw on a common stock of inherited literary topics in heroic and romance literature, as well as on contemporary experience. The siege represents a theme in which contemporary realities can be recognized but also transcended, as they are translated in literature into a world of legend, crusading glory, and myth.

The Siege of Jerusalem emphasizes throughout the theme of total destruction wrought by siege, and the destiny behind the violence inflicted

---

[19] J. A. W. Bennett, *Middle English Literature*, ed. and completed by D. Gray (Oxford, 1986), 199.

on Jerusalem. Like Richard's army at the Third Crusade, Vespasian's soldiers are described as an inexorable force, bringing low the rich towns
of the East:

> Was noght bot roryng & ruth   in alle the riche tounnes,
> & red laschyng lyeth   alle the londe ouer;
> Token toun & tour,   teldes ful fele,
> Brosten gates of brass   & many borwe wonnen.
>
> (303–6)

Such apocalyptic imagery is frequently repeated with regard to the final
assault, which is to be for the Romans a violent cleansing rite, as Vespasian foresees: 'For or this toun be tak & this toures heye / Michel torfere
& tene vs tides on hande' (861–2). The strength and richness of Jerusalem and the towns of the East are mentioned to point out the difficulty of the siege and the devastation it will cause. Besieged cities are
described as human 'wrecchys', punished by Christ for gaining false
power and wealth. Biblical echoes may be detected in the threatening,
doom-laden prophecy of the Roman leader:

> Suree, Cesaris londe,   thou may seken euer,
> Ful mychel wo mon be wroghte,   in thy wlonk tounes,
> Cytees vnder Syon,   now is your sorow uppe:
> The deth of the dereworth Crist   der schal be yolden.
> Now is, Bethleem, y bost   y-broght to an ende;
> Jerusalem & Ierico,   for-juggyd wrecchys,
> Schal neuer kynge of your kynde   with croune be ynoyntid,
> Ne Jewe for Jesu sake   iouke in you more.
>
> (293–300)

Descriptions of pitched battles outside Jerusalem continue this tone of
doom and general destruction. One of the ways in which the poet
achieves this is the use of various images of the ground or earth, dust
being the end of soldiers and cities alike. Knights fall to the 'cold',
'blake', 'hard' earth, each adjective carrying strong associations of mortality. The armies are surrounded by the dust they have raised from the
desert, again a reminder of the calamity caused by the siege: 'Doust
drof vpon lofte,   dymedyn alle aboute, / As thonder & thicke rayn,
throwolande in skyes' (531–2). The theme of the devouring earth appears again when Jerusalem has finally been destroyed:

> Nas no ston in the stede   stondande alofte,
> Morter ne mode walle   bot alle to mulle fallen —

> Nother tymbr ne tre,   temple ne other,
> Bot doun betyn & brent   into blake erthe.

(1285–8)

The language of death and destruction associated with the siege
is contrasted with the colourful and lavish descriptions of the Roman
army, with its decorated tents in the field, gleaming armour, emblem of
a golden eagle on a globe, and the belfry, which shines like the sun over
the beleaguered city. The passage lays stress on the light coming from
the Roman belfry, expressing the power and illumination of the Romans and also perhaps implying the spiritual darkness of the Jews; it also
illustrates the creative and decorative aspects of the description of siege
warfare in contrast to the apocalyptic imagery previously encountered:

> Ibrytaged aboute   the belfray was thanne
> With a tenful tour,   that ouer the toun gawged.
> The best by the brightnesse   burnes myght knowe
> Four myle ther fro,   so the feldes schonen;
> & on eche pomel wer pyght   penseles hyghe
> Of selke & sendel,   with seluere ybetyn.
> Hit glitered as gled fur,   ful of gold riche,
> Ouer al the cite to se,   as the sonne bemys.

(409–16)

The picture created here, and in the description of the Roman eagle of
shining gold and splendid decoration, recalls images of armies at sieges
in French epics.[20] The spectacular element in battle description lends
drama and significance to the event, giving it the feeling of a ritual:
ornate pennants and emblems can suggest both superior force and a
morally dubious luxury. In *La Destructioun de Rome* Saracens as well as
Romans are described in a rich setting, perhaps to emphasize the havoc
which is about to take place (398–400). Poets describing sieges build the
drama out of extremes, whether moral, physical, or emotional.

Around the theme of the siege, the author of *The Siege of Jerusalem*
consequently creates a pattern of contrasting images and ideas: the
gleaming arms and the sky over the battlefield darkened by dust; colourful images of the elephants and rich robes worn by the priests in the
battles outside the city next to the gruesome descriptions of agony and
death; the construction of the palatial Roman tents and the demolition
of Jerusalem itself. This technique of 'contrasting sensory or emotional
effects' continually presents the reader with starkly opposed images and

---

[20] See, e.g. Ambroise, ll. 3973–90. *Le Siège de Barbastre*, ll. 3910 (banners), 3950–3 (eagle).

concepts of warfare.[21] The siege is at one moment an occupation for noblemen who ride into the fields to hunt, at another—as when Caiphas and his scribes are flayed alive and hung up outside the walls covered in honey—a barbaric enterprise. Our readings of other sieges suggest that this particular contrast might not have been perceived so strongly as such by a medieval audience. The depictions of Richard, Arthur, and Vespasian as commanders combine cruelty, piety, and a strong practical military sense with little evident awareness of juxtaposition of opposed qualities.

Of all the sieges so far considered, that of Jerusalem is perhaps the one which would have had the strongest claim to be just for a medieval audience: all the violence exercised by the Romans is simply the expression of the divine will, a visitation on the persecutors of Christ of the same degree of violence which they themselves perpetrated. The execution of the Saracen prisoners at Acre had to be sanctioned by the appearance of an angel urging Richard to execute them, suggesting at least a feeling that such a massacre needed justification. In the case of Jerusalem, however, there is no moral ambiguity since God had warned of the siege and fall of the city through His prophets. The poet has ample scope to indulge in descriptions of torture and execution after the siege, and his audience can similarly enjoy identifying with the Romans' brutal demonstration of power. The final image of the siege is that of the burning of Caiphas and his scribes outside the city walls 'on the wynde syde, / & alle a-brod on the burwe blewen the powder' (717–18). Reference to dust recurs here, reminding us that the siege is a symbol of mortality and of the transience of earthly glory. *The Siege of Jerusalem* conveys the feeling of a short campaign, describing battles, storms, and the final massacre with little space given to the kind of digressions on various subjects made in *Titus and Vespasian*. The violence employed is balanced by the compelling depictions of the two armies and their accoutrements, in particular perhaps the dromedaries of the Jews. In general, the siege is treated as an event of heroic crusading warfare, with enough local detail to enable a contemporary audience to catch echoes of contemporary sieges they may have experienced more directly themselves.

Both the violence and the technicalities of siege warfare are explored in the final text we shall consider here, the *English Bible*. The depiction of the siege reflects the sources of the work in Josephus and other

---

[21] A. C. Spearing, *Readings in Medieval Poetry* (Cambridge, 1987), 165–72 (169).

historical writings and the heroic poetry of crusading warfare. It also reveals a strong interest in practical matters; more than *Titus and Vespasian* or the alliterative romance, the *English Bible* gives a vivid and informed picture of late medieval siege practices. The encounter is updated to include at least a mention of fifteenth-century elements such as guns, and the author seems anxious to include as much information on siege warfare as can be accommodated in the space. At the same time, these modernizing elements are combined with motifs derived from earlier heroic literature. As a prose description of a siege, the treatment of the destruction of Jerusalem in the *English Bible* shares several features with the similarly detailed passages in *The Prose Siege of Thebes* and Kaye's rendering of Caoursin's chronicle of the defence of Rhodes. Other aspects of the description resemble the elements of heroic portraiture considered earlier in various romances. The *English Bible* also describes with macabre detail the violence supposedly sanctioned by God, giving rise to some of the same issues of conduct in victory at a siege as were raised by the alliterative *Morte Arthure*.

The *English Bible* begins the section on 'How that Vaspasian bisegid and destrued Ierusalem' with a brisk account of Vespasian's arrival in the Holy Land and the start of the campaign: 'He destrued alle the tovnes and castellis about Ierusalem & sloug as many of the Iuwes as he might mete with and bisegid the cite manli and forcibly with much and many dyverse and gret ordinauncis vpon euery side' (ch. 20, pp. 75–6). The suggested interest in the details of the 'ordinauncis' used is revealed later in the description of an assault on the city. Jerusalem itself is again imagined as a fortress: this is clear from passages in which Vespasian's humiliated messengers are sent back to Vespasian with the Jews' message of defiance, in which they 'passid the drawbriggis and the dichis without the barbicans of the cite'. The topic of the humiliation of messengers sent to negotiate during a siege is a common one in French crusading epic.[22]

The depiction of Vespasian in the *English Bible* has much in common with the presentation of commanders such as Arthur or Richard the Lionheart. The scene is one of the busy preparations for an assault by siege which might have taken place during a campaign in the Hundred Years War: outraged by the treatment of his messengers, who have been bound and anointed with ashes, Vespasian has them washed,

---

[22] In *Ogier le Danois* Charlemagne's messengers are sent home shaven of their beards and moustaches, and in Gui de Cambrai's *Vengement Alixandre* Antipater's face is blackened with charcoal: examples given in *English Bible*, Introduction, 28.

and aftir toke togidir counseil that eche man shuld be armed the day by the morow, redy to assaile the cite, and anone sent knightis and seriauntis thurgh alle the host that euery man shuld make redy theire armures and their harneys for to make assaut on the morow to the Iuwes.

Than the knightis and the seriauntis made hem redy and harneysid hem with their hauberkis and their helmes and alle their othir harneys and were alle redy, sum on horsbake and sum on fote. And when the morow was comen Vaspasian lete crie aboute in the host that eche man were redy armed & come to his tent for to defende it. And whan the host was redy armed, thei com afore Vaspasian. Than he divided and departid his host & made scaling laddirs and divisid .iiij. ladders ageyn the maistirs gate of Ierusalem. And in that one was Vaspasian himselue in the middis of his host ageyn the strengist and the grettist gate of Ierusalem ... (ch. 20, p. 78)

The commander of the army is at the centre of this description, issuing directions, supervising the strategy of assault, and, like Richard, leading the army from the centre against the most difficult point. As in the romance of Richard, the siege tower is a focus of attention. The Roman standard, described at some length, is part of the great belfry or tower which appears in *The Siege of Jerusalem*: 'And in the same standard was .xij. whelis and .xiiij. horsis that were made aboue the toure and [carneaux], which was alle fulle withyn and without of shildis and speris and armures' (ch. 20, p. 79).

The defences are described at even greater length. The passage in which the Jews charge out of the city at the Roman army while leaving the walls defended gives a vivid description of this aspect of siege warfare, and illustrates the combination of technical detail and interest in the unusual military practices in the East which characterizes the description of a crusading siege in this and other texts:

Next folowing this whan that noble prince, the brothir of themperoure of Rome, had thus ordeyned his host in .x. wardis and dressid his standard ayens the Iuwes, the which lete crye by alle the cite of Ierusalem that euery man shuld to harneis and to armure. The Iuwes than manly issuid out ayens Vaspasian, which were nombrid mo than an .C.M. without the smalle peple & were armed strongly. And then thei brought out their olyuantis, camelles, and dromadories, with their bastellis, gunnes, and engines, tribiettis, quillyuers, shildis, targis, rivaudis, garetis, speris, paveis, axis, springaldis, and al maner of othir habilementis for the werre. (ch. 21, pp. 79–80)

Trebuchets (tribiettis) and guns are of the later medieval period, indicating that the description is being adapted to changing practices of warfare. Differences between the Roman and Jewish, or Western and

Eastern, 'habilementis' and strategies are evidently a matter of interest here, and the passage provides an illustration of Western imagination of the animals of the East. The passage goes on to list the Jewish 'ordin-aunce', which includes: 25 elephants, each bearing a castle with 100 knights; 100 dromedaries carrying fifty armed men in a 'garet' (as in the 'garetis' in the passage above); 140 camels with fifty men each in a tur-ret; 100 chariots 'and in euerych of them myght fight .xv. men harneisid with glayvis, axis, and speris', and 20,000 horses. This fantastic cavalry leaves the city to face the Romans while the infantry remains to guard the city:

And alle the wallis, the touris, gatis, and posterns were wele ordeyned and fortified, enforcid, and stuffid with men of armes and habilementis for the werre defensibles, vitail, and al maner artillery. (ch. 21, p. 80)

The besieged Jews themselves use siege weapons from the castles mounted on their elephants. Just as the Roman commander leads from a belfry (siege tower) carrying the standard of Rome, symbolizing the imperial strength, so the defenders also deploy a symbolic mobile castle: the tabernacle, with the ornamented chair of the high priest Caiphas, is borne in the largest tower. The siege expresses a deeper conflict between the powers of Rome, strengthened by Christ, and the anti-Christian force represented by the tabernacle and its ministers. Again we see, in the reference to drawbridges, that the besieged city has become an archetypal fortress in the mind of the author:

Then went out of the Iuwes on horsebak, wel armed, ten thousand at one frunt togidirs, and then issuid out alle the gret armye of the olivauntis, drom-madories, and camellis at .iiij. parties of that cite. And they were alle passid the draubriggis, the gatis, and the diches, and com without at theire large and dis-plaied theire baners, standardis, gitons, and pensilles, and sette gret shotte of quilliuers, [balastirs], and springaldis in the grettist [castelle] of the olivauntis, which was solemply made by sotel artificers in wise of a curious tabernacle of grete defence in which ther was .xij. gret pilers of siluer that supported it. (ch. 21, pp. 80–1)

The echoes of the description of the building of the Ark of the Coven-ant become clearer in the description of Caiphas. Here he appears wear-ing what seem to be the horns of Moses as described in the Book of Exodus (37: 25–9), though there is no sense that the allusion in any way softens the perception of him as being covetous and aggressive: 'And in the myddis of hys brest he had a plate of the finest gold of Arabie, garnysshid with .xij. precious stones ful passingly riche and of feire entaile. And vpon his hede eke had this busshop Caiphas a corone of gold with .ij. short hornes & sharp aboue his eris' (ch. 21, p. 81).

Caiphas and the Jews are shown by such imagery to be adhering stubbornly and ostentatiously to the Old Law, and rejecting the revelation of Christ. For the writer and his audience, such descriptions emphasize the significance of the siege as a holy action, performed under a moral imperative to avenge Christ's death and enforce His Law. In his speech before battle, Vespasian differs from the starkly practical Richard the Lionheart in his pious enthusiasm. He reminds his army of the suffering of Christ and urges them to fight in 'oure Lordis quarelle'. His soldiers respond by promising to avenge Christ and the martyrs. The crusading siege is portrayed as an act of heroism and possible self-sacrifice in the name of the Lord: 'Lat us hardily go upon hem in Goddis behalue ayens his enemyes, and he shal be oure help' (ch. 21, p. 82).

The main battle is fought outside the city, and is described with familiar literary elements such as the gleaming armour and helmets of the Romans, which light up the sky, and the slaughter of the cavalry, given a touch of brutal realistic detail as the Romans approach the elephants and dromedaries 'and they went vndir their wombis and smote hem with sharp glayvis and bare hem to the hert with ther wepens and made hem to falle to the erth' (ch. 21, p. 82). Caiphas and the priests are captured and the Jewish army retreats into Jerusalem, leaving many dead behind them. Where other accounts of the siege include description of a blockade and its results on the populace, the *English Bible* describes a siege assault immediately following the defeat of the Jewish cavalry in pitched battle. Once again the scene could be that of a besieged castle in Western Europe at any time in the later Middle Ages:

And then they brake the drawbriggis and went up into the barbicans and upon kiornelles of Ierusalem and garnysshid hem with stones and engines, balastirs, and quarels alle about and made their ladders aboue upon the toures of the cite. And they hourdisid and garnyshid them of alle that was nedefulle in as much as they might, so that the Iuwes might haue no strength to issue out of the cite to fight. (ch. 21, p. 83)

A later list adds 'gunnes' to the list of weapons involved (ch. 22, p. 87), but no guns are used, although, as has been noted, they were in regular use at sieges in the later fifteenth century, when the *English Bible* was composed. As with other texts, a conservative tendency seems to be at work: though in other respects, such as the mention of the trebuchet,

the siege is made to conform with later medieval practice, there is still a
hesitancy over the use of firearms, perhaps out of a feeling that the
chivalric code as exemplified by the Romans would be obscured or
complicated by this development. Other technological aspects of siegecraft interest the writer greatly, however. On the morning after the
battle, a full-scale assault is laid. Vespasian's leadership is admiringly described, as is the range of artillery employed:

And then lete he dresse ayens the maistir gate of Ierusalem anothir castel of
tymbir, high, strong, and large for .v.M. men to fight in. And he made to cast and
shote from thens quarels firid and envenymed upon the Iuwes at the toures and
corners, by the which they destrued much peple and brent & bette doun alle
the toures and touretis and garetis and assailed the cite on eche side and dressid
theire scaling ladders ayens the height of the wallis, that were full high and
strong and thicke, and shotte up quarellis ayenst hem on high. Then lete Vaspasian avale the laddirs and lete cast stones an high on eche side of the wallis and
made shote tribgettis and engynes and quarellis federid with brasse and hedis of
speris. (ch. 21, p. 84)

The final assault on the city is described at even greater length, and
provides a model description of various aspects of medieval siege warfare: weapons are again listed, and this time guns make another appearance in the culverins which were mentioned in Ferrer's roughly
contemporary poem on the defence of Rhodes. The scaling ladders are
fitted with iron hooks, and despite the presence of numerous engines
the main combat seems to be hand-to-hand. Poisoned bolts are once
again employed, as is wild fire. The passage moves from a description of
the assault to a eulogy of Roman knightly conduct. Here the congru-
ence of cruelty and chivalry is startlingly evident: indeed, the destruction and atrocities wrought by the Romans, including the horrific
murder of children, seem to be offered as examples of the nobility of the
besieging commanders, who are fulfilling a biblical prophecy. These
subjects associated with the theme of siegecraft—military detail, the
figure of the commander, chivalry, and cruelty—are unified in the
lengthy description, which is here given in full.

And on the morow at prime Vaspasian comaundid to assaile the cite fercely on
euery side. And with springaldis, tribiettis, gunnes, balastirs thei mightily cast
out stones and quarellis ayens the touris, the wallis, and the gatis, and the Iuwes
for enfamyn were feint and ferd and hid hem. Than Vaspasian made his host to
arme hem & leid strong wardis about the city on eche side, and lete serce the
cite by alle the gatis, postern, dichis, & caves, and made dresse up his scaling
laddirs ayens the wallis, and made bring targis, pauysis, and long trees with

crokis of iren for to hang and fasten on the wallis & the touris, and with al maner shotte of gunnes, culuerynes, engines, tribiettis, springaldis, bowis of brake, bal-astirs, and al maner othir habilementis and ordinaunces for the werre enforcid hem to assaile the Iuwes at the wallis and the bretismentis, the toures and the tourettis and garetis of the cite, and to shote wilde fire with arrowis envenymed, that thassaut and the mellee of without and withynne was a wundir to here and to se, and a gret hidour to thinke and to se the contrauersy & the slaughtir, which was so mightily and manly continued with the cheualrous men of werre and so mightily done by the host of Vaspasian, so fiers and chiualrous ayens the Iuwes, that by the help of almighty God Vaspasian toke the cite and alle thei withyn yilden to his wille, and made his men of his host to sette fire on alle parties of the cite and brent and destrued and bete it alle doun, the temples, the toun, and the wallis into the hard erthe so that ther left not one stone upon an-othir: *Quia non relinquetur lapis super lapidem.* And alle the Iuwes that he founde withyn went to the swerd and to slaughtir. And the Iuwes that were hidde for fere in cavis or in any othir privee placis, thei were brent to dethe. And alle the litle yong children that were founden alyue, he made take hem by the leggis and armes and bete their hedis and ther bodies ayens the wallis and brak their bones and bete out their braynes—not one escapid ne saued, but alle slayne. (ch. 22, pp. 87–8)

In describing this scene of total destruction and slaughter the writer adopts a tone suggestive of a chronicler: apart from the reference to Roman chivalry, which itself is stated as a fact, the text reads as the dis-passionate report of a historian, though one might catch an underlying tone of excitement and exultation. A modern journalist might use the same method of selecting telling details such as the Jews in hiding burn-ing to death, to stress the full horror of the scene and the might of the Roman army. As we have seen, such scenes were not unknown in the Middle Ages, particularly when the defending commander had refused to surrender: in the treatments of the siege of Jerusalem, this refusal also implies a refusal to repent or to convert, thus increasing—according to medieval theory—the justification for total assault when the siege is won. Elsewhere in the *English Bible* are further reminders of the terrible fate of the Jews, as in the torture of Caiphas, or the continued campaign in the Holy Land after the siege in Jerusalem in which the Romans 'brent, disempirid, and destrued alle theire castellis and forteressis, citees, tovnes, and villagis' (ch. 23, p. 89). The determination to bring down the towns of 'Iuwery' is as much a positive quality of Vespasian as is his distribution of the rich spoils of war to his army, an important attribute of other siege commanders such as Richard the Lionheart. The destruction of the Temple is in interesting contrast to *Titus and*

Vespasian, where it is left standing: the symbolic smashing of religious statues, as occurs in the romance of Richard and in *The Sege of Melayne*, is a frequent topic in crusading romances. Laying low the inner sanctum is less usual, and is similar to some romances of Troy, where emphasis is placed on the temple of false gods within Ilion, and the damage inflicted upon it. The fall of the main tower and temple seems to be a mark of total destruction which goes beyond routine assault. It is finally such descriptions of the atrocities of siege warfare in the *English Bible*, and the supposed justification for them, which make it both a memorable and a repellent work for the modern reader.

The treatments in Middle English of the matter of the capture and destruction of Jerusalem illustrate the variations that could be made on the theme of the siege by writers. Material which had evolved from a mixture of historical and religious writings of the early medieval period appealed to later audiences for several reasons: the story of the siege combines piety and religious meaning with a narrative of crusading warfare and chivalry, in which God is seen to triumph over his enemies. While accepting the basic idea of the siege as God's vengeance, writers responded to the different aspects of the siege in different ways. The author of *Titus and Vespasian* places greatest emphasis on the symbolism of the siege and the miraculous legends associated with it. In *The Siege of Jerusalem* the drama and spectacle of the siege are the features which most interest the author, who also clearly incorporates elements of later Western warfare in his account, mixing the exotic and the familiar. A similar approach is taken in the *English Bible*, the text which offers the most detailed description of siege assault and its aftermath and in which the concept of chivalry is apparently divorced from that of compassion.

The writings considered in this chapter also embrace topics discussed earlier: in its detail, its chronicle-like style, and its focus on the commander, the *English Bible* has much in common with the *Prose Siege of Thebes* considered in Chapter 1. Sickness among commanders has already been noted as a frequent theme, making the siege part of a private recovery as well as a larger, more spiritual healing process. The figure of Vespasian in all three texts, combining military prowess with fervent belief and the capacity for great cruelty, recalls that of Richard in *Richard Coeur de Lion*, while the emphasis on historical truth and the attention paid to the miraculous are elements shared by the texts on the historical sieges of Rhodes and Belgrade.

One aspect of the theme of the siege which arises from a consideration of the siege of Jerusalem alongside that of Troy is the idea of calamity. Both subjects illustrate disasters of a magnitude which reveals the shape of history: the siege of Troy is an exemplum of 'the cryinges of tragedyes' caused by 'the dedes of Fortune, that with unwar strook overturneth the realmes of greet nobleye', while the fall of Jerusalem is not 'unwar' but predicted and fulfilled as part of a divine scheme.[23] In both, destruction follows creativity: the fall of Troy answers the splendour of its construction, while there seems to be a symmetry between the supremely creative act of miraculous healing and the later act of destructive vengeance in the accounts of the siege of Jerusalem. The siege of Troy illustrates the ephemeral nature of human power and achievement, while that of Jerusalem reveals the ineluctable and terrible avenging power of an offended God. It is notable that the patterns of tragedy, according to both secular and Church history, should be represented in two popular matters of medieval literature, both culminating in a great siege. The siege as a theme involves profound ideas of human tragedy and destiny beyond the immediate pleasures afforded by an exciting narrative. At the heart of the vision of besieged Troy or Jerusalem is the idea of a purging experience, a painful rite of passage in which a great cultural or spiritual change is effected. This notion of beleaguerment and transformation could also be exercised on an individual level. Sieges outside history, existing on the timeless plane of allegory, express further fundamental medieval concepts of the soul and the self.

[23] Chaucer, *Boece*, Prose 2, ll. 68–70.

6

Allegorical Sieges

THE image of the siege appears in many allegorical texts of the Middle Ages: in religious writings it most often represents the soul, or the enclosing body; in love allegories it usually symbolizes the heart of the beloved or of the lover, in their different ways beleaguered by love. In addition to its literary manifestations, the figure is also found in drama and pageantry and in the visual arts. The texts and spectacles in which the siege is used as a model or an image to express ideas are too numerous to discuss comprehensively here. Consideration of selected instances, however, provides some insight into several areas of medieval thought. The changing usages of the allegorical siege illustrate some of the preoccupations in spiritual writings in the course of the medieval period; in the appearances of the image in texts with an amorous theme, we see both the development of ideas on love and the adaptation of the imagery of spiritual texts in other kinds of writing. The allegorical siege is a versatile literary trope, and contributes to developing conceptions of the soul, the self, and types of love from the erotic to the spiritual during the Middle Ages and beyond.

In this chapter we shall first consider the use of the image or idea of the siege in spiritual writings, an important aspect of the larger subject of the allegorical fortress.[1] Sieges in non-spiritual writings concerning love will be separately discussed, together with examples from art and civic and courtly pageantry. The siege of the soul and the siege of love are not always easy to distinguish: the two literary traditions developed at the same time, and the representations of sieges of love owe much in style and imagery to spiritual writings. Conversely, some religious texts employing the siege as an allegorical model also use the language of courtly love to help expound ideas on the soul, and the distinction between spiritual and human love in some works is consequently not always clear. None the less, for all their mutual influence, the traditions of the siege of the soul and the siege of love can usually be regarded as

---

[1] See R. D. Cornelius, *The Figurative Castle* (Bryn Mawr, 1930).

separate, differing in their main emphases even though closely similar at times in their imagery and structure.

THE SIEGE OF THE SOUL

As an image used in spiritual exposition, the siege is part of a wider rhetoric of warfaring terms, developed from suggestions in such texts as St Paul's 'Induite universam illam armaturam Dei, ut possitis stare adversus artes Diaboli' ('Put on the whole armour of God, that ye may be able to stand against the wiles of the devil', *Ephesians*, 6: 11). The idea of the beleaguered fortress as a defence against the devil is congruent with the symbolic armour of the breastplate of righteousness, the shield of faith, the helmet of salvation, and the sword of the Spirit described by St Paul in the same text. St Cyprian (*c*.200–58) employs the image of the besieged or fortified place when explaining sin in his *Liber de zelo et livore*, where he compares the approaches of the devil to those of an enemy attempting to break into a protected place:

Circuit ille nos singulos, et tamquam hostis clausos obsidens, muros explorat, et tentat an sit pars aliqua murorum minus stabilis et minus fida, cujus aditu ad interiora penetretur.

He goeth about every one of us; and even as an enemy besieging those who are shut up [in a city], he examines the walls, and tries whether there is any part of the walls less firm and less trustworthy, by entrance through which he may penetrate to the inside.[2]

St Cyprian goes on to list the sins which will help the devil undermine the constancy of the Christian: the passage is an early instance of the use of the siege to illustrate the Seven Deadly Sins, a popular theme in later homiletic writings.[3]

The pressures on Rome and its Empire in the fourth century perhaps influenced writers of the period to use the image of the threatened or besieged place in treatments of spiritual and moral issues. In the *Hamartagenia* of Prudentius (348–*c*.410), for example, the place under attack is used as a figure for the soul, which is assailed by an army of personified vices including Anger, Thirst of Blood, Envy, Adultery, Cheating, and Violence. The same text characterizes Rome as Sodom, a

---

[2] St Cyprian, *Liber de zelo et livore*, II; *PL* 4, col. 639, pp. 664–5. *The Writings of Cyprian, Bishop of Carthage*, ed. and trans. R. E. Wallis, 39–51 (40).
[3] See M. W. Bloomfield, *The Seven Deadly Sins* (Michigan, 1952), 135–41.

morally corrupt place which, like the soul, is liable to fall before the devil or a vengeful God; the association of Troy with Sodom made by Gerald of Wales, noted earlier, follows the same logical line.[4] A similar view is expressed by Prudentius' contemporary, St Augustine (354–430): in *De civitate dei*, he sees in the fall of Rome to Alaric an illustration of the weakness of the fortress of the soul against the powers of darkness when it is left undefended by moral strength:

Romam quippe partam ueterum auctamque laboribus foediorem stantem fecerant quam ruentem, quando quidem in ruina eius lapides et ligna, in istorum autem uita omnia non murorum, sed morum munimenta atque ornamenta ceciderunt, cum funestioribus eorum corda cupiditatibus quam ignibus tecta illius urbis arderent.

Rome was founded and extended by the labours of those men of old; their descendants made Rome more hideous while it stood than when it fell. For in the ruin of the city it was stone and timber which fell to the ground; but in the lives of those Romans we saw the collapse not of material but of moral defences, not of material but of spiritual grandeur. The lust that burned in their hearts was more deadly than the flame which consumed their dwellings.[5]

The notion of the city falling through its own moral weakness links the spiritual citadel of homiletic and exegetical writings with subjects of secular romance such as Troy or Rome. Similarly, the siege of Jerusalem was also regarded as the just end for a morally corrupt city. Romances of the sieges of the great cities of antiquity, with their emphasis on wrongdoing and calamity, reflect the spiritual tradition of the menaces lurking about the fortress of the soul, which is threatened by vice. In a later passage, St Augustine writes that Rome was defended in the wrong way, with an appeal to false gods:

Quando quidem ut auerteretur quod metuebatur ab hoste in corporibus, eo modo dii conciliabantur, quo uirtus debellaretur in mentibus, qui non opponerentur defensores oppugnatoribus moenium, nisi prius fierent expugnatores morum bonorum.

To ward off the dreaded assaults of the enemy upon their bodies, men tried to win the gods' favour by means which utterly overthrew virtue in their minds. For the gods would not drive off those who assailed the walls of Rome from outside unless they themselves first drove out all morality from within the city.[6]

---

[4] The Rome–Sodom identification is observed by D. Pearsall, *Old and Middle English Poetry* (London, 1977), 29.

[5] St Augustine, *De civitate dei*, II. 2; *CCSL* 47, p. 36; trans. Bettenson, 49.

[6] Ibid. II. 27; *CCSL* 47, p. 63; trans. Bettenson, 84–5. See J. F. Doubleday, 'The Allegory of the Soul as Fortress in Old English Poetry', *Anglia*, 88 (1970), 503–8 (505).

The fall of Rome and other cities of the Empire is suggested by the imagery of other writings, such as the consideration of the threats to monastic devotion in the *De institutibus coeniborum* by St Cassian (*c.*360–433):

Haec uero cum infelicem possederit mentem, ut quidam saeuissimus tyrannus sublimissima capta arce uirtutum universam funditus ciuitatem diruit atque subuertit…

But this one [vice] when once it has taken possession of some unfortunate soul, like some most brutal tyrant, when the lofty citadel of the virtues has been taken, utterly destroys and lays waste the whole city.[7]

Patristic writers and poets in the period before and during the fall of Rome thus used the siege as an image of the soul threatened by sin, and associated the idea of the soul as a protected place with the images from real experience of Christian cities falling to pagan enemies. This articulation of an abstract idea by reference to common experience helps to explain the frequent occurrence of the image in spiritual and allegorical works: poets and preachers could refer to historical sieges to draw their audience from real life into the imagined or figurative worlds of romance and theology.

In the sixth century St Gregory (c.540–604) elaborates the image of the siege of the soul in several writings. In his homilies on the gospels, he writes of the cloister of the soul being infiltrated and damned by the vice of Pride.[8] The image of the siege is developed at greater length in an interpretation of the text of *Ezekiel* 4: 1–2: 'Sume tibi laterem, et pones eum coram te, et describes in eo civitatem Jerusalem. Et ordinabis adversus eam obsidionem, et aedificabis munitiones, et comportabis aggerem, et dabis contra eam castra, et pones arietes in gyro' ('[Thou also, son of man], take thee a tile, and lay it before thee, and portray upon it the city, even Jerusalem. And lay siege against it, and build a fort against it, and cast a mount against it; set the camp also against it, and set battering rams against it round about'). The tile is explained as the image of the Holy City which the teacher implants in the mind of his disciple, in order that he may withstand the temptations of the world.[9] In the *Liber regulae pastoralis* St Gregory elaborates on the same text in his development of the theme of the Christian beleaguered by sin. Here again it is

---

[7] St Cassian, *De institutis coenibiorum*, XII. 3; *CSEL* 17, p. 207; *The Twelve Books on the Institutes of the Coenobia*, trans. E. C. S. Gibson, 201–90 (280, col. 2).

[8] St Gregory, *Homiliarum in Evang.* 7; *PL* 76. 1100.

[9] St Gregory, *Homiliarum in Ezechielem*, I. 12, 25; *PL* 76. 930–2.

used as a picture of pedagogy: the teacher must impress the idea of the divine city on the mind of his pupil, and then assail it with tempting thoughts:

Sancti quippe praedicatores obsidionem circa laterem, in quo Jerusalem civitas descripta est, ordinant, quando terrenae menti, sed jam supernam patriam requirienti, quanta eam in hujus vitae tempore vitiorum impugnet adversitas, demonstrant.

For holy preachers order the siege about the tile on which is portrayed the city of Jerusalem, when they shew to the earthly soul, which nevertheless already seeketh the country above, how great is the enmity of sin which assaileth it in the season of this life.[10]

Siege imagery is also used extensively in St Gregory's commentary on the book of Job. Here it is used exegetically, while being imagined realistically, as in this elaboration upon the words 'Omnia Satanae machinamenta contra Job erecta', in which the strength of Job in resisting the trials of temptation is praised:

Ecce quot obsidionum machinamenta circumposuit; ecce quot percussionum tela transmisit: sed in his omnibus mansit mens imperterrita, stetit civitas inconcussa.

See, what numberless beleaguering enemies he set about him! See how many weapons of assault he let fly, but in all his mind continued undaunted, the city stood unshaken.[11]

The identification of the mind with the city, surrounded by enemies, recurs in a gloss on Job 22:25:'Eritque omnipotens lectissimum aurum tuum;et argentum viresque tibi' ('Yea,the Almighty shall be thy defence, and thou shalt have plenty of silver'). Real sieges of the time were generally of towns;the imagery here reflects the state of contemporary military practice.In other texts,such as the prose account of the siege of Jerusalem in the previous chapter,cities are imagined as castles. The defence and definition of town walls gave towns an extra sense of unity as a fortress. Mind, fortress, and city could be easily linked in the imagination:

Quos magis alios hostes patimur quam malignos spiritus, qui in nostris nos cogitationibus obsident,ut civitatem valeant nostrae mentis irrumpere,eamque sub sui jugo dominii captam tenere?

---

[10] St Gregory, *Liber regulae pastoralis. St Gregory on the Pastoral Charge: The Benedictine Text with an English Translation*, ed. and trans. H. R. Bramley, part 2, ch. 10 (pp.118–19).

[11] St Gregory, *Moralia in Job*, Preface, 4: 10; *PL* 75. 522; *CCSL* 143; trans. *Morals on the Book of Job*, i. 23.

What other enemies are we more subject to than evil spirits, who in our thoughts besiege us, that they may break into the city of our minds, and hold it, taken captive, under the yoke of their dominion?[12]

The dominant idea of the mind or soul as an enclosed urban place to be defended is reiterated by St Gregory in a gloss on Proverbs 4:23:'Omnia custodia serva cor tuum, quia ex ipso vita procedit' ('Keep thy heart with all diligence; for out of it are the issues of life'). Again the space imagined is that of a strongly protected town or city. There is little suggestion that the mind could break out of these walls, but every danger that besieging evil could find its way in:

Si qua etenim civitas contra insidiantes inimicos magno valletur aggere, fortibus cingatur muris, ex omni parte insomni muniatur custodia, unum vero in ea foramen tantummodo immunitum per negligentiam relinquatur; inde procul dubio hostis ingreditur, qui undique exclusus videbatur.

For if against plotting enemies a city be encompassed by a great rampart, be girt with strong walls, on every side defended by a sleepless watch, yet a single opening only be left therein undefended through neglect, from this quarter surely the enemy enters in, who seemed to be every way shut out.[13]

Numerous other passages in patristic writings demonstrate the vitality of the image of the siege in treatments of sin. The idea also appears in vernacular religious writings and poetry. By the time of the composition of Beowulf, perhaps the early eighth century or later, it is commonplace.[14] The situation of Heorot in this poem is similar to that of the allegorical places under siege in patristic writings: it stands as a symbol of civilization, in a wilderness from which evil forces emanate and infiltrate a fortress which is also a living space. St Gregory's picture of Pride stealing up on the unvigilant mind lies behind Hrothgar's sermon on the happy man assailed by wickedness. The soul now has a guardian assigned to it, here represented by the watchman in the night. It is the growth of pride, and the relaxation of the watchman of conscience, which lets in the murderous enemy (lines 1739–44). A similar passage occurs in Vainglory (?800–50), which follows closely the Gregorian analysis of sin in describing how the fortress of the soul, defended on behalf of a greater ruler, is betrayed to the enemy of Pride, who lets

[12] Ibid., ch.18: 23; PL 75. 1131; trans. ii. 238.
[13] Ibid. 21: 33; PL 76. 118–19; trans. ii. 423.
[14] See D. Whitelock, The Audience of Beowulf (Oxford, 1951), 8.

loose his arrows to cause the spiritual wound of sin (lines 35–9).[15] The passage is part of a longer discourse on the process by which the soul is entered and corrupted by sin, and shares with patristic texts the association of monastic and spiritual devotion with physical combat. The emphasis on feudal obligation to a ruler, who owns the besieged place and on whose behalf it is to be defended, illustrates the combination of derived imagery and allusion to contemporary practices. Similar references to feudal tenancy and obligation occur in *Juliana* by Cynewulf (active 775–825). Imprisoned for her faith, Juliana captures the devil sent to tempt her and forces him to describe his methods for beguiling and tempting the Christian. The speech again follows St Gregory's scheme of the different stages of moral corruption, through 'suggestio', 'delectatio', 'consensus', and 'defenso audacia'. The devil describes how he assaults the wall's gate, pierces the covering tower, and sends arrows of temptation into the now captive soul, seized from the fiefdom of Christ's law (lines 401–11).[16]

While the siege was thus established as an image of the soul beleaguered by sin, further elaborations on the idea were made by later homilists, commentators, and poets. Two developments in particular emerge: first, there is greater interest taken in the description of the place besieged. In place of general references to walls and cities, complex interiors are imagined and architectural terms are employed. Such imagery in ecclesiastical writings develops at the same time as the rise in castle building and real sieges of castles during the twelfth century. Another new variation is the extension of the idea of the fortress of the soul to other allegorical castles or enclosures, such as the Virgin's womb which received Christ at the Incarnation, or the corporeal castle of human life.

Several of the new tendencies in images of sieges in spiritual allegory are illustrated by expositions of Luke 10: 38: 'Intravit Jesus in quoddam castellum: et mulier quaedam, Martha nomine, excepit illum in domum suam' ('[Now it came to pass, as they went, that] he entered into a certain village: and a certain woman named Martha received him into her

---

[15] See C. A. Regan, 'Patristic Psychology in the Old English "Vainglory"', *Traditio*, 26 (1970), 324–35. For further discussion of these images in Old English poetry, see E. G. Stanley, 'Old English Poetic Diction and the Interpretation of *The Wanderer*, *The Seafarer*, and *The Penitent's Prayer*', *Anglia*, 73 (1956), 413–66; repr. in id., *A Collection of Papers with Emphasis on Old English Literature*, Publications of the Dictionary of Old English (Toronto, 1987), 234–80.

[16] See J. F. Doubleday, 'The Allegory of the Soul as Fortress in Old English Poetry', 503–8. E. R. Anderson, *Cynewulf: Structure, Style, and Theme in his Poetry* (London and Toronto, 1983), 90.

house'). The suggestions of 'castellum', which was interpreted to mean both 'village' and 'castle', are explored by various writers, who also elaborate on the idea of the female interior. There is also extensive Marian imagery, as when the Virgin is identified with the protecting, unpenetrated castle as a shield for the soul, or in references to the spotless womb which protected Christ. Similarities between religious and love allegory become apparent: the association of the besieged fortress with exemplary virginity, the female, and the female interior is common both to spiritual allegories of the beleaguered soul and to erotic sieges in romances, love lyrics, and allegories. We see a further shift in siege imagery employed for religious instruction towards ideas of spiritual consummation, from which much of the rhetoric of love yearning in the sieges of love is derived. Whereas St Gregory used the image of the siege essentially as a practical didactic aid, a new, less plainly doctrinal tone emerges in eleventh- and twelfth-century writings through which the image is an inspiration to devotion. The siege becomes expressive of mystical unions with Christ and with perfect love as well as of confrontations with the devil. A homily attributed to St Anselm provides an example of this kind of treatment. The passage begins with a useful image of the castle as a tower protected by a wall, two essential elements which are present in many variations on the allegorical siege:

Castellum enim dicitur quælibet turris, et murus in circuitu ejus. Quae duo sese invicem defendunt, ita ut hostes per murum ab arce, et a muro per arcem arceantur. Hujusmodi castello non incongrue Virgo Maria assimilatur, quam virginitas mentis et corporis, quasi murus, ita undique vallavit, ut nullus unquam libidini ad eam esset accessurus, nec sensus ejus aliqua corrumperentur illecebra.

Any tower surrounded by a wall is called a castle. These two defend each other in turn, so that enemies are kept away from the tower by the wall, and from the wall by the tower. It would not be inappropriate to compare the Virgin Mary to a castle of this kind. Purity of mind and body so protect her on all sides, like a wall, that no one may ever approach her with desire, nor may his senses be corrupted by any enticement.[17]

The elements of the Virgin, the castle, a siege, and the devil's wiles are also combined in a homily by Godfrey of Admont on the same text. Both writers adumbrate some of the images employed in allegorical

---

[17] St Anselm, *Homiliae*, 9, PL 158. 644–9 (645); trans. S. Anderson (private correspondence).

sieges of love and romances, where the chaste beloved lady is perceived in a fortress:

'Intravit Jesus in quoddam castellum'. Castellum ubi pro tuitione construitur, munitione muri per circuitum undique cingitur, et, turre in medio eminente, ipsa muri constructio desuper protegitur, ut vicissim et a turre murus defend-atur, et a muro turris muniatur. Hujus ergo castelli nomine intemerata beatae Mariae virginitas convenienter figuratur, cujus et vita sub magisterio sancti Spiritus constituta, tota continentiae munitione mirabiliter roboratur, et ipsa incomparabili et inexpugnabili humilitatis arce contra omnia diabolicae sug-gestionis jacula humiliter defensatur.

'Jesus entered into a certain village'. When a castle is constructed for defence, it is surrounded on all sides by a circular fortifying wall, and with the tower stand-ing high in the middle, the very construction of the wall is protected from above, so that in turn the wall is defended by the tower, and the tower fortified by the wall. This castle, then, provides a suitable allegory for the unspotted virginity of the Virgin Mary, and her life, too, established beneath the power of the Holy Ghost, is wonderfully strengthened by the total fortification of chast-ity, and is humbly defended against all the darts of the devil's temptations by that same incomparable and impregnable tower of humility.[18]

St Ailred of Rievaulx (1109–67), in a sermon on the same text, com-pares the Virgin's womb to the spiritual home of Christ which should be found in the heart of every Christian: 'Et nos, fratres, si habuerimus in nobis hoc spiritale castellum de quo loquimur, sine dubio ad nos in-trabit spiritaliter Jesus. Sed ad beatam Mariam non solum spiritaliter, sed etiam corporaliter intravit, quia in ea et ex ea corpus assumpsit' ('And if, brothers, we have in us this spiritual castle, about which we are speak-ing, without a doubt Jesus will enter into us in the spirit. But he entered the blessed Mary not only spiritually but also bodily, because he as-sumed his body in her and from her').[19] Further variations on the nature of the besieged place appear in numerous sermons on the text of Matthew 21: 2, where Christ prepares for his entry into Jerusalem: 'Ite in castellum quod contra vos est' ('Go into the village over against you'). The castle-city which Christ commands his followers to enter was in-terpreted as the world or human life in a sermon by St Bernard amongst many others.[20] Honorius of Autun uses the image of the fortress of

---

[18] Godfrey of Admont, *Homiliae Festivales*, Homily 65; *PL* 174. 959–71 (964); trans. S. Anderson.

[19] St Ailred of Rievaulx, *Sermones i–xlvi*: Sermon 19, pp. 147–54 (150–1); trans. S. Anderson.

[20] 'Mundus est castellum, cuius vallum superbia et munitiones cetera vita': Paris, BN, MS lat. 10695, fos. 80–129. See B. Hauréau, *Notices et extraits de quelques manuscrits latins de la*

human life to expound the idea that life itself is a struggle similar to a castle's attempts at defence. The topic of a threat from within aiding the enemies without recalls the writings of the Fathers at the time of the fall of Rome and anticipates the theme of treachery in the romances on Troy:

Cujusque autem fidelis corpus hujus civitatis castellum praedicatur, quod ab anima principe et populo virtutum inhabitatur, in qua contra exercitum vicio-rum decertatur. Hoc castellum a turba hostium exterius obsidetur, a factione civium interius commovetur dum proximi exteriora damna ei inferunt, vicia autem et carnis desideria interiora bona obruunt.

Moreover the body of every faithful man is like a castle of this city, because it is inhabited by a virtuous prince and people, the soul, in which battle is done against an army of vices. This castle is beset from without by a throng of enemies, and is shaken from within by the faction of its citizens; whilst its neighbours inflict external losses upon it, vices and the lusts of the flesh over-whelm its inner virtues.[21]

Many other homilists and preachers of the time employ, with increasing elaboration, the image of the castle of the world, surrounded by Pride and other sins and protected by virtues.[22]

A further important development in the imagery of sieges and fort-resses in the twelfth century is the composition of edifying narratives around the central idea of the siege. In the Latin text *De custodia interioris hominis*, sometimes ascribed to St Anselm, the idea of the body as the habitation of the soul is explored. This concept was readily turned to by homilists and poets writing on the fortress of mansoul.[23] Narrative treatments of the siege of the soul within the body developed the idea of personified virtues guarding the soul from the world, the flesh, and the devil. Five parables ascribed to St Bernard of Clairvaux (1090–1153) deal with the theme of psychomachia, or battle between the virtues and the vices. A summary of the first parable illustrates the complex

Bibliothèque Nationale, 6 vols. (Paris, 1890–3), ii. 19. For references to sermons on this text by Philip the Chancellor, Hugh of St Victor, Hugh of St Caro and Nicholas of Aquavilla see ibid. v. 41. D. Bloch *et al.*, *Catalogue generale des manuscrits latins: Tables des tomes iii à vi (nos. 2693 à 3775b). II. Table des Incipit A–M* (Paris, 1983), 492.

[21] Honorius of Autun, *Speculum ecclesiae*, 'In conventu populi': *PL* 172. 1097; trans. S. Anderson. See Cornelius, *The Figurative Castle*, 58.

[22] See G. R. Owst, *Literature and Pulpit in Medieval England* (Cambridge, 1933; revised 2nd edn. Oxford, 1961), 77–85.

[23] For the influence of the *De custodia*, see J. A. W. Bennett, *Middle English Literature*, ed. and completed by D. Gray (Oxford, 1986), 275–6. On literary instances, see C. L. Powell, 'The Castle of the Body', *SP* 16 (1919), 197–205.

narrative strands which could be woven around the central idea of the siege of the soul by sin:

[This parable] tells of a King who had three daughters, Fides, Spes, and Caritas, whom he puts in charge of the town of Mansoul, in which are three castles, Rationabilitas, Concupiscibilitas, and Irascibilitas. To each daughter is assigned a castle, and each sets a guardian with attendants to watch over it. Fides appoints Prudentia and gives her as associates Obedientia, Patientia, Dispensatio, Ordo, and Disciplina; Spes appoints Sobrietas and gives her Discretio, Continentia, Constantia, and Humilitas, with Silentium as doorkeeper; Caritas appoints Pietas (who is accompanied by Munditia Corporis and 'congruas exercita-tiones, videlicet lectiones, meditationes, orationes, et spirituales affectiones') and Beatitudo, with Peace as doorkeeper. The whole town is governed by Liberum Arbitrium. These arrangements having been made, the daughters re-tire, and the town is attacked by the Adversary at the head of an army of wickedness. They gain entrance by the doors of Rationabilitas and Concup-iscibilitas, Liberum Arbitrium is bound, and Blasphemia, Luxuria, and Superbia hold sway. The three daughters seek help from their father, who sends Timor and Gratia with an army of Virtues. Liberum Arbitrium is liberated, and, it is hoped, will remain under the dominion of Gratia forever.[24]

Here a complex allegory is constructed with recognizable images of royal power, with castles across a kingdom and extensive familial rela-tions. A similar combination of edifying intent and everyday imagery occurs in *Sawles Warde* (*c.*1200), the Middle English rendering of the *De custodia interioris hominis*, in which the house of man's mind ('consci-entia' in the Latin) is guarded by Wit and Will with the aid of the senses against the Devil's wiles: local and colloquial phrases concerning such matters as servants and noise enliven the familiar image of the symbolic fortress within which the mind or soul is threatened by adverse forces outside.

A siege appears more directly in the texts of the Katharine Group in the *Ancrene Wisse* (*c.*1200), where the imagery of chivalric romance is used to add colour to the allegory. The soul is depicted as a lady besieged in an earthen castle by her enemy the Devil, a situation similar to the story of later English romances such as *Le Bone Florence of Rome*, in which the beautiful and virtuous heroine is besieged in a wealthy city by the wicked Byzantine king, or *The King of Tars*, in which the siege again expresses the lust of an unscrupulous Eastern potentate for an immaculate princess.[25] The author of the *Ancrene Wisse* adds realistic detail such as the earthen castle in which the lady is beleaguered (alluding perhaps to the 'earth upon earth' tradition of texts on mortality as well as the earthen mottes on which earlier castles were constructed) and the army summoned by the King—Christ—who is in love with the lady and determined to rescue her:

A leafdi wes mid hire fan biset al abuten, hire lond al destruet, & heo al poure, inwith an eorthene castel. A mihti kinges luue was thah biturned up on hire swa unimete swithe thet he for wohlech sende hire his sonden, an efter other, ofte somet monie; sende hire beawbelez bathe feole & feire, sucurs of liuene, help of his hehe hird to halden hire castel. (vii. 9–15)

Here, the siege of the soul and the siege of love are combined to great effect: both the enemy and Christ wish to enter the castle, the one to ravage the soul, the other to rescue it. The trope of entering or relieving a fortified place is an important one in the siege imagery of love allegories which will be discussed later. The soul in *Ancrene Wisse* must choose which of the two powers who beset her—one with weapons, the other with gifts—is to be accepted, and wrongly decides to reject Christ's offers despite being provided with guidance in the form of the prophets symbolized by the King's 'sonden' (messengers) and the 'sucurs' of the Gospels. The idea of the soul being fought over appears in other writings, but the element of the siege is not always present: analogous texts depict the forces of good and evil fighting for a personified female soul before the castle, while she looks out at the battle. In the *Ancrene Wisse* the inner tensions of mind or soul are explored more dramatically: the lady-soul foolishly spurns Christ's offer of love, but so powerful is His love that He defeats her enemies by sacrificing Himself. The Passion is allegorized as the lover-knight dying in battle for his lady, as Christ sacrificed Himself on the Cross to redeem the soul of mankind beleaguered by sin.[26] A similar image of the siege of love which is also the siege of the soul is used in the *Chasteau d'amour* of Robert Grosseteste (c.1175–1253), where the virtuous soul is beleaguered by an army of vices led by the Devil. Both works show the scope there is for original handling of a familiar set of literary types.

[25] See also H. Newstead, 'The Besieged Ladies in Arthurian Romance', *PMLA* 63 (1948), 803–30.
[26] See W. Gaffney, 'The Allegory of the Christ-Knight in *Piers Plowman*', *PMLA* 46 (1931), 155–68. R. Woolf, 'The Theme of Christ the Lover-Knight in Medieval English Literature', *RES*, NS 13 (1962), 1–16.

The fusing in *Ancrene Wisse* of the siege as a model for exegesis with ideas concerning chivalry is echoed in texts more directly concerned with chivalric conduct. An early example occurs in the writing of Ramon Llull (*c.*1232–*c.*1315), who uses the siege as a simile for noble fortitude in his treatise on chivalry (*c.*1275):

Ausberg significa castell e mur contra vicis e falliments; car enaixí con castell e mur és enclòs environ per ço que hom no hi pusca entrar, enaixí ausberg és per totes parts enserrats e tancats, per ço que dó significança a lo noble coratge de cavaller, con no pusca entrar en ell traïció ni ergull ni deslleialtat, ni null altre vici.

The hauberke sygnefyeth a castel & fortresse ageynst vyces & deffaultes / For al in lyke wyse as a castel and fortresse ben closed al aboute / In lyke wyse an hauberke is ferme & cloos on al partes / to thende that gyve sygnefyaunce to a noble knyght / that he in his courage ought not to entre in to Treason / ne none other vyce.[27]

As a practitioner as well as theorist of the art of chivalry, Henry of Lancaster (*c.*1300–1361) had experience of siege warfare as well as an evident knowledge of the image of the soul protected by the castle of the body as developed in homiletic writings. In his devotional treatise, *Le Livre de seyntz medicines*, he describes sin entering the fortress of the body when the defence of the senses is weak and corrupting the mind or soul within. In this treatment of the idea, knowledge of the processes of a real assault appears in references to ransom and mining, invigorating a commonplace figure:

Ore vous ai jeo, Sire, selonc l'eide de vous et mon petit sene, recordee et moustree coment les sept mortels pecchez sont entreez mon chastel par le meure ausi com par les portes avant ditez. Et touz sont ensi entrez pur robber et enporter vostre tresor—c'est l'alme —, si en vous, douz Sire, ne soit meilloure la rescouce q'ele ne soit en moi.

Et tout ensi come ces sept pecchez sont entrez par les mayns qe jeo signyfie al meure du chastel, ausi sont entrez ils par les pieez, ou poynt de porte n'y ad, mes un malveis fieble meure sicom l'autre. Et ceo meure est si tendre et si mol et si tenu, qe les sept enemys devant ditez y entront sanz gairez de destourber ou defense trover qe acontre face. Ceaux sont mynours qe brisent le meure al piee desouz et par la y entront ausi pleinement come par un de portez et sanz contredit de moy. (p. 70)

---

[27] R. Llull, *Llibre de l'orde de cavalleria*, 70; trans. W. Caxton, *The Book of the Ordre of Chyvalry*, 78. Caxton uses an intermediary French translation, but his rendering is close to the original.

Now, Lord, according to your aid and my small understanding, I have recorded for you and shown how the Seven Deadly Sins have entered my castle by the wall just as they did by the doors mentioned earlier. And they have thus entered to rob and carry off your treasure—that is, the soul —, if in you, sweet Lord, there be no better rescue than there is in me.

And just as the Seven Sins have entered by my hands, which I signify as the wall of the castle, so they have also entered by the feet, where there is no door, but a wall as poor and feeble as the other. And that wall is so fragile and so soft and so frail, that the Seven enemies aforesaid will enter there without encountering scarcely any obstacle or defence raised against them. They are miners who bring down the wall to the feet beneath and there they will enter as freely as by one of the doors and without any denial on my part.

A close parallel to this passage is provided by the poem known as *Le Songe du castel*, in which a castle representing body and soul, constructed on two pillars like a body on legs, is besieged by the seven deadly sins; the siege is eventually only ended by death. A later example is William Nevill's *The Castle of Pleasure* (1518), in which once again the beleaguering army is made up of the sins.[28] The allegorical figure is suited to various forms of writing, from dream allegory to spiritual autobiography to the sermon: similarly precise imagery of siege warfare is present in a macaronic passage from a fourteenth-century sermon in which the castle of the Virgin becomes the castle of paradise, a fortress 'so sikurli set per nequid undermynid ita forte per non gunne ut machina parte illud wynyd'.[29]

Later medieval drama presents further versions of the siege of Mansoul. The most ambitious and best known of these is the morality play, *The Castle of Perseverance* (*c.*1400–25), in which the figure forms the basis for a long and involved narrative. A drawing in the manuscript of this work reveals the centrality of the image of the siege in the play. A single tower, representing a castle, is surrounded by a ditch or barricade, outside which there are five scaffolds: apart from the eastern one, which points to Jerusalem and God, the others all point to enemies without.[30] The play depicts the siege of Mansoul by the Seven Sins (together with Pleasure and Folly), led by the three enemies of Man—the World, the

[28] See E. J. Arnould, *Étude sur le Livre des saintes médecines du duc Henri de Lancastre* (Paris, 1948), 98–101.
[29] Oxford, Bodleian Library, MS Bodley 649, fos. 124–129r. Cited by Owst, *Literature and Pulpit in Medieval England*, 78.
[30] Washington, DC, Folger Shakespeare Library, MS V. a. 354, fo. 191v. See R. Southern, *The Medieval Theatre in the Round: A Study of the Staging of the Castle of Perseverance and Related Matters* (London, 1957).

Flesh, and the Devil. Defence is earned by penitence and provided by the Seven Virtues, a continuation of the Gregorian image of the soul finding salvation through the struggle of fending off besieging vices. After a long battle, the Virtues defeat the Vices by throwing from the battlements roses, emblems of Christ's blood. When Mankind is deceived by the enemy within (Avarice) the dominant theme becomes that of penitence. He dies contrite and his soul is saved thanks to the intercession of the Four Daughters of God—Mercy, Peace, Justice, and Truth—who plead for him after a debate.

The Castle of Perseverance realizes the potential for drama and spectacle in the siege of Mansoul. Like the author of *Ancrene Wisse* or Henry of Lancaster, the dramatist links this figure effectively with the complementary subjects of penitence and salvation, though here the form of salvation is different, effected by the intercession of the daughters rather than through the redeeming sacrifice of Christ. The siege recurs in other works as a basis of dramatic imagery and structure, though there are no other cases comparable to *The Castle of Perseverance*, in which the idea dominates the entire staging. A century after this play, the idea is found in Henry Medwall's *Nature, I and II* (*c.*1516–20). In *Nature II* Reason describes the tactics of the World, the Flesh, and the Devil and compares Man's life to a castle under attack:

> Whom to impugn laboreth incessantly
> The world, the fleshe, the enemy—these thre—
> Hym to subdue and bryng into captyvyte.[31]

A comparable usage occurs in the *Digby Mary Magdalene* (*c.*1500). Here the castle of Maudelyn is besieged by the Seven Deadly Sins: the internal drama of the spirit is again realized as a theatrical spectacle, using verbal and visual motifs which could be understood by literate and non-literate alike, and which continued into the Tudor and post-Reformation period.

THE SIEGE OF LOVE

It has been observed that 'the assault on a fortress is a fundamental image of love-conquest'.[32] Certainly the image is a popular one in many

---

[31] Cited by G. Wickham, *Early English Stages 1300 to 1660*, 3 vols. (London, 1959–81), iii. 87.

[32] W. Calin, *A Muse for Heroes: Nine Centuries of the Epic in France* (Toronto, 1983), 123.

different kinds of writing and artistic production. In some respects the tradition of the siege of love in all its forms in the medieval period is harder to trace than that of the siege of the soul, since many possible instances of its use, in folk festivals and song or in proverbial and colloquial speech, are unrecorded.[33] The evidence available, however, suggests that the figure of the siege, drawn largely from the imagery of homiletic writings, became a frequent element not only in works of art and literature concerning love but also as a more general, readily comprehensible metaphor for the experience of love and desire.

One possible source for medieval conceptions of the siege as an expression of erotic desire is the poetry of Ovid, who uses the idea twice in the *Amores*, first when he addresses his beloved as 'ianitor', imploring her to open the gates and let him enter while it is still night:

> urbibus obsessis clausae munimina portae
> prosunt; in media pace quid arma times?
> quid facies hosti, qui sic excludis amantem?
> tempora noctis eunt; excute poste seram!
>
> (I. vi. 29–32)

It is towns beleaguered that look for protection to the closing of their gates; you are in the midst of peace, and why fear arms? What will you do to an enemy, who thus exclude a lover? The hours of the night are going; away with the bar from the door![34]

In another passage, Ovid compares the lover to a soldier and uses the imagery of warfare to describe the rigours of courtship:

> mittitur infestos alter speculator in hostes;
> in rivale oculos alter, ut hoste, tenet.
> ille graves urbes, hic durae limen amicae
> obsidet; his portas frangit, at ille fores.
>
> (I. ix. 17–20)

The one is sent to scout the dangerous foe; the other keeps his eyes upon his rival as a foeman. The one besieges mighty towns, the other the threshold of an unyielding mistress; the other breaks in doors, the one, gates.

---

[33] An early treatment of the subject is E. Muret, *Le Château d'amour* (Lausanne, 1908). See also J. Murray, 'Le Château d'amour' (dissertation, Paris, 1918). General use has been made in this chapter of R. S. Loomis, 'The Allegorical Siege in the Art of the Middle Ages', *AJA*, 2nd ser. 23 (1919), 255–69. See also K. Sajavaara (ed.), *The Middle English Translations of Robert Grosseteste's 'Chateau d'amour'*, Mémoires de la Société Néophilologique de Helsinki, 32 (Helsinki, 1967), 'The Allegory of the *Castle of Love*', 90–7. A popular song on the conquest of the castle of love is recorded in 19th-cent. Vaud and Fribourg, where a civic pageant involving a siege of love was continued into the 18th cent.: mentioned by Loomis, 'Allegorical Siege', 258. [34] Trans. G. Showerman, 337–9.

The image is developed more fully in medieval love lyrics, where the beleaguered town is often recast as a besieged fortress. In a poem by the Provençal troubadour Giraut de Borneil, the image becomes an extended simile. In this instance, love is depicted in a very different fashion from that offered by Ovid. The lover is no longer an aggressive soldier attempting to break down the defences of the object of his desire, but a sensitive onlooker, a victim more than an aggressor, assailed by the thoughts of the beauty of his beloved. The use of the terms of siegecraft in the poem relates the private experience of the lover to the contemporary conditions of castle-building and warfare:

> Domna, aissi cum us chasteus
> Qu'es assejatz per fortz senhors,
> Can la peirer'abat las tors,
> E.ls chalabres e.ls manganeus,
> Et es tan greus
> La guerra devas totas partz
> Que no lor te pro genhs ni artz,
> E.l dols e.l critz es aitan fers
> De cels dedins quez an grans gers,
> Sembla.us ni.us par
> Que lor ai'obs merce clamar?
> Aissi.us clam merce umilmens,
> Bona domna, pros e valens.

Lady, as when a castle is besieged by grim barons, when the siege-engine topples the towers—and the catapult and the mangonel—and the onslaught is so fierce from every side that neither cunning nor guile avails them, and the suffering and the cries are so terrible of those within who are in great anguish, does it not seem and appear to you that there's need for them to cry mercy? In the same way I humbly cry mercy of you, good lady, noble and worthy.[35]

Here the lady, whose looks so torment the lover, is also the one who can rescue him from his state. The idea of surrender—envisioned by Ovid as female submission to the male will—is in this poem related to the lover's desire to give himself up entirely to his mistress and to be accepted by her in an act of mercy.

Festivals and pageants involving a siege of love are recorded from an early period, implying that the image was widespread in its manifestations outside religious or courtly literature. An example of the siege in

[35] A. R. Press (ed. and trans.), *Anthology of Troubador Lyric Poetry*, Edinburgh Bilingual Library, 3 (Edinburgh, 1971), 136–7. See also J. J. Salverda de Grave, *Observations sur l'art lyrique de Giraut de Bornelh*, Mededeenlingen der Koninklije Nederlandsche Akademie van Wetenschapen, Afd. Letterkund, 1 (1938), 57.

a civic pageant is that described by Roland of Padua at the Festival of Treviso in 1214, not long after Giraut de Borneil was writing. Venetians and Paduans were invited to participate in this Festival in a spirit of common harmony. Twelve of the fairest ladies of Padua represented a 'Court of Solace and Mirth' within a symbolic fortress which was then besieged by the amorous youths of both republics:

Factum est enim ludicrum quoddam castrum, in quo posite sunt dompne cum virginibus sive domicellabus et servitricibus earundem, que sine alicuius viri auxilio castrum prudentissime defenderunt. Fuit eciam castrum talibus municionibus undique premunitum: scilicet variis et griseis et cendatis, purpuris, samitis et ricellis, scarletis et baldachinis et armerinis. Quid de coronis aureis, cum grisolitis et iacantis, topaciis et smaragdis, piropis et margaritiis omnisque generis ornamentis, quibus dompnarum capita tuta forent ab impetu pugnatorum? Ipsum quoque castrum debuit expugnari et expugnatum fuit huiuscemodi telis et instrumentis: pomis, datalis et muscatis, tortellis, piris et coctanis, rosis, liliis et violis, similiter ampullis balsami, amphii et aque rosee, ambra, camphora, cardamo, cinamo, gariofolis, melegetis, cunctis immo florum vel specierum generibus, quecunque redolent vel splendescunt.

A fantastic castle was built and garrisoned with dames and damsels and their waiting women, who without help of man defended it with all possible prudence. Now this castle was fortified on all sides with skins of vair and sable, sendals, purple cloths, samites, precious tissues, scarlet, brocade of Bagdad, and ermine. What shall I say of the golden coronets, studded with chrysolites and jacinths, topaz and emeralds, pearls and pointed headgear and all manner of adornments wherewith the ladies defended their heads from the assaults of the beleaguerers? For the castle itself must needs be assaulted; and the arms and engines wherewith men fought against it were apples and dates and muscat-nuts, tarts and pears and quinces, roses and lilies and violets, and vases of balsam or ambergris or rosewater, amber, camphor, cardamons, cinnamon, cloves, pomegranates, and all manner of flowers or spices that are fragrant to smell or fair to see.[36]

For all its delicacy and fragrance, this particular pageant siege unfortunately descended into a brawl between the Venetians and Paduans, and the Court of Solace and Mirth ended in unseemly disharmony.

Other thirteenth-century examples of the siege of love include most notably the siege of the castle of Jealousy where Fair Seeming and the rose are held in Jeun de Meun's continuation of *Le Roman de la rose* (c.1275). This episode, though it forms only a small part of the whole

[36] Rolandini Patavini, *Cronica in factis et circa facta Marchie Trivixane*, Bk. 1, ch. 13, pp. 24–5; trans. G. G. Coulton, *A Medieval Garner* (London, 1910), 268–70.

poem, is one of the most distinctive and interesting allegorical sieges in medieval literature. Though many of the individual elements in the description are traditional, their development and association makes the episode an original and complex examination of the psychology of erotic love; in addition it provides a comically irreverent variation on the solemn symbolic systems we have previously met. The later siege is prepared for in the first part of the poem by Guillaume de Lorris, who uses a mixture of allegorical types and a surprisingly detailed realism: first the rose-bushes of the beloved are rendered inaccessible by thorns and brambles and the Lover is struck by the five arrows of the God of Love (Beauty, Simplicity, Courtesy, Company, and Fair Seeming). The Lover is imprisoned by the God of Love, to whom he willingly surrenders, and Jealousy imprisons Fair Welcoming and the Rose in a Castle. With these developments, the opening idea of love as a quest in the garden is transformed into the depiction of love as a combat between two armies, with the castle as a centrepiece. There are suggestions in the First Part that Love will eventually capture the castle, and in his continuation Jean de Meun develops chiefly the belligerent and erotic themes implicit in an allegorical siege of love, taking up the story at a much later point in the poem with the assault on the castle by the God of Love and his forces, and its eventual incineration by Venus.[37]

Though Jean de Meun's continuation of *Le Roman de la rose* is in many ways strikingly different to the courtly tone of the first part, there are points of contact in the handling of the subject of the siege by both writers. They share, for example, a tendency to use realistic terminology when dealing with military architecture and battle. When the God of Love captures the Lover, who describes his heart as being imprisoned by a garrison that will guard it, the language of their pact seems naturalistic; similar feudal images and phrases are employed by Jean de Meun, when the God of Love summons his barons to a parliament and asks practical counsel on the strategy they should use to capture the castle. The Castle itself appears very real indeed. In a long description of its construction, Guillaume departs from any apparent allegorical scheme to include as much realistic detail as possible: thus we are told of the cost of moats, the

---

[37] The arrows are described in ll. 1679–87. Imprisonment: 1898–991. Castle of Jealousy: 3797–947. In ll. 3502 it is suggested that Love will later recapture the castle. For discussion of arrow imagery relating to love, see R. Cline, 'Heart and Eyes', *RPh* 25 (1972), 263–97. The present discussion owes much to the analysis by H. Arden, 'The Slings and Arrows of Outrageous Love in the *Roman de la Rose*', in I. A. Corfis and M. Wolfe (eds.), *The Medieval City under Siege* (Woodbridge, 1995), 191–206.

payment of masons, the crenellated walls, and a 'donjon' or central tower strong enough to withstand missiles. We are even given the ingredients of the mortar used (quicklime soaked in vinegar). The strictly allegorical garrison—Shame, Fear, Foul Mouth—are armed with very unallegorical mangonels and arbalests, which are visible over the battlements. Viollet-le-Duc argued that the accumulation of such details, particularly the unusual element of four gates, is sufficient to allow us to identify the Castle as the Louvre of Philippe-Auguste. It is certainly the case that the description of the castle and its defences has diverted Guillaume from his allegorical scheme, rather as the redactor of the siege of Thebes turns from his narrative to exhaustive realistic description when the city-fortress appears in the story. Jean de Meun does not present a description rivalling Guillaume's in detail, but in the account of the initial skirmish between the armies outside the castle, the arms used and blows exchanged are recounted with a vivid and vigorous realism.[38]

The theme of aggression and violence, which has turned the central metaphor for love from quest to combat, is introduced by Guillaume and taken further by Jean de Meun. Cupid's arrows, derived from Ovid and expanded by Guillaume, carry with them the suggestion of Love as a violent force, as does the physical imprisonment of the Lover, albeit with his eager consent. There is an early mention of the rose-bush being protected by stones and crossbow bolts in the account of the arrows of love. These early suggestions of Love as a battle are developed by Jean into the full-scale military engagement later in the poem. The experience of Love itself, in Raison's account, is an irrational one of contending emotional states: 'C'est faus deliz, c'est tristour lie, / C'est leece la corroucie; / Douz maus, douceur malicieuse' (4308–10) ('False delight, joyous sorrow, enraged happiness, sweet ill, malicious sweetness'). The narrative schemes of pitched battle, assault on the Castle of Jealousy, and its final destruction further establish the basic idea of Love as by nature combative and aggressive, involving attack, surrender, and conquest—a process as perilous and testing as the protection of the fortress of the soul against its enemies.

[38] The siege engines are described in ll. 3853–9. God of Love summons barons: 10430 ff.; asks their advice: 10679–82. The skirmish (15511–674) is analysed by T. Bouché, 'Burlesque et renouvelement des formes: L'Attaque du château dans le *Roman de la rose* de Jean de Meun', in *Hommage à Jean-Charles Payen: Farai chansone ta novele. Essai sur la liberté créatrice au Moyen Age* (Caen, 1989), 87–98. On the possible use of the Louvre as a model, see E. Viollet-le-Duc, *Dictionnaire raisonné de l'architecture française du xie au xvie siècle* (Paris, 1857), iii. 122–8. Cited by Arden, 'Slings and Arrows', 199.

An important feature of the siege in the second part of the poem, and the area in which Jean most dramatically departs from Guillaume, is the erotic element. If the ongoing battle represents tensions in the minds of the lover and the beloved, the castle is the female body protected—or prevented—from the threatening or liberating powers of love by social conventions which Jean de Meun apparently deplores. When the final assault on the castle is declared, Venus makes a threatening speech reminiscent of those of real commanders, describing the fate of the rose after it has been captured (or rescued): 'Tuit i queldront sanz nul delai / Boutons et roses, clerc et lai, / Religieus et seculer' (20,755–7) ('Everyone, lay or cleric, religious or secular, will there gather buds and roses without hindrance'). In this passage, as an editor of the work notes, 'la rose se confond de plus en plus avec une réalité bien concrète'.[39] Detached from the language of allegory, the rose becomes more plainly the sexuality of the female which the Lover longs to possess. The castle not only symbolizes the body but represents it physically, when Venus aims her firebrand at a slit in the tower, which, we are deliberately told, is placed not at the side but at the front, above and between two pillars— a description which has led one critic to say that the tower is 'nothing but a glorified vagina', though it closely resembles the towers of other bodily castles such as that in *Le Songe du castel*.[40] The explicitly erotic imagery is continued with the lover's final approach to the rose, with his pilgrim's staff and sack.

It is this frankness of description which distinguishes the siege of *Le Roman de la rose* from other allegorical love sieges. The allegory here leads not to any further refinement of the concept of love but to the physical act of intercourse, alluded to in an energetically bawdy tone. Throughout the description of the castle, the pitched battles, and the siege, the texture of the poem is a varied one of allegory mixed with realism. When the castle is captured, the fortress of courtly allegory is finally subdued by the less sophisticated sensual desires of the body. Jean de Meun takes the inherited metaphors of love as a military engagement, and deliberately subverts them to show the unchivalric, even coarse state of male sexual desire on which the allegorical edifice is founded. The siege of Jealousy is also a defiant secularization of the contrived spiritual sieges such as those previously discussed. Elements

[39] Strubel's edn., p. 1189. Dahlberg's translation of lines quoted.
[40] A. S. Bernardo, 'Sex and Salvation in the Middle Ages: From the *Romance of the Rose* to the *Divine Comedy*', *Italica*, 67 (1990), 305–18 (311).

such as doorkeepers and generals are shared, and these similarities serve to point out the great contrast in tone; as spiritual writers tirelessly point out the perils of bodily temptations, Jean de Meun's work, using the same basic symbolic system, celebrates the triumphs of the body over artifice, returning us to the aggression and zest of Ovid.

Further variations on the idea of the siege of love occur in several works of the French allegorical tradition: an example is Messire Thibaut's *Roman de la poire* (thirteenth century), where, as in Giraut de Borneil's poem, it is the lover who is besieged in a tower by Love: the lover submits entirely to Love after a parley with Biauté, Cortoisie, Noblece, and Franchise. Again the idea of complete surrender is important, while the deputation sent by the God of Love recalls the messengers sent before by Christ in the *Ancrene Wisse*.

While the allegory may be varied and extended, the conception of the siege is usually realistic. Far from leading into abstractions, symbolic complexity seems to intensify the sense of a real place and concrete objects. This is clear from manuscript illuminations of the battle for the rose in *Le Roman de la rose*, in which close attention is often paid to the detailed depiction of siege weapons.[41] The popularity of the image of a siege of love outside the context of a particular narrative is suggested by illustrations in other manuscripts. In the late thirteenth-century Peterborough Psalter, for example, there is a marginal picture of a castle occupied and defended by ladies against an assault by knights. The ladies defeat the knights attempting to scale the castle by throwing and shooting flowers, a detail which recalls the roses thrown in *The Castle of Perseverance*; their attackers are depicted collapsing, presumably with the same seizures of love as that experienced by the lover in the first part of the *Roman de la rose*. The castle is presided over by a crowned figure, possibly the God of Love. In Walter de Milemete's treatise *De nobilitatibus sapientiis, et prudentiis regum* (1326), important for its detailed pictures of siege weapons, there is an illustration of a castle guarded by four ladies regarded by knights on the facing page who make gestures of despair. The Luttrell Psalter (*c*.1340) contains a similar marginal image in which knights attacking the fortress with real weapons are thrown into confusion by a shower of roses thrown from the battlements. Sieges of a castle of love are found in numerous French and English objects such as ivory mirror caskets and metalwork in the fourteenth century, and inventories record tapestries of sieges of love owned by the

[41] See e.g. Oxford, Bodleian Library, MS Douce 332.

aristocracy.[42] Such images associate the siege with the rhetoric and emotional states described in writings on courtly love: the siege expresses the violence of desire and the state of being lovestruck, the psychological wounding caused by delicacy and beauty (in the defence of flowers), and the unambiguous erotic ideas of approach, surrender, and entrance.

Allegorical treatments of the siege of love were not confined to the French romance tradition. A siege of love which reflects in several of its aspects the figurative sieges of homiletic writings is the siege in *Die Minneburg* (1325–50). Here the castle symbolizes the pure woman, containing love and honour, and beleaguered by slanderous malice. The idea of words, either malicious or seductive, as artillery in the siege of woman is repeated by Chaucer's Wife of Bath. In lines suggestive of the *Roman de la rose* she accuses one of her unfortunate husbands of being over-protective and ascribes to him the idea, 'Thou seist men may nat kepe a castel wal, / It may so longe assailed been over al' (III (D), 263–4).

Representations of sieges of love tend to keep the object of desire silent and let the men do the talking. While beleaguered ladies are often besieged by verbal blandishments and material offerings, the image of the lover usually shows him assaulted by the sight, rather than the speeches, of his beloved. In the poem 'Lo Setge d'amor' by the Valencian poet Jordi de Sant Jordi (*c*.1390–*c*.1421), for example, the lover is afflicted by the evidence of his senses and his memories of the beauties of his beloved rather than by anything she has said. The beloved is mute and distant while the lover complains eloquently of his anguish. The poem shows the continuation of the main ideas in Giraut de Borneil's lyric discussed earlier:

> Ajustat vey d'amor tot lo poder
> e sobre me ja posat son fort siti,
> si que no.m val força, .njeny ne sauber;
> tant suy destrets que no.m tinch gens per quiti
> de perdre.l cors, l'arma e tots los bes,

[42] Peterborough Psalter: Brussels, Royal Library, MSS 9961–2, fo. 90r. Walter de Milemete: Oxford, Christ Church, MS 92, fos. 3v–4r. Luttrell Psalter: London, British Library, MS Add. 42130, fo. 75v. For examples of other art works, see Loomis, 'Allegorical Siege', 258–66. On the ivory caskets and mirror-cases, see also: M. O. Dalton, *Catalogue of the Ivory Carvings of the Christian Era . . . in the British Museum* (London, 1909), nos. 368, pp. 125–7, pl. 86; nos. 381–2, p. 130, pl. 89; R. Koechlin, 'Les Ivoires profanes: Les valves de boîtes à miroir', in *Les Ivoires gothiques français*, 3 vols. (Paris, 1968), i. 359–415; R. Van Marle, *Iconographie de l'art profane au Moyen Age et à la Renaissance*, 2 vols. (New York, 1971), i. 415–26 and figs. 450 and 451.

car ja no puch sofrir la vida streta
ne.l tresnuytar; tan fort carrech ay pres
per que la fi me covendra que.m reta.

I see all the power of love and his strong siege laid around me, in such a way that strength, skill and knowledge cannot help me; I am so constrained that I cannot see what can save me from losing my body, my soul and all my goods, for I can no longer endure the straitened life, nor the nocturnal invasions; I have taken up a burden which is too heavy, for which ultimately I shall have to surrender.[43]

Like Giraut, Jordi de Sant Jordi makes use of accurate military terminology. In the second stanza, he compares his weakened state to that of a fortified castle or town, which would only be able to resist such a strong assault with ample resources and stout defenders:

> Mas eu, qui suy tan flachs per defensar,
> sens mur, sens vall, sens merlet ne verdescha,
> que de mes gens no pusch gayre fiar,
> veyats si stich en so que tost perescha.

But I, who am of such weak defence, without a wall, without a ditch, without a merlon or 'verdescha' [wooden construction attached to wall or tower to cover defenders from enemy fire], who can scarcely trust my people, see if I am not in a position to die soon.

The remainder of the poem develops the twin themes of attack from without and betrayal from within; as in the siege by Sin as expounded in homiletic writings, it is the inner weakness of the stronghold against external forces which causes its downfall. The poet's defences are meagre: his sighs are crossbow bolts and his groans are mortars sent out against 'ley que puny que.m destroescha' ('she who exerts herself to destroy me', line 20). He is betrayed by his five senses, who have plotted his death with the enemy. His eyes and heart (making the number of betrayers up to seven) soon follow by placing him in the enemy's power. Finally, in a gesture similar to that of the captive lover in the *Roman de la rose*, he surrenders as a captain in the enemy's tent, on condition that he is granted his life—if not, he cunningly points out, she will not win a good ransom. Here the laws and diplomacy of warfare as well as its actual conduct are used as metaphors; such specific and precise language gives the central conceit greater force and a feeling of authenticity.

---

[43] Jordi de Sant Jordi, *Les Poesies*, 'Lo Setge d'Amor', pp. 105–13 (108–9).

The tradition of the besieged lover continues in verse of the fifteenth century. Other Hispanic poets who make use of it include the Marqués de Santillana (1398–1458), who begins a poem on the castle of love with the words 'Sitio de amor con grand artelleria, / me veo en torno, e con poder inmenso' ('The siege of love, with large artillery, I see around me, immensely powerful'). In the 'Castillo d'amor' ('Castle of Love') by Jorge Manrique (1440–79) ideas of tenancy and obligation are again invoked: the poet-lover is likened to a fort under the control of his beloved, which could never fall to anyone else. The symbolism of fortress and defences has much in common not only with earlier love allegories but with the religious writings on the castle of the soul. Walls are of love reinforced with loyalty, the moat is dug in a loyal heart, the drawbridge expresses faith, and the windows constantly bring to the viewer the dangerous sight of the beloved. From the tower of homage a standard proclaims that the lover is his lady's vassal. With the strength of love now inside it, the fortress of the heart could withstand a siege of two thousand years. An admission of male weakness before the threat of uncontrollable emotions is thus transformed into an affirmation of strength built on the virtues of courtly love—a secular version of the Seven Virtues which protect the stronghold of the spirit against sin, and of the protection of the castle by a greater, providential power. The religion of love is also celebrated in fifteenth-century French texts such as Martin le Franc's *Le Champion des dames* (*c.*1442), in which the castle is a fortified temple administered by priests of love who defend it against critics of women, or in the beautifully illustrated *Livre du cuers d'amour espris* by René d'Anjou (1409–80), where love is seized, held captive, and eventually rescued.

In such treatments of the siege of love, psychological violence, depicted through military images, is ritualized and made graceful by art. A similar effect is created by civic and ceremonial displays using the same basic pattern of fortress and assailant. Here the siege takes on political and communal connotations, as in some Royal Entries where the king is invited into a castle or dale of pleasure, and in some of the 'pas d'armes' where a fortress is defended against all comers. In a 'pas d'armes' held at Saumur in 1448, for example, a castle structure was beleaguered and defended, as it was at Ghent in 1469, when a knight defended the Queen of the wild men and her people, who watched from a castle behind him. The associations of civic identity and security with the image of the fortress were strong: 'The suitability of the castle for this purpose is obvious. In a feudal world the castle was the ultimate stronghold, to lose which was to lose all. Communities clustered round it. Little imagination was needed then for it to represent the city itself, prosperity or safety.'[44]

As court pageants became more sophisticated, it was the technological accomplishments achieved in the making of mock castles as well as the spectacle of the siege itself which drew admiration and comment. A spectacular pageant siege of the fifteenth century is described in *Tirant lo Blanc* (1460–8). This occurs early in the work, when Tirant is staying at the English court. The siege may not have a specific historical event as its source, but it is likely to have been based on the personal experiences of the author Joanot Martorell (*c.*1413/1415–68), who was himself at the English court between March 1438 and February 1439.[45] Tirant, having participated in the celebrations of the wedding of the English king, meets a hermit on his return to Brittany and recounts some of his experiences at the court:

'Enmig de la praderia trobam una gran roca feta de fusta per subtil artifici tota closa; e sobre la roca se demostrà un gran e alt castell ab forniment de molt bella muralla, on havia cinc-cents hòmens d'armes qui el guardaven, tots armats en blanc.

'Aplegà primer lo Duc ab tota la gent d'armes e manà que obrissen les portes de la roca; e los qui estaven dins digueren que per negú ells no obririen, per ço com llur senyor no ho volia, sinó que tornassen atràs. "Sus !—dix lo Duc —, tothom faça lo que jo faré." Davallà del cavall e mès-se lo primer de tots, e los seus feren lo que ell havia fet; ab les espases en les mans e ab les llances combateren molt fort la dita roca. Los qui estaven alt en la muralla llançaven de grans canteres e bombardes, colobrines e espingardes, barres que semblaven de ferro, e pedres; e tot açò era de cuiro negre, e les pedres de cuiro blanc, on n'hi havia de grans e de poques, e totes eren plenes dins d'arena: emperò senyor, si dava a negun home d'armes, plegat lo metia per terra. E certament fon un combat molt gentil: e los qui no ho sabíem pensam, en lo primer combat, que anava de veres, e molts descavalcam e ab les espases en les mans cuitam allà; emperò prestament coneguem que era burla.'

'In the middle of that meadow, we found a big rock made of wood so cunningly crafted that it made one continuous surface, and on the rock stood a high castle with mighty walls, guarded by five hundred men in shining armour.

First the Duke rode up with all his men, demanding that the doors to the rock be opened. Those inside refused, claiming their lord had forbidden it.

[44] Wickham, *Early English Stages*, i. 43. The 'pas d'armes' is discussed on pp. 17–43.

[45] See J. Entwistle, 'Observacions sobre la dedicatòria i primera part del *Tirant lo Blanch*', trans. J. Rubió Balaguer, *Revista de Catalunya*, 7 (1927), 381–98.

"Have at them !" cried the Duke. "Everyone follow me !" He dismounted and his soldiers followed him, drawing their swords and assailing the rock. Those guarding the walls fired catapults, muskets, and cannon. They hurled bars that looked like iron but were made of black leather, just as the stones were white leather, some big and some small. They were filled with sand, and if they hit a soldier they could fell him. Certainly it was a most genteel battle, but at the first we thought it real. Many of us dismounted, drew our swords, and hastened to aid the Duke, but then we realized that it was only a masque.'[46]

The defenders refuse entrance to the castle to all comers, including the King. At length, the Queen approaches with her consort of maidens and asks who the lord of the castle is. On being told that it is the God of Love, she curtsies and, in a formal address, requests that as one of his slaves she be allowed to see the bliss and delights which are concealed within. With a crash of thunder, the door in the rock opens, and all the members of the court enter a courtyard decorated with tapestries showing stories. The God of Love then replies to the Queen, giving her power as his daughter to rule over and punish those who sail in 'la mar d'amor' ('the sea of love'). Finally, the tapestries disappear and the rock splits into four, each part being elaborately and fantastically decorated and housing a different set of guests of the court.

The siege in this case has served as an initiation to the mysteries of the Castle of Love, and evidently belongs to the same tradition as the allegorical sieges of love poetry. As in those texts, an image with strong Christian theological ramifications has been endowed with meanings from the alternative religion of courtly love. In both text and pageant, the Castle of Love cannot be forced open physically but is vulnerable to the power of words, when expressed with the proper devotion and humility. For all the ludic and fantastic qualities of the event which Tirant describes, the pageant siege clearly carries political meaning (love democratizes the court and makes a slave of the monarchs) and represents an examination of the contracts of fidelity and obedience to which both lovers and servants of the court are bound. A more straightforward image of the siege of love occurs later in the work in a briefer, metaphorical form, in a chapter heading introducing one of the hero's sexual conquests as 'Com Tirant vencé la batalla e per força d'armes entrà lo castell' ('How Tirant won the battle and by force of arms entered the castle', ch. 436).

The mixture of solemnity and spectacle in events like that described in *Tirant lo Blanc* made the Castle of Love a popular courtly game.

---

[46] J. Martorell, and M. Joan de Galba, *Tirant lo Blanc*, ch. 53, i.86–7; trans. Rosenthal, 64.

Occasional poems like Walter of Bibbesworth's 'Chastel de leal amour', in which a lover is quizzed on the meanings of the various parts of the castle, set such festivals in a context of elegant riddles and conversation. The tradition of pageant sieges continued into Tudor times along with the models and metaphors of beleaguered castles in literature. A drawing exists of an attack on the gateway of 'Castle Loyall', constructed for a 'pas d'armes' at the English court in 1510.[47] At the court of Henry VII in 1501, to form part of the celebrations of the marriage of Prince Arthur, a castle was drawn into the hall, containing eight ladies and children singing. After a parley, knights from the 'Mount of Love' assailed the fortress until it yielded. A similar edifice made an appearance at court festivities on New Year's night in 1512. A castle named 'La Fortrese dangerus', occupied by six ladies, was carried about the hall, and then, 'after the quene had behelde it, in came the kyng with five other . . . These VI. assaulted the castle, the ladies seyng them so lustie and coragious, were content to solace with them and upon further communication, to yeld the castle, and so thei came doune and daunced a long space.' The tradition was continued in a pageant given by Cardinal Wolsey in 1522, 'where the castle was held by the ladies Beautie, Honor, Perseveraunce, and other noble qualities who occupied the towers, and by Daungier, Gelousie, Scorne, and other shrewish qualities who occupied the lower walls of the fortress. Ardent desire led seven other gentlemen to an attack with comfits and was victorious, driving the shrews away. After this a dance followed.'[48] Some midsummer popular English pageants from the early sixteenth century included an acted siege against the Moors. Two mock assaults on castles were staged in different entertainments for Edward VI in 1548 and 1550, and part of Henry VIII's entertainments for the Scottish Embassy was a fortress constructed for mock assault and other combats in Greenwich in 1524.

In other Tudor and Jacobean pageants involving sieges the political subtext is stronger. In 1581 Queen Elizabeth I, possibly in an allusion to her refusal of marriage offers from the Duke of Anjou, took part in a pageant in which she sat in the 'Castle of Perfect Beauty' while the Four Children of Desire (including Sir Philip Sidney) laid claim to it as their inheritance. Being defied, they showered it with flowers and rosewater,

---

[47] Walter of Bibbesworth: see Bibliography. J. Huizinga, *The Waning of the Middle Ages*, trans. F. Hopman (London, 1924), 117. Drawing: London, British Library, MS Harley 69 ('The Book of Certain Triumphs'), fo. 20v. Printed in Wickham, *Early English Stages*, i. 28.

[48] Both examples given by Loomis, 'Allegorical Siege', 256.

and on the next day confessed their presumption and surrendered to 'Perfect Beauty'.[49]

The popularity of the figurative siege in the Middle Ages was in part the result of the spread of castle-building from the twelfth century and the consequent frequency of real sieges: homilists and poets could express their ideas by using the images of common experience. Another possible reason for the appeal of the image was the wide range of significance that could be attached to the castle or beleaguered stronghold. In previous chapters we have seen how the besieged place could represent larger communities such as the nationality of the Scots at the siege of Berwick in Barbour's *Bruce*, or the wider community of Christendom in the sieges which took place at its edges, at Rhodes or Belgrade. In the romances of Troy, the besieged city stands for a whole culture and civilization, later to be reborn in the West, while Jerusalem when under siege suggests to writers both the natural base of Christianity, as the place where Christ died, and the weak fortress of the false faith of the Jews. The siege is an image of any force that might test or threaten to destroy the coherence of these entities.

In the figurative sieges considered in this chapter, the beleaguered place takes on a further level of significance as a symbol of the inner self. The mind of Man is identified as the essence enclosed by walls in St Gregory's analysis of sin or in *Sawles Warde*. Through the image of the siege, the spiritual centre of being, the soul, or the vulnerable emotions of human love are perceived as defended and beautiful objects of desire. As the symbolic and allegorical siege is varied in the writings and works of art discussed over the medieval period, a concept of the private self emerges, as an individual essence protecting its spiritual treasure from the temptations without and its uniqueness and beauty from the turbulent forces of love which threaten to storm it. Through the figure of the siege we can trace a developing sense of privacy and identity, as religious writers and poets use the image to explore worlds of inner feeling.

The allegorical siege is renewed and re-created in later literary works: Spenser in *The Faerie Queene* draws on the rich tradition of metaphors and symbols in the siege of the castle of Alma (Bk. II, canto ix), and still later there is a full-scale battle over the castle of the soul in Bunyan's *The Holy War* (1682). The innumerable sieges of fiction and

---

[49] See S. Anglo, *Spectacle, Pageantry, and Early Tudor Policy* (Oxford, 1969), 299–300 (Edward VI); 177 (pageant sieges); 115 (Henry VIII). Loomis, 'Allegorical Siege', 256–8.

films frequently carry with them the connotations of spiritual and ideological battles without using an explicit symbolism, in much the same way that the sieges of medieval romances can seem resonant with implied significance without apparently being used for ends other than continuing and enlivening the story. To read the romances in the context of such writings as we have considered is to be reminded of the potency of certain themes and images which work by suggestion rather than direct statement.

As a literary theme, the siege brings together disparate subjects, from the practical techniques described in military manuals and crusading romances, to the analysis of sin and the refined sensibility of love in patristic and poetic texts. In all its manifestations, though, the siege is above all an image of suffering. Writers use the theme to show us the afflictions endured by the faithful, and the violence they can inflict in the name of religion on their enemies. National as well as religious identity is forged and affirmed in a trial by siege. The physical suffering of charismatic leaders draws together private and public struggles, and turns the event into a process of painful moral and physical progress. The siege denotes a test of faith, or, in the Troy romances, an examination of the permanence of great human achievements. In allegorical writings, it depicts spiritual growth as a process of endurance and resistance, and love as a psychological combat, whose implicit violence needs to be controlled by the rituals of symbol and ceremony.

As an image of testing and tribulation, the siege is an appropriate theme in the mode of romance, which is often characterized by forms of questing, trial, and pursuit of material or spiritual ends. In turn, the narratives of romance and allegory make a siege a meaningful part of a greater story, transforming a familiar image of destruction into a means towards fulfilment. The fall of a city ensures that another will rise, the righteous, beleaguered by their enemies, will find salvation, and the tested soul is shown to withstand the predatory evils that assail it. There is always the promise of treasure after the assault: the castle of the rose, when at last through the aid of Venus it is captured, will yield to the victor the delights of love.

Bibliography

PRIMARY TEXTS

ABBO, *Le Siège de Paris par les Normands: Poème du ixe siècle*, ed. and trans. H. Waquet, CHFMA (Paris, 1942).

Acta Pilati: Gesta Pilati, in *Evangelia Apocrypha*, ed. L. F. C. Tischendorf (Leipzig, 1876), 333–88.

AENEAS, TACTICUS, *On Siegecraft*, ed. L. W. Hunter, rev. S. A. Handford (Oxford, 1927).

—— *How to Survive under Siege*, trans. with introduction and commentary by D. Whitehead (Oxford, 1990).

AILRED OF RIEVAULX, ST (AELREDIS RIEVALLENSIS), *Opera omnia, Corpus christianorum continuatio mediaevalis* (Turnhout, 1971–): *Sermones i–xlvi*, ed. G. Raciti, vol. 2A (Turnhout, 1989).

AMBROISE, *L'Estoire de la Guerre Sainte*, ed. G. Paris, Collection des documents inédits sur l'histoire de France, 11 (Paris, 1897).

—— *L'Estoire de la Guerre Sainte*, in *Three French Chronicles of the Crusades*, ed. and trans. E. N. Stone, University of Washington Publications in the Social Sciences, 10 (Seattle, 1939), 1–160.

Ancrene Wisse. Parts Six and Seven, ed. G. Shepherd (London, 1959).

ANSELM, ST, *Opera omnia*, ed. F. S. Schmitt, 6 vols. (Edinburgh, 1946–62).

—— *Homiliae, PL* 158.

—— *Memorials of St Anselm*, ed. R. W. Southern and F. S. Schmitt (London, 1969).

L'Art d'archerie: Publié avec notes d'après un manuscrit du xve siècle, ed. H. Galice (Paris, 1901).

AUGUSTINE, ST, *De civitate dei, CCSL* 47.

—— *City of God*, trans. H. Bettenson, Penguin Classics (Harmondsworth, 1972).

BARBOUR, J., *Barbour's Bruce*, ed. M. P. McDiarmid and J. A. C. Stevenson, 3 vols., STS, 4th ser. 12, 13, 15 (Edinburgh, 1980–5).

—— 'Siege of Berwick', extract, in K. Sisam (ed.), *Fourteenth Century Verse and Prose* (Oxford, 1921; rev. edn. 1975), 107–14.

BARCLAY, A., *The Shyp of Folys of the Worlde*, ed. T. H. Jamieson (Edinburgh, 1874).

BENOÎT DE SAINTE-MAURE, *Le Roman de Troie*, ed. L. Constans, 5 vols., SATF 61 (Paris, 1904–12).

Beowulf and the Fight at Finnsburg, ed. F. Klaeber (London, 1922).

BERNARD, ST, *Opera*, ed. J. Leclercq *et al.*, 8 vols. (Rome, 1957–77).

—— *Opera omnia, PL* 182–5.

BOCCACCIO, G., *De casibus virorum illustrium* (Paris, 1520).

Le Bone Florence of Rome, ed. C. F. Heffernan, Old and Middle English Texts (Manchester, 1976).

BONET, H., *L'Arbre des batailles*, ed. E. Nys (Brussels, 1883).

—— *The Tree of Battles*, ed. and trans. G. W. Coopland (Liverpool, 1949).

BOSIO, J., *Dell'istoria della sacra religione et illustrissima militia di San Giovanni Gierosolimitano*, 2 vols. (Rome, 1594–1602).

The Brut or the Chronicles of England, ed. F. W. D. Brie, 2 vols., EETS OS, 131, 136 (London, 1906–8).

BUNYAN, J., *The Holy War*, ed. R. Sharrock and J. F. Forrest (Oxford, 1980).

CAOURSIN, G., *Descriptio obsidionis urbis Rhodie* (Venice, 1480).

—— *Descriptio obsidionis urbis Rhodie: Bretning om belejringen af byen Rhodos*, ed. J. Isager, Forening for Boghaandvaerk Fynsafdelingen (Trykt and Odense, 1982).

See also KAYE, J.

Capystranus: W. A. Ringler (ed.), 'Capystranus (an anonymous English epic poem printed in London in 1515)', *NHQ* 27/104 (1986), 131–40.

—— extract, in D. Gray (ed.), *The Oxford Book of Late Medieval Verse and Prose* (Oxford, 1985), 199–203, 459–60.

CASSIAN, ST, *De institutis coenibiorum*, ed. M. Petschenig, *CSEL* 17.

—— *The Twelve Books on the Institutes of the Coenobia*, trans. E. C. S. Gibson, A Select Library of Nicene and Post-Nicene Fathers of the Christian Church, 2nd ser. 11 (Oxford and New York, 1894).

The Castle of Perseverance, in *The Macro Plays: The Castle of Perseverance, Wisdom, Mankind*, ed. M. Eccles, EETS OS, 262 (London, 1969).

CAXTON, W.: see CHRISTINE DE PISAN; LLULL, R.

CHANDOS HERALD, *La Vie du Prince Noir*, ed. D. B. Tyson (Tübingen, 1975).

La Chanson d'Antioche, ed. S. Duparc-Quioc, Documents relatifs à l'histoire des Croisades publiés par l'Académie des Inscriptions et Belles-Lettres, 11 (Paris, 1976).

Chanson de la Croisade Albigeoise, ed. E. Martin-Chabot, 3 vols., CHFMA (Paris, 1931–61).

CHAUCER G., *The Riverside Chaucer*, ed. L. D. Benson, 3rd edn. (Oxford, 1987).

CHRISTINE DE PISAN, *L'Arte de chevalerie selon Végèce* (Paris, 1488).

—— *The Book of Fayttes of Armes and of Chyvalrye*, trans. W. Caxton, ed. A. T. P. Byles, EETS OS, 189 (London, 1932).

COMNENA, A., *The Alexiad of Anna Comnena*, trans. E. R. A. Sewter, Penguin Classics (Harmondsworth, 1969).

COMMYNES, PHILIPPE DE, *Mémoires*, ed. J. Calmette, 3 vols., CHFMA (Paris, 1924–5).

The Crusade and Death of Richard I, ed. R. C. Johnston, ANTS 17 (Oxford, 1961).

CURTI, G. DE, 'Relazione del Sacerdote Giacomo De Curti, intitolata "La città de Rodi assediata dai Turchi il di 23 Maggio 1480" diretta a suo fratello Francesco', in *Le Guerre di Rodi: Relazioni di diversi autori sui due grandi assedi di Rodi (1480–1522)*, ed. and trans. E. F. Mizzi (Turin, 1934), 66–87.

CYNEWULF, *Cynewulf's Juliana*, ed. R. Woolf (London, 1955).

CYPRIAN, ST, *Liber de zelo et livore*, *PL* 4.

—— *The Writings of Cyprian, Bishop of Carthage*, ed. and trans. R. E. Wallis, Ante-Nicene Christian Library: Translations of the Writings of the Fathers down to AD 325, ed. A. Roberts and J. Donaldson, 13 (Edinburgh, 1869).

DARES PHRYGIUS, *De excidio Troiae*, ed. G. Marcello (Rome, 1967).

—— *Anonimi historia troyana Daretis Frigii: Untersuchungen und kritische Ausgaben*, ed. J. Stohlmann (Wuppertal, 1968).

—— in *The Trojan War: The Chronicles of Dictys of Crete and Dares the Phrygian*, trans. R. M. Frazer (Bloomington, Ind. and London, 1966), 133–68.

De custodia interioris hominis, in *Memorials of St Anselm*, ed. R. W. Southern and F. S. Schmitt (London, 1969), 354–60.

De expugnatione Lyxbonensi: The Conquest of Lisbon, ed. and trans. C. W. David, Columbia University Records of Civilization, 24 (New York, 1936).

De Pylato: summary in F. J. More, *Anzeiger für Kunde der deutschen Vorzeit*, 7 (Karlsruhe, 1838), cols. 626–9.

—— trans. in E. du Méril (ed.), *Poésies populaires du Moyen Âge* (Paris, 1847), 359–68.

Destrucción de Jerusalén auto en langua Mexica (Anónimo) Escrito con letra de fines del siglo xvii, ed. and trans. F. del Paso y Troncoso, Biblioteca Náutal, i, *El Teatro* (Florence, 1907).

La Destruccion de Jérusalen: A. Micha (ed.), 'Une rédaction de la *Vengeance de Notre Seigneur*', in *Mélanges offerts à Rita Lejeune* (Gembloux, 1969), ii. 1291–8.

La Destructioun de Rome: Version de Hanovre, ed. L. Formisano (Florence, 1981).

Destruction of Troy: The Gest Hystoriale of the Destruction of Troy, ed. G. E. Panton and D. Donaldson, EETS 39 and 56 (London, 1869 and 1874).

DICTYS CRETENSIS, *Ephemeridos belli Troiani*, ed. W. Eisenhut (Leipzig, 1958).

—— *The Trojan War: The Chronicles of Dictys of Crete and Dares the Phrygian*, trans. R. M. Frazer (Bloomington, Ind. and London, 1966), 19–119.

Digby Plays: The Late Medieval Religious Plays of MSS Digby 133 and E Museo 160, ed. D. C. Baker et al., EETS OS, 283 (Oxford, 1982).

The Dystruccyon of Iherusalem by Vespazian and Tytus, pub. Wynkyn de Worde (1507).

EINHARD, *The Life of Charlemagne*, trans. L. Thorpe, Penguin Classics (Harmondsworth, 1969).

EIXIMENIS, F., *Dotzè del Chrestià o Regiment de Prínceps e de Comunitats* (València, 1484).

Eneas: Antikisierender Roman des 12 Jahrhunderts, ed. R. Baehr, Sammlung Romanischer Ubungstexte, 53 (Tübingen, 1969).

English Bible: The Middle English Prose Translation of Roger d'Argenteuil's Bible en françois, ed. P. Moe, Middle English Texts, 6 (Heidelberg, 1977).

ERMOLD LE NOIR [ERMOLDUS NIGELLUS], *In Honorem Hludowici: Poème sur Louis le Pieux et épitres au Roi Pepin*, ed. and trans. E. Faral, CHFMA 14 (Paris, 1932).

Estoire del Saint Graal: Le Roman de l'Estoire dou Graal, ed. W. A. Nitze, CFMA 37 (Paris, 1927).

EUSEBIUS, *The Ecclesiastical History*, ed. K. Lake *et al.*, trans. K. Lake, 2 vols., Loeb Classical Library (London, 1957–9).

Excidium Troiae: E. B. Atwood (ed.), 'The Rawlinson *Excidium Troiae*', *Speculum*, 9 (1934), 379–404.

FANTOSME, JORDAN, *Jordan Fantosme's Chronicle*, ed. R. C. Johnston (Oxford, 1981).

FERRER, F., *Romanç dels actes e coses que l'armada del gran Soldà féu en Rodes: Obra completa*, ed. J. Auferil, Els Nostres Clàssics, Col.lecció A, 128 (Barcelona, 1989), 254–68.

—— L. Nicolau d'Olwer (ed.), 'Un Témoignage catalan du siège de Rhodes en 1444', *EUC* 12 (1927), 376–87.

FROISSART, J., *Œuvres: Chroniques*, ed. K. de Lettenhove, 25 vols. (Brussels, 1870–7).

—— *The Chronicle of Froissart Translated out of French by Sir John Bourchier Lord Berners*, ed. with introduction by W. P. Ker, 6 vols., The Tudor Translations, 27–32 (London, 1901–3).

—— *Chronicles*, selection trans. G. Brereton, Penguin Classics (Harmondsworth, 1968).

FRONTINUS, *Juli Frontini Stratagemata*, ed. R. I. Ireland (Leipzig, 1990).

GEOFFREY OF BRETEUIL, *Epistles, PL* 205.

GEOFFROY DE CHARNY, *Livre de chevalerie*: printed in J. Froissart, *Œuvres: Chroniques*, ed. K. de Lettenhove, 25 vols. (Brussels, 1870–7), vol. i, part 3, 463–533.

GERALD OF WALES (GIRALDUS CAMBRENSIS), *Opera*, ed. J. S. Brewer *et al.*, 8 vols., Rolls Series, 21 (London, 1861–91).

—— *The Journey through Wales and the Description of Wales*, trans. with introduction by L. Thorpe, Penguin Classics (Harmondsworth, 1978).

Gesta Francorum et aliorum Hierosolimitanorum, ed. and trans. R. Hill, Nelson's Medieval Texts (Oxford, 1962).

GIRAUT DE BORNEIL, 'Domna, aissi cum us chasteus', in A. R. Press (ed. and trans.), *Anthology of Troubador Lyric Poetry*, Edinburgh Bilingual Library, 3 (Edinburgh, 1971), 136–7.

GODFREY OF ADMONT, *Homiliae Festivales, PL* 174.

GOWER, J., *Vox Clamantis*, in *Complete Works*, ed. G. C. Macaulay, 4 vols. (Oxford, 1899–1902), vol. iv.

—— *The Major Latin Works of John Gower*, ed. and trans. E. W. Stockton (Seattle, 1962).

GRAY, SIR T., *Scalacronica*, ed. J. H. Stevenson (Edinburgh, 1836).

GREGORY, ST, *Homiliarum in Evangelium, PL* 76.

—— *Homiliarum in Ezecheliem*, ed. M. Adriaen, *CCSL* 142; *PL* 76.

—— *Liber regulae pastoralis, PL* 77.

—— *St Gregory on the Pastoral Charge: The Benedictine Text with an English Translation*, ed. and trans. H. R. Bramley (Oxford and London, 1874).

—— *Moralia in Job*, ed. M. Adriaen, *CCSL* 143; *PL* 75–6.

—— *Morals on the Book of Job*, translated by various hands, A Library of the Fathers of the Holy Catholic Church, 18, 21, 23, 31 (Oxford, 1844–50).

GROSSETESTE, R., *Le Château d'amour*, ed. J. Murray (Paris, 1918).

—— *The Middle English Translations of Robert Grosseteste's 'Chateau d'amour'*, ed. K. Sajavaara, Mémoires de la Société Néophilologique de Helsinki, 32 (Helsinki, 1967).

Le Guerre de Rodi: Relazioni di diversi autori sui due grandi assedi di Rodi (1480–1522), ed. and trans. E. F. Mizzi (Turin, 1934).

GUIDO DE COLUMNIS, *Historia destructionis Troiae*, ed. N. E. Griffin (Cambridge, Mass., 1936).

—— *Historia destructionis Troiae*, trans. with introduction and notes by M. E. Meek (Bloomington, Ind. and London, 1974).

GUILLAUME DE LORRIS and JEAN DE MEUN, *Le Roman de la rose*, ed. E. Langlois, 5 vols., SATF 61 (Paris, 1914–24).

—— *Le Roman de la rose*, ed. A. Strubel, Lettres gothiques (Paris, 1992).

—— *The Romance of the Rose*, trans. C. Dahlberg (Hanover and London, 1971).

HEGESIPPUS, *Historiae libri v*, ed. V. Ussani, *CSEL* 66.

HENRY OF LANCASTER, *Le Livre de seyntz medicines: The Unpublished Devotional Treatise of Henry of Lancaster*, ed. E. J. Arnould, ANTS 2 (Oxford, 1940).

Histoire ancienne jusqu'à César: extracts in P. Meyer (ed.), 'Les Premières compilations françaises d'histoire ancienne. II. Histoire ancienne jusqu'à César', *Romania*, 14 (1885), 36–81.

HONORIUS OF AUTUN, *Speculum ecclesiae, PL* 172.

Itinerarium peregrinorum et gesta regis Ricardi, ed. W. Stubbs, Rolls Series, 38/1 (London, 1864).

JAUME I, *Crònica o llibre dels feits*, ed. F. Soldevila, Les Millors Obres de la Literatura Catalana, 86 (Barcelona, 1982).

—— *Crònica o llibre dels feits*, in *Les quatre grans Cròniques*, ed. F. Soldevila (Barcelona, 1971).

—— *Chronicle*, ed. and trans. J. Forster, 2 vols. (London, 1883).

JEAN DE BUEIL, *Le Jouvencel*, ed. L. Lecestre and C. Favre, 2 vols., SHF (Paris, 1887–9).

JEAN DE MEUN, *Li Livres de confort de philosophie*: V. L. Dedeck-Héry (ed.), 'Boethius' *De Consolatione* by Jean de Meun', *MS* 14 (1952), 165–275.

—— *L'Art de chevalerie: Traduction du 'De re militari' de Végèce*, ed. U. Robert, SATF (Paris, 1897).

—— Jean de Meun, Li Abregemenz noble homme Vegesce Flave René des establisse-menz apartenanz a chevalerie, ed. L. Löfstedt (Helsinki, 1977).

See also GUILLAUME DE LORRIS.

JEAN PRIORAT, Li Abrejance de l'Ordre de Chevalerie. Mise en vers de la traduction de Végèce de Jean de Meun par Jean Priorat de Besançon, ed. U. Robert, SATF (Paris, 1897).

JORDI DE SANT JORDI, Les Poesies, ed. M. de Riquer and L. Badia, Tres i Quatre Biblioteca d'estudis i investigacions (València, 1984).

JOSEPHUS, F., Flavii Josephi opera omnia, ed. S. S. Naber, 6 vols., Bibliotheca scrip-torum Graecorum et Romanorum Teubneriana (Leipzig, 1888–96).

—— The Jewish War, trans. with introduction by G. A. Williamson, Penguin Classics (Harmondsworth, 1959).

Journal d'un bourgeois de Paris, ed. C. Beaune, Lettres gothiques (Paris, 1990). Trans. J. Shirley, A Parisian Journal (1405–1449) (Oxford, 1968).

KAYE, J., The Dylectable Newesse and Tithynges of the Glorious Victorye of the Rhodyans agayenst the Turkes (London, 1482).

—— Gulielmus Caorsin: 'The Siege of Rhodes' (1482), The English Experience, 236 (Amsterdam, 1970).

—— 'The Siege of Rhodes' (1482) Translated by John Kaye and 'The Book of Subtyl Histories and Fables of Esope' (1484), facsimile reproductions with an intro-duction by D. Gray, Scholars' Facsimiles & Reprints (New York, 1975).

—— extract from The Siege of Rhodes, in D. Gray (ed.), The Oxford Book of Late Medieval Verse and Prose (Oxford, 1985), 23–5, 422.

—— Caoursin's Account of the Siege of Rhodes in 1480, Translated into English by John Kay, the Poet-Laureate to King Edward IV, ed. H. W. Fincham, with intro-duction by E. J. King, Library Committee, OSJJ, Historical Pamphlets, 2 (London, 1926).

King Alisaunder, ed. G. V. Smithers, EETS OS, 227 (London, 1952).

King of Tars, ed. J. Perryman, Middle English Texts, 12 (Heidelberg, 1980).

The Knight of Curtesy, in D. Gray (ed.), The Oxford Book of Late Medieval Verse and Prose (Oxford, 1985), 185–99.

Knyghthode and Bataile: see VEGETIUS, F. R.

The Laud Troy Book: A Romance of about 1400 AD, ed. J. E. Wülfing, 2 vols., EETS 121, 122 (London, 1902–3).

LLULL, R., Llibre de l'orde de cavalleria, ed. M. Gustà (Barcelona, 1980).

—— The Book of the Ordre of Chyvalry, trans. W. Caxton, ed. A. T. P. Byles, EETS OS, 168 (London, 1926).

The Luttrell Psalter, facsimile, ed. with introduction by E. G. Millar (London, 1932).

LYDGATE, J., Lydgate's Siege of Thebes, ed. A. Erdmann and E. Ekwall, 2 vols., EETS ES, 108, 125 (London, 1911–30).

LYDGATE, J., Lydgate's Troy Book, ed. H. Bergen, 4 vols., EETS ES, 97, 103, 106, 126 (London, 1906–35).

LYDGATE, J., *The Fall of Princes*, ed. H. Bergen, 4 vols., EETS ES, 121–4 (London, 1924–7).

MAILLART, J., *Le Roman du Comte d'Anjou*, ed. M. Roques, CFMA 67 (Paris, 1974).

MANRIQUE, J., *Poesia*, ed. J.–M. Alda Tesan, 6th edn. (Madrid, 1980).

MANUEL, DON JUAN, *El Conde Lucanor*, ed. J. M. Blecua (Madrid, 1982).

MARTORELL, J., and JOAN DE GALBA, M. *Tirant lo Blanc*, ed. M. de Riquer, 2 vols., Les Millors Obres de la Literatura Catalana, 99–100 (Barcelona, 1983; 3rd edn. 1988).

—— *Tirant lo Blanc*, trans. with foreword by D. H. Rosenthal (London, 1984).

MEDWALL, H., *The Plays of Henry Medwall*, ed. A. H. Nelson, Tudor Interludes, 2 (Cambridge and Totowa, NJ, 1980).

THOMAS MORE, ST, *A Dialogue of Comfort Against Tribulation*, in *Complete Works of St Thomas More*, ed. L. L. Martz and F. Manley, 16 vols., vol. xii (New Haven, 1976).

Morte Arthure: A Critical Edition, ed. M. Hamel, Garland Medieval Texts, 9 (New York and London, 1984).

—— *King Arthur's Death: The Middle English 'Stanzaic Morte Arthure' and 'Alliterative Morte Arthure'*, ed. L. D. Benson (Exeter, 1986).

—— extracts in *Morte Arthure*, ed. J. Finlayson, York Medieval Texts (London, 1967).

MUNTANER, R., *Crònica*, ed. M. Gustà, 2 vols., Les Millors Obres de la Literatura Catalana, 19–20 (Barcelona, 1979).

—— *The Chronicle of Muntaner*, trans. Lady Goodenough, Hakluyt Society, 2nd ser. 47 and 50 (London, 1920–1).

A Myrroure for Magistrates, ed. L. B. Campbell (Cambridge, 1938).

NEVILL, W., *The Castell of Pleasure*, ed. R. D. Cornelius, EETS OS, 179 (London, 1930).

OVID, *Heroides and Amores*, ed. and trans. G. Showerman, Loeb Classical Library, 41 (London and Cambridge, Mass., 1914).

PAGE, J., 'The Siege of Rouen', in *The Brut or the Chronicles of England*, ed. F. W. D. Brie, 2 vols., EETS OS, 131 and 136 (London, 1906–8), ii. 404–22.

—— *The Historical Collections of a Citizen of London in the Fifteenth Century*, ed. J. Gairdner, Camden Society (London, 1876), pp. x–xvi, 1–46.

Le Pas Saladin: F. E. Lodeman (ed.), 'Le Pas Saladin', *MLN* 12 (1897), 21–34, 84–96, 209–29, 273–81.

PETER OF VAUX-DE-CERNAY, *Hystoria Albigensis*, ed. P. Guébin and E. Lyon, 3 vols. (Paris, 1926–39).

Peterborough Psalter: *Le Psautier de Peterborough*, facsimile, ed. J. van den Gheyn (Haarlem, 1905).

PHILIPPE DE MÉZIÈRES, *Le Songe du vieil pèlerin*, ed. G. W. Coopland, 2 vols. (Cambridge, 1969).

The Poem of the Cid: A Bilingual Edition with Parallel Text, ed. I. Michael, trans. R. Hamilton and J. Perry, Penguin Classics (Harmondsworth, 1984).

Poésies populaires latines du Moyen Age, ed. E. du Méril (Paris, 1847).

PRESS, A. R. (ed. and trans.), Anthology of Troubadour Lyric Poetry, Edinburgh Bilingual Library, 3 (Edinburgh, 1971).

La Prise de Damiette: P. Meyer (ed.), 'La Prise de Damiette en 1219: Relation inédite en Provençal', BEC 38 (1877), 497–571.

—— extract in P. Meyer (ed.), 'Relation du siège de Damiette', in Recueil d'anciens textes bas-latins provençaux et français (Paris, 1877), i. 138–41.

—— extract, in P. Bec (ed.), Anthologie de la prose occitane du Moyen Age (xiie–xve siècle), Les Classiques d'Oc (Avignon, 1977), 63–9.

The Prose Siege of Jerusalem: A. Kurvinen (ed.), The Siege of Jerusalem in Prose, Mémoires de la Société Néophilologique de Helsinki, 34 (Helsinki, 1969).

The Prose Siege of Thebes: see The Prose Siege of Troy.

The Prose Siege of Troy: F. Brie (ed.), 'Zwei mittelenglische Prosaromane: The Sege of Thebes und The Sege of Troy', Archiv, 130 (1913), 40–52, 269–85.

—— Griffin, N. E. (ed.), 'The Sege of Troye', PMLA 22 (1907), 157–200.

PRUDENTIUS, Opera, ed. and trans. H. J. Thomson, Loeb Classical Library (Cambridge, Mass., 1949).

Registrum Abbatiae Johannis Whethamstede, ed. H. T. Riley, 2 vols., Rolls Series (London, 1872–3).

RENÉ D'ANJOU, Le Livre du cueur d'amours espris, facsimile, ed. F. Unterkircher (London, 1975).

Richard Coeur de Lion: K. Brunner (ed.), Der mittelenglisch Versroman über Richard Löwenherz, WBEP 42 (Vienna and Leipzig, 1913).

ROBERT DE BALSAC, La Nef des princes et des batailles de noblesse (Lyon, 1502).

ROBBINS, R. H. (ed.), Historical Poems of the XIVth and XVth Centuries (New York, 1959).

ROLANDINO OF PADUA, Cronica in factis et circa facta Marchie Trivixane, ed. A. Bonardi, Rerum Italicarum Scriptores, 8/1 (Città di Castello, 1905).

Le Roman de la rose: see GUILLAUME DE LORRIS

Le Roman de Troie en prose, ed. F. Vielliard, Bibliotheca Bodmeriana, Textes, IV (Cologny-Geneva, 1979).

—— ed. L. Constans and E. Faral, CFMA 29 (Paris, 1922). [Different text]

St Erkenwald, ed. T. Turville-Petre, in Alliterative Poetry of the Later Middle Ages (London, 1989), 101–19.

SALE, A. DE LA, Le Reconfort de Madame de Fresne, ed. I. Hill, Textes littéraires, 34 (Exeter, 1979).

—— La Salade, vol. i of Œuvres complètes, ed. F. Desonay, 2 vols. (Paris, 1935).

SANTILLANA, MARQUÉS DE, Poesia, ed. M. Duran (Madrid, 1975).

Sawles Warde, ed. R. M. Wilson (Leeds, 1938).

Scottish Troy Fragments: C. Horstmann (ed.), *Barbour's, des schottischen National-dichters, Legendsammlung nebst den Fragmenten seines Trojanerkrieges*, 2 vols. (Heilbronn, 1881), ii. 215–308.

The Seege of Troye: M. E. Barnicle (ed.), *The Seege or Batayle of Troye*, EETS OS, 172 (London, 1927).

—— ed. C. H. A. Wager (New York, 1899).

The Sege of Melayne: in *Six Middle English Romances*, ed. M. Mills (London, 1973), 1–45.

—— S. J. Herrtage (ed.), *The Sege off Melayne*, EETS ES, 35 (London, 1880).

Le Siège de Barbastre, ed. J.-L. Perrier, CFMA 54 (Paris, 1926).

The Siege of Caerlaverok, in *Eight Thirteenth Century Rolls of Arms in French and Anglo-Norman Blazon*, ed. G. J. Brault (University Park, Philadelphia and London, 1973), 101–25.

'The Siege of Calais': in R. H. Robbins (ed.), *Historical Poems of the XIVth and XVth Centuries* (New York, 1959), 78–83.

—— R. A. Klinefelter (ed.), ' "The Siege of Calais": A New Text', *PMLA* 67 (1952), 888–95.

The Siege of Jerusalem, ed. E. Kölbing and M. Day, EETS OS, 188 (London, 1932).

Sir Ferrumbras, ed. S. J. Herrtage, EES ES, 34 (London, 1879; repr., 1966).

Sir Gawain and the Green Knight, ed. J. R. R. Tolkien and E. V. Gordon, 2nd edn., rev. N. Davis (Oxford, 1967).

Le Songe du castel: R. D. Cornelius (ed.), 'Le Songe du castel', *PMLA* 46 (1931), 321–32.

SPENSER, E., *The Faerie Queene*, ed. J. C. Smith, 2 vols. (Oxford, 1909).

STUART, BÉRAULT, *Traité sur l'art de guerre*, ed. E. de Comminges (The Hague, 1976).

SUGER, *Vie de Louis VI le Gros*, ed. and trans. H. Waquet, CHFMA 11 (Paris, 1929).

THIBAUT, M., *Le Roman de la poire par Tibaut*, ed. C. Marchello-Nizia, SATF (Paris, 1984).

Titus and Vespasian, ed. J. A. Herbert, Roxburghe Club (London, 1905).

—— R. Fischer (ed.), 'Vindicta Salvatoris', Archiv, 111 (1903), 285–98; 112 (1904), 25–45.

TURVILLE-PETRE, T. (ed.), *Alliterative Poetry of the Middle Ages* (London, 1989).

Vainglory, ed. and trans. T. A. Shippey, in *Poems of Wisdom and Learning in Old English* (Cambridge, 1976), 54–7.

VEGETIUS, F. R., *Epitoma rei militari*, ed. L. F. Stelten (New York, 1990).

—— *Vegetius: Epitome of Military Science*, trans. N. P. Milner (Liverpool, 1993).

—— *The Earliest English Translation of Vegetius' De re militari*, ed. G. Lester, Middle English Texts, 21 (Heidelberg, 1988).

—— *Knyghthode and Bataile: A XVth Century Verse Paraphrase of Flavius Vegetius Renatus' Treatise 'De re militari'*, ed. R. Dyboski and Z. M. Arend, EETS OS, 201 (London, 1935).

See also JEAN DE MEUN, JEAN PRIORAT.

Venjance Nostre Seigneur: in A. Graf (ed.), *Roma nella memoria e nelle imaginazioni del medio evo,* 2 vols.(Turin, 1882; 2nd edn. 1923), i. 285–373.

—— *The Oldest Version of the Twelfth-Century Poem 'La Venjance Nostre Seigneur',* ed. L. Gryting, University of Michigan Contributions in Modern Philology, 19 (Ann Arbor, 1952).

—— A. Micha (ed.), 'Une rédaction de la *Vengeance de Notre Seigneur',* in *Mélanges offerts à Rita Lejeune* (Gembloux, 1969), ii. 1291–8.

—— *La Venjance de Nostre-Seigneur: The Old and Middle French Prose Versions: The Version of Japheth,* ed. A. E. Ford, Pontifical Institute of Medieval Studies, Studies and Texts, 63 (Toronto, 1984).

VILLEHARDOUIN, G. DE, *La Conquête de Constantinople,* ed. E. Faral, 2 vols., CHFMA 18, 19 (Paris, 1961).

—— *The Conquest of Constantinople,* in M. R. B. Shaw (ed. and trans.), *Chronicles of the Crusades,* Penguin Classics (Harmondsworth, 1963).

Vindicta Salvatoris: in *Evangelia Apocrypha,* ed. L. F. C. Tischendorf (Leipzig, 1876), 471–86.

—— R. Fischer (ed.), 'Vindicta Salvatoris', *Archiv,* 111 (1903), 285–98, 112 (1904), 25–45.

VIOLLET-LE-DUC, E. *Dictionnaire raisonné de l'architecture française du xie au xvie siècle* (Paris, 1857).

VITRUVIUS, *On Architecture,* ed. F. Granger, 2 vols. (London, 1931, 1934).

WALTER OF BIBBESWORTH, 'Chastel de Leal Amour', printed in J. Froissart, *Œuvres: Chroniques,* ed. K. de Lettenhove, 25 vols. (Brussels, 1870–7), vol. i, part 1, 554–6.

WALTER DE MILEMETE, *The Treatise of Walter de Milemete De nobilitatibus sapientiis, et prudentiis regum,* facsimile, ed. M. R. James, Roxburghe Club (London, 1913).

The Wars of Alexander, ed. H. N. Duggan and T. Turville-Petre, EETS SS, 10 (London, 1989).

WAURIN, J. DE, *Anciennes cronicques d'Engleterre,* ed. Mlle Dupont, SHF, 3 vols. (Paris, 1858–63).

—— N. Iorga (ed.), 'Les Aventures "sarrazines" des français au Bourgogne au xve siècle', in C. Marinesco (ed.), *Mélanges d'histoire générale* (Cluj, 1927), i. 30–5. [Anonymous addition to Waurin's chronicle]

WIDUKIND, *Rerum gestarum Saxonicarum,* ed. G. Waitz and K. A. Kehr, MGH Scriptores, 60 (Hanover, 1904).

William of Palerne: An Alliterative Romance, ed. G. H. V. Bunt, Mediaevalia Groningana, fasc. 6 (Groningen, 1985).

Wynnere and Wastoure, ed. S. Trigg, EETS OS, 297 (London, 1990).

SECONDARY TEXTS

ACKERMAN, R. B., 'Armor and Weapons in the Middle English Romances', *RSSCW* 7/2 (June 1939), 104–18.

ADAM-EVEN, P., 'Les Fonctions militaires des hérauts d'armes', *AHS* 71 (1957), 2–33.

ALLMAND, C. T. (ed.), *War, Literature and Politics in the Late Middle Ages* (Liverpool, 1976).

ANDERSON, E. R., *Cynewulf: Structure, Style and Theme in his Poetry* (London and Toronto, 1983).

ANDREW, M., 'The Fall of Troy in *Sir Gawain and the Green Knight* and *Troilus and Criseyde*', in P. Boitani (ed.), *The European Tragedy of Troilus* (Oxford, 1989), 75–93.

ANGLO, S., *Spectacle, Pageantry and Early Tudor Policy* (Oxford, 1969).

ARDEN, H., 'The Slings and Arrows of Outrageous Love in the *Roman de la rose*', in I. A. Corfis and M. Wolfe (eds.), *The Medieval City under Siege* (Woodbridge, 1995), 191–206.

ARNOLD, E. J., *Étude sur le Livre des saintes médecines du duc Henri de Lancastre* (Paris, 1949).

ARTONNE, A., 'Froissart Historien: Le Siège et la prise de la Roche-Vendeix', *BEC* 110 (1952), 89–107.

ATWOOD, E. B., 'The *Excidium Troiae* and Medieval Troy Literature', *MP* 35 (1937–8), 115–28.

BAIN, R. N., 'The Siege of Belgrade by Muhammed II, July 1–23, 1456', *EHR* 7 (1892), 235–42.

BARNIE, J., *War in Medieval English Society: Social Values and the Hundred Years War 1337–99* (London, 1974).

BARRON, W. R. J., '*Trawthe* and *Treason: The Sin of Gawain Reconsidered* (Manchester, 1980).

—— *English Medieval Romance* (London and New York, 1987).

BAUGH, A. C., 'The Middle English Romance: Some Questions of Creation, Presentation and Preservation', *Speculum*, 42 (1967), 1–31.

BAYOT, A., *La Légende de Troie à la cour de Bourgogne* (Bruges, 1908).

BEER, J. M. A., *Villehardouin: Epic Historian*, Études de philologie et d'histoire, 7 (Geneva, 1968).

BENNETT, J. A. W., *Middle English Literature*, ed. and completed by D. Gray (Oxford, 1986).

BENSON, C. D., 'Chaucer's Influence on the Prose "Sege of Troy"', *N&Q* 216, NS 18 (1971), 127–30.

—— *The History of Troy in Middle English Literature* (Woodbridge, 1980).

BENSON, L. D., 'The Alliterative *Morte Arthure* and Medieval Tragedy', *TSL* 11 (1966), 75–87.

BERNARDO, A. S., 'Sex and Salvation in the Middle Ages: From the *Romance of the Rose* to the *Divine Comedy*', *Italica*, 67 (1990), 305–18.

BILLINGS, M., *The Cross and the Crescent* (London, 1987).

BLOCH, D., *et al.* (eds.), *Catalogue generale des manuscrits latins: Tables des tomes iii à vi (nos. 2693 à 3775b)*. *II. Table des incipit A–M* (Paris, 1983).

BLOOMFIELD, M. W., The Seven Deadly Sins (Michigan, 1952).

BORNSTEIN, D., 'The Scottish Prose Version of Vegetius' *De re militari*', *SSL* 8 (1971), 174–83.

—— 'Military Strategy in Malory and Vegetius' *De re militari*', *CLS* 9 (1972), 123–9.

—— 'Military Manuals in Fifteenth-Century England', *MS* 37 (1975), 469–77.

BOSSUAT, R., 'Jean de Rouvroy, traducteur des Stratagèmes de Frontin', *BHR* 22 (1960), 273–86, 469–89.

BOUCHÉ, T., 'Burlesque et renouvelement des formes: L'Attaque du château dans le *Roman de la rose* de Jean de Meun', in *Hommage à Jean-Charles Payen: Farai chansone ta novele. Essai sur la liberté créatrice au Moyen Age* (Caen, 1989), 87–98.

BRADBURY, J., 'Greek Fire in the West', *History Today*, 29 (1979), 326–31, 344.

—— *The Medieval Siege* (Woodbridge, 1992).

BRADFORD, E., *The Great Siege: Malta 1565* (London, 1961).

—— *The Shield and the Sword: The Knights of Malta* (London, 1972).

BRAULT, G. J., 'Heraldic Terminology and Legendary Material in the *Siege of Caerlaverok (c.1300)*', in U. T. Holmes (ed.), *Romance Studies in Memory of Edward Billings Ham*, California State College Publications, 2 (Hayward, Calif., 1967), 5–20.

BROCKMAN, E., *The Two Sieges of Rhodes, 1480–1522* (London, 1969).

BROUGHTON, B. B., *The Legends of King Richard I Coeur de Lion: A Study of the Sources and Variations to the Year 1600*, Studies in English Literature, 25 (Paris and The Hague, 1966).

BUCHTHAL, H., *Historia Troiana: Studies in the History of Mediaeval Secular Illustration*, Studies of the Warburg Institute, 32 (London, 1971).

BURROW, J. A., *Medieval Writers and their Work: Middle English Literature and its Background 1100–1500* (Oxford, 1982).

CALIN, W., *A Muse for Heroes: Nine Centuries of the Epic in France* (Toronto, 1983).

CAMUS, J., 'Notice d'une traduction française de Végèce faite en 1380', *Romania*, 25 (1896), 393–400.

CATHCART-KING, D. J., 'The Trebuchet and other Siege-Engines', *Château Gaillard Études de castellologie médiévale*, 9–10, *Actes de Colloques internationaux tenus à Basel (1978) et à Durham (1980)* (Caen, 1982), 457–70.

CHESNEY, K., 'A Neglected Prose Version of the *Roman de Troie*', *MÆ* 11 (1942), 46–67.

CHIÀNTERA, R., *Guido delle Colonne* (Naples, 1955).

CHILDRESS, D., 'Between Romance and Legend: "Secular Hagiography" in Middle English Literature', *PQ* 57 (1978), 311–22.

CLINE, R., 'Heart and Eyes', *RPh* 25 (1972), 263–97.

COCKLE, M. J., *A Bibliography of English Military Books up to 1642*, ed. H. D. Cockle (London, 1900).

COHEN, G., *Études d'histoire du théâtre en France au Moyen Age et à la Renaissance* (Paris, 1956).

COMBELLACK, C. R. B., 'The Composite Catalogue of *The Sege of Troye*', *Speculum*, 26 (1951), 624–34.

CONTAMINE, P., 'The War Literature of the Late Middle Ages: The Treatises of Robert de Balsac and Béraud Stuart, Lord of Aubigny', in C. T. Allmand (ed.), *War, Literature and Politics in the Late Middle Ages* (Liverpool, 1976), 102–21.

—— 'Froissart: Art militaire, pratique et conception de la guerre', in J. J. N. Palmer (ed.), *Froissart: Historian* (Woodbridge and Totowa, NJ, 1981), 132–44, 180–1.

—— *War in the Middle Ages*, trans. M. Jones (Oxford, 1984).

COOPLAND, G. W., 'Le Jouvencel (Revisited)', *Symposium*, 5 (1951), 137–86.

CORFIS, I. A., and WOLFE M. (eds.), *The Medieval City under Siege* (Woodbridge, 1995).

CORNELIUS, R. D., *The Figurative Castle* (Bryn Mawr, 1930).

COULTON, G. G., *A Medieval Garner* (London, 1910).

CURTIUS, E. R., *European Literature and the Latin Middle Ages*, trans. W. R. Trask (original German publication, Berne, 1948; trans., London, 1953).

DALTON, M. O., *Catalogue of the Ivory Carvings of the Christian Era . . . in the British Museum* (London, 1909).

DENHOLM-YOUNG, N., 'The Song of Carlaverok and the Parliamentary Roll of Arms as found in Cott. MS. Calig. A. XVIII in the British Museum', *PBA* 47 (1961), 251–62.

DOBSCHÜTZ, E., *Christusbilder: Untersuchungen zur christlichen Legende*, in O. Gebhardt and A. Harnack (eds.), *Texts und Untersuchungen zur Geschichte der altchristen Literatur*, Neue Folge, vol. iii (Leipzig, 1899).

DOUBLEDAY, J. F., 'The Allegory of the Soul as Fortress in Old English Poetry', *Anglia*, 88 (1970), 503–8.

DOUTREPONT, G., *Les Mises en prose des epopées et des romans chevaleresques du xive au xvie siècle* (Brussels, 1939).

DOYLE, I., 'The Manuscripts', in D. Lawton (ed.), *Middle English Alliterative Poetry and its Literary Background* (Cambridge, 1982).

DUFFY, C., *Siege Warfare: The Fortress in the Early Modern World 1494–1660* (London, 1979).

EDWARDS, J. G., 'The *Itinerarium Regis Ricardi* and the *Estoire de la Guerre Sainte*', in J. G. Edwards *et al.* (eds.), *Historical Essays in Honour of James Tate* (Manchester, 1933), 59–77.

ENTWISTLE, J., 'Observacions sobre la dedicatòria i primera part del *Tirant lo Blanch*', trans. J. Rubió Balaguer, *Revista de Catalunya*, 7 (1927), 381–98.

ESDAILE, A., *A List of English Tales and Prose Romances Printed before 1740* (London, 1912).

FARAL, E., *Recherches sur les sources latines des contes et roman courtois au Moyen Age* (Paris, 1913), 169–87.

FINLAYSON, J., 'Rhetorical "Description" of Place in the Alliterative *Morte Arthure*', *MP* 61 (1963), 1–11.

—— '*Morte Arthure*: The Date and a Source for Contemporary References', *Speculum*, 42 (1967), 624–38.

FINÓ, J.-F., *Forteresses de la France médiévale: Construction—ataque—défense* (Paris, 1967).

FLEISCHMAN, S., 'On the Representation of History and Fiction in the Middle Ages', *History and Theory*, 22 (1983), 278–310.

FRYE, N., *The Secular Scripture: A Study of the Structure of Romance* (Cambridge, Mass. and London, 1976).

FURNEAUX, R., *The Roman Siege of Jerusalem* (London, 1973).

GAFFNEY, W., 'The Allegory of the Christ-Knight in *Piers Plowman*', *PMLA* 46 (1931), 155–68.

GARCÍA GUAL, C., *Primeras Novelas Europeas* (Madrid, 1990).

GILLINGHAM, J., *Richard the Lionheart* (London, 1978; 2nd edn. 1989).

—— 'Some Legends of Richard the Lionheart: Their Development and their Influence', in *Ricardo Cuor di Leone nella storia e nella leggenda: Accademia Nazionale dei Lincei, colloquio italo-britannico*, Accademia Nazionale dei Lincei, Problemi attuali di scienza e di cultura, 253 (Rome, 1981), 35–50. Reprinted in *Richard Coeur de Lion: Kingship, Chivalry and War in the Twelfth Century*, 181–92.

—— 'Richard I and the Science of War in the Middle Ages', in J. Gillingham and J. C. Holt (eds.), *War and Government in the Middle Ages: Essays in Honour of J. O. Prestwich* (London, 1984), 78–91. Reprinted in *Richard Coeur de Lion: Kingship, Chivalry and War in the Twelfth Century*, 211–26.

—— *Richard Coeur de Lion: Kingship, Chivalry and War in the Twelfth Century* (London, 1994).

GIST, M. A., *Love and War in the Middle English Romances* (Philadelphia, 1947).

GODMAN, P., *Poets and Emperors: Frankish Politics and Carolingian Poetry* (Oxford, 1987).

GOFFART, W., 'The Date and Purpose of Vegetius' *De re militari*', *Traditio*, 33 (1977), 65–100.

GÖLLER, K. H. (ed.), *The Alliterative Morte Arthure: A Reassessment of the Poem* (Cambridge, 1981).

GOLUBEVA, O., 'The Saltykov-Schedrin Library, Leningrad', *The Book Collector*, 4 (1955), 99–109.

GOODWIN, C. W., *The Anglo-Saxon Legends of St Andrew and St Veronica* (Cambridge, 1851).

GORDON, G., 'The Trojans in Britain', *E&S* 9 (1923), 9–30.

GRAF, A., *Roma nella memoria e nelle imaginazioni del medio evo* (Turin, 1882; 2nd edn. 1923).

GRAY, D., 'A Scottish "Flower of Chivalry" and his Book', *Words: Wai-te-ata Studies in English*, 4 (1973), 22–34.

—— (ed.), *The Oxford Book of Late Medieval Verse and Prose* (Oxford, 1985).

GRIFFIN, N. E., 'Un-Homeric Elements in the Medieval Story of Troy', *JEGP* 7 (1907), 32–52.

—— *Dares and Dictys: An Introduction to the Study of Mediaeval Versions of the Story of Troy* (Baltimore, 1907).

GRILLO, A., *Tra filologia e narratologia: Dai poemi omerici ad Apollonio Rodio, Ilias Latina, Ditti-Settimo, Darete Frigio, Draconzio*, Bibliotheca Athena, NS 4 (Rome, 1988).

GUDDAT-FIGGE, G., *Catalogue of Manuscripts Containing Middle English Romances* (Munich, 1976).

GUIETTE, R., 'Chanson de geste, chronique et mise en prose', *Cahiers*, 6 (1963), 423–40.

HALE, J. R., 'International Relations in the West: Diplomacy and War', ch. 9 of *The New Cambridge Modern History*, i, *The Renaissance 1493–1520*, ed. G. R. Potter (Cambridge, 1971), 259–91.

HARNEY, M., 'Siege Warfare in Medieval Hispanic Epic and Romance', in I. A. Corfis and M. Wolfe (eds.), *The Medieval City under Siege* (Woodbridge, 1995), 177–90.

HAUER, S. R., 'Richard Coeur de Lion: Cavalier or Cannibal', *MFR* 14 (1980), 88–95.

HAURÉAU, B., *Notices et extraits de quelques manuscrits latins de la Bibliothèque Nationale*, 6 vols. (Paris, 1890–3).

HIGHET, G., *The Classical Tradition* (Oxford, 1949).

HOGG, I., 'Siege Techniques' and 'Siege and Siegecraft Fortifications', chs. 4 and 7 of H. W. Koch (ed.), *Medieval Warfare* (London, 1978), 45–55, 77–85.

HOGG, O. F. G., *English Artillery, 1326–1716* (London, 1963).

HUDSON, H., 'Middle English Popular Romances: The Manuscript Evidence', *Manuscripta*, 28 (1984), 67–78.

HUIZINGA, J., *The Waning of the Middle Ages*, trans. F. Hopman (London, 1924).

JÄGER, G., *Aspekte des Krieges und der Chevalerie im XIV. Jahrhundert in Frankreich: Untersuchungen zu Jean Froissarts Chroniques*, Geist und Werk der Zeiten, 60 (Berne and Frankfurt, 1981).

JENTSZCH, F., 'Die mittelenglische Romanze Richard Coeur de Lion und ihre Quellen', *Eng. Stud.* 15 (1891).

JONES, T., *Chaucer's Knight: Portrait of a Medieval Mercenary* (London, 1980).

KAEUPER, R. W., *War, Justice, and Public Order: England and France in the Later Middle Ages* (Oxford, 1988).

KEEN, M. H., *The Laws of War in the Late Middle Ages*, Studies in Political History (London and Toronto, 1965).

—— 'Chivalry, Nobility and the Man-at-Arms', in C. T. Allmand (ed.), *War, Literature and Politics in the Late Middle Ages* (Liverpool, 1976), 32–45.

—— 'Chivalry, Heralds and History', in R. H. C. Davis and J. M. Wallace-Hadrill (eds.), *The Writing of History in the Middle Ages: Essays Presented to Richard William Southern*, (Oxford, 1981), 393–414.

—— 'Chaucer's Knight, the English Aristocracy and the Crusades', in V. J. Scattergood (ed.), *English Court Culture in the Later Middle Ages* (New York, 1983), 45–61.

—— *Chivalry* (New Haven, 1984).

KEISER, G. R., 'Edward III and the Alliterative *Morte Arthure*', *Speculum*, 48 (1973), 37–51.

—— 'Narrative Structure in the Alliterative *Morte Arthure*, 26–720', *ChRev*, 9 (1974–5), 130–44.

—— 'The Theme of Justice in the Alliterative *Morte Arthure*', *AM* 16 (1975), 94–109.

KELLY, D., 'Translatio studii: Translation, Adaptation and Allegory in Medieval French Literature', *PQ* 57 (1978), 287–310.

KNOWLES, C., 'A 14th Century Imitator of Jean de Meung: Jean de Vignai's Translation of the *De re militari* of Vegetius', *SP* 53 (1956), 452–8.

KOECHLIN, R., *Les Ivoires gothiques français*, 3 vols. (Paris, 1968).

KURVINEN, A., 'MS Porkington 10: Description with Extracts', *Neu. Mitt.* 54 (1953), 33–67.

LANGLOIS, E., 'Chronologie des romans de Thèbes, d'*Eneas* et de *Troie*', *BEC* 66 (1905), 107–20.

LAWTON, D. A., 'The *Destruction of Troy* as Translation from Latin Prose: Aspects of Form and Style', *SN* 52 (1980), 259–70.

LEGGE, M. D., 'The Lord Edward's Vegetius', *Scriptorium*, 7 (1953), 262–5.

LE GOFF, J., 'Warriors and Conquering Bourgeois: The Image of the City in Twelfth-Century French Literature', in *The Medieval Imagination*, trans. A. Goldhammer (Chicago and London, 1988), 151–76.

LEVY, B. J., 'Pèlerins rivaux de la 3ème croisade: Les Personnages des rois d'Angleterre et de France, d'après les chroniques d'Ambroise et d'"Ernoul" et le récit anglo-normand de la *Croisade et Mort Richard Coeur de Lion*', in D. Buschinger (ed.), *La Croisade: Realités et fictions: Actes du Colloque d'Amiens 18–22 mars 1987*, Göppinger Arbeiten zur Germanistik, 503 (Göppingen, 1989), 143–55.

LEWIS, C. S., *The Discarded Image: An Introduction to Medieval and Renaissance Literature* (Cambridge, 1964).

LOOMIS, L. H., 'Secular Dramatics in the Royal Palace, Paris, 1378, 1389, and

Chaucer's "Tregetoures"', *Speculum*, 33 (1958), 242–55. Reprinted in J. Taylor and A. H. Nelson (eds.), *Medieval English Drama: Essays Critical and Contextual* (Chicago, 1972), 98–115.

LOOMIS, R. S., 'Richard Coeur de Lion and the Pas Saladin in Medieval Art', *PMLA* 30 (1915), 509–28.

—— review of Brunner's edition of *Richard Coeur de Lion, JEGP* 15 (1916), 455–66.

—— 'The Allegorical Siege in the Art of the Middle Ages', *AJA*, 2nd ser. 23 (1919), 255–69.

LUMIANSKY, R. M., 'The Story of Troilus and Briseida according to Benoit and Guido', *Speculum*, 29 (1956), 727–53.

—— 'Dares' *Historia* and Dictys' *Ephemeris*: A Critical Comment', in E. B. Atwood and A. A. Hill (eds.), *Studies in Language, Literature and Culture of the Middle Ages and Later* (Austin, Tex., 1969), 200–9.

—— 'Legends of Troy', in Severs and Hartung (eds.), *Manual*, i. 118–19.

MACCRACKEN, H. N., 'Vegetius in English: Notes on the Early Translations', in E. S. Sheldon *et al.* (eds.), *Anniversary Papers by Colleagues and Pupils of George Lyman Kittredge* (Boston and London, 1913), 389–403.

MAHONEY, D. B., 'Malory's Great Guns', *Viator*, 20 (1989), 291–310.

MARINESCO, C., 'Du nouveau sur *Tirant lo Blanc*', *ER* 4 (1953–4), 137–203.

MATTHEWS, W., *The Tragedy of Arthur* (Berkeley and Los Angeles, 1960).

MAYER, H. E., *The Crusades*, trans. J. Gillingham (Oxford, 1972).

MEHL, D., *The Middle English Romances of the Thirteenth and Fourteenth Centuries* (London, 1968).

MEYER, P., 'Les Anciens Traducteurs français de Végèce et en particulier Jean de Vignai', *Romania*, 25 (1896), 401–23.

MOE, P., 'The French Source of the Alliterative *Siege of Jerusalem*', *MÆ* 39 (1970), 147–54.

—— 'On Professor Micha's *Vengeance de Notre Seigneur*, Version II', *Romania*, 95 (1974), 555–60.

MONGEAU, R. G. B., 'Thirteenth-Century Siege Weapons and Machines in *L'Art de chevalerie*', *Allegorica*, 7/2 (1987), 123–43.

MORRIS, C., 'Geoffrey de Villehardouin and the Conquest of Constantinople', *History*, 53 (1968), 24–34.

MURET, E., *Le Château d'amour* (Lausanne, 1908).

MURRAY, J., 'Le Château d'amour' (dissertation, Paris, 1918).

MUSCATINE, C., *Poetry and Crisis in the Age of Chaucer* (Notre Dame, Ind. and London, 1972).

NEEDLER, G. H., *Richard Coeur de Lion in Literature* (Leipzig, 1890).

NEILSON, G., *Huchown of the Awle Ryale* (Glasgow, 1902).

—— '*Morte Arthure* and the War of Brittany', *N&Q*, 9th ser. 10 (1902), 161–5.

—— 'The Baulked Coronation of Arthur in *Morte Arthure*', *N&Q*, 9th ser. 10 (1902), 381–3, 402–4.

NEILSON, W. A., *The Origins and Sources of the 'Court of Love'*, Studies and Notes in Philology and Literature, 6 (Boston, 1899).

NELSON, J. (ed.), *Richard Coeur de Lion in History and Myth* (London, 1992).

NEWARK, T., *Medieval Warfare* (London, 1979).

NEWSTEAD, H., 'The Besieged Ladies in Arthurian Romance', *PMLA* 63 (1948), 803–30.

NORMAN, A. V. B., and POTTINGER, D., *English Weapons and Warfare 449–1660* (London, 1979).

OLIVER, T. E., *Jacques Milet's Drama 'La Destruction de Troye la Grant': Its Principal Source: Its Dramatic Structure* (Heidelberg, 1899).

OMAN, C., *A History of the Art of War: The Middle Ages from the Fourth to the Fourteenth Century* (London, 1898).

OWST, G. R., *Literature and Pulpit in Medieval England* (Cambridge, 1933; revised 2nd edn. Oxford, 1961).

PANOFSKY, E., *Renaissance and Renascences in Western Art* (Stockholm, 1960; 2nd edn., London, 1970).

—— and Saxl, F., 'Classical Mythology in Mediaeval Art', *Metropolitan Museum Studies*, 4 (1933), 28–80.

PARIS, G., 'Le Roman de Richard Coeur de Lion', *Romania*, 26 (1897), 353–93.

PARSONS, A. E., 'The Trojan Legend in England: Some Instances of its Application to the Politics of the Times', *MLR* 24 (1929), 253–64.

PATTERSON, L., *Negotiating the Past: The Historical Understanding of Medieval Literature* (Madison, Wis. and London, 1987).

PEARSALL, D., *John Lydgate* (London, 1970).

—— 'The English Romance in the Fifteenth Century', *E&S*, NS 29 (1976), 56–83.

—— *Old and Middle English Poetry* (London, 1977).

The Penguin Dictionary of Architecture, ed. J. Fleming *et al.* (Harmondsworth, 1966).

PETROVICS, I., and SZÓNYI, G., '*Capystranus*, a Late Medieval English Romance on the 1456 Siege of Belgrade', *NHQ* 27/104 (1986), 141–6.

PICKERING F P., *Literature and Art in the Middle Ages* (London, 1970).

PORTER, E., 'Chaucer's Knight, the Alliterative *Morte Arthure*, and Medieval Laws of War: A Reconsideration', *NMS* 27 (1983), 56–78.

—— 'The Conduct of War as Reflected in Certain Middle English Romances, with Special Reference to the Alliterative *Morte Arthure*' (thesis, Queen's University of Belfast, 1985).

POWELL, C. L., 'The Castle of the Body', *SP* 16 (1919), 197–205.

PRESTWICH, J. O., 'Richard Coeur de Lion: Rex Bellicosus', in *Ricardo Cuor di Leone nella storia e nella leggenda: Accademia Nazionale dei Lincei, colloquio italo-britannico*, Accademia Nazionale dei Lincei, Problemi attuali de scienza e di cultura, 253 (Rome, 1981), 1–15.

RAYNAUD DE LAGE, G., 'Du *Roman de Troie* de Benoit au *Roman de Troie* en prose', in T. G. S. Combe and P. Rickard (eds.), *The French Language: Studies presented to Lewis Charles Harmer* (London, 1970).

REGAN, C. A., 'Patristic Psychology in the Old English "Vainglory"', *Traditio*, 26 (1970), 324–35.

RICE, J. A., *Middle English Romance: An Annotated Bibliography, 1955–1985*, Garland Reference Library of the Humanities, 545 (NewYork and London, 1987).

RICHÉ, P., 'Les Représentations du palais dans les textes littéraires du Haut Moyen Age', *Francia*, 4 (1976), 161–71.

RIQUER, M. de, *Aproximació al Tirant lo Blanc*, Quaderns Crema, Assaig, 8 (Barcelona, 1990).

ROACH, W. A., 'The Modena Text of the Prose *Joseph d'Arimathie*', *RPh* 9 (1955–6), 313–42.

ROBBINS, R. H., 'Good Gossips Reunited', *BMQ* 27 (1964), 12–15.

ROBERTSON, D. W., 'The Concept of Courtly Love as an Impediment to the Understanding of Medieval Texts', in F. X. Newman (ed.), *The Meaning of Courtly Love* (NewYork, 1968), 1–19.

ROGERS, R., *Latin Siege Warfare in the Twelfth Century* (Oxford, 1992).

RONA, E., 'Hungary in a Medieval Poem: "Capystranus", a Metrical Romance', in M. Brahmer *et al.* (eds.), *Studies in Language and Literature in Honour of Margaret Schlauch* (Warsaw, 1966), 343–52.

RUIZ DOMÉNEC, J. E., 'El asedio de Barcelona, según Ermoldo el Negro (Notas sobre el carácter de la guerra en la alta Edad Media)', *BRABLB* 37 (1977–8), 146–68.

RUSSELL, F. H., *The Just War in the Middle Ages* (Oxford, 1975).

—— 'Love and Hate in Medieval Warfare: The Contribution of Saint Augustine', *NMS* 31 (1987), 108–24.

SABLONIER, R., *Krieg und Kriegertum in der Crònica des Ramon Muntaner: Eine Studie zum spätmittelalterlichen Kriegswesen aufgrund Katalanischer Quellen*, Geist und Werk der Zeiten, 31 (Berne and Frankfurt, 1971).

SALVERDA DE GRAVE, J. J., *Observations sur l'art lyrique de Giraut de Bornelh*, Mededeenligen der Koninklije Nederlandsche Akademie van Wetenschapen, Afd. Letterkund, 1 (1938).

SANDER, E., 'Der Belagerungskrieg im Mittelalter', *HZ* 165 (1941), 99–110.

SAXL, F., 'The Troy Romance in French and Italian Art', in *Lectures*, 2 vols. (London, 1957), i. 125–38.

SCHERER, M. R., *The Legends of Troy in Art and Literature* (NewYork and London, 1963).

SCHRADER, C. R., 'A Handlist of Extant Manuscripts containing the *De re militari* of Flavius Vegetius Renatus', *Scriptorium*, 33 (1979), 280–303.

SETTON, K. M., *The Papacy and the Levant (1204–1571)* (Philadelphia, 1978).

SEVERS, J. B., and HARTUNG, A. E. (eds.), *A Manual of the Writings in Middle English* (New Haven, 1967–).

SEZNEC, J., *La Survivance des dieux antiques: Essai sur le rôle de la tradition mythologique dans l'humanisme et dans l'art de la Renaissance*, Studies of the Warburg Institute, 11 (London, 1940).

SHEPHERD, S. H. A., '"This grete journee": *The Sege of Melayne*', in M. Mills *et al.* (eds.), *Romance in Medieval England* (Cambridge, 1991), 113–31.

SILVERSTEIN, T., '*Sir Gawain*, Dear Brutus and Britain's Fortunate Founding: A Study in Comedy and Convention', *MP* 62 (1965), 189–206.

SISAM, K. (ed.), *Fourteenth Century Verse and Prose* (Oxford, 1921; rev. edn. 1975).

SMAIL, R. C., *Crusading Warfare 1097–1193* (Cambridge, 1956).

SMALLEY, B., *Historians in the Middle Ages* (London, 1974).

SMITHERS, G. V., 'Notes on Middle English Texts', *LMS* 1 (1937–8), 208.

SOMMER, H. O., *The Recuyell of the Historyes of Troye* (London, 1894).

SOUTHERN, R., *The Medieval Theatre in the Round: A Study of the Staging of the Castle of Perseverance and Related Matters* (London, 1957).

SPEARING, A. C., *Readings in Medieval Poetry* (Cambridge, 1987).

SPRINGER, M., 'Vegetius im Mittelalter', *Philologus*, 123 (1979), 85–90.

SPRUNG, A., 'The "Townes Wal": A Frame for "Fre Chois" in Chaucer's *Troilus and Criseyde*', *Medievalia*, 14 (1988), 127–42.

STANLEY, E. G., 'Old English Poetic Diction and the Interpretation of *The Wanderer, The Seafarer, and The Penitent's Prayer*', *Anglia*, 73 (1956), 413–66. Reprinted in *A Collection of Papers with Emphasis on Old English Literature*, Publications of the Dictionary of Old English (Toronto, 1987), 234–80.

STEINER, G., *The Death of Tragedy* (London, 1961).

STEVENS, J., *Medieval Romance: Themes and Approaches* (London, 1973).

STOKOE, W. C., 'The Work of the Redactors of *Sir Launfal, Richard Coeur de Lion* and *Sir Degaré*' (dissertation, Cornell University, 1947).

STROHM, P., 'Storie, Spelle, Geste, Romaunce, Tragedie: Generic Distinctions in the Middle English Troy Narratives', *Speculum*, 46 (1971), 348–59.

SUCHIER, W., 'Über das altfranzösische Gedicht von der *Zerstörung Jerusalems (La Venjance Nostre Seigneur)*, *ZRP* 24 (1900), 161–98; 25 (1901), 94–109, 256.

SUMPTION, J., *The Hundred Years War: Trial by Battle* (London, 1990).

TAMIZEY DE LARROQUE, P. (ed.), 'Notice sur Robert de Balsac: Le Chemin de l'ospital et ceulx qui en sont possesseurs', *Rev*, 3rd ser. 16 (1886), 276–300.

TAYLOR, A., *The Welsh Castles of Edward I* (London, 1986).

THOMPSON, J. J., *Robert Thornton and the London Thornton Manuscript*, Manuscript Studies, 2 (Cambridge, 1987).

THORPE, L., 'Mastre Richard, a Thirteenth-Century Translator of the *De re militari* of Vegetius', *Scriptorium*, 6 (1952), 39–50.

TURVILLE-PETRE, T. (ed.), *Alliterative Poetry of the Later Middle Ages* (London, 1989).

TUVE, R., *Allegorical Imagery: Some Mediaeval Books and their Posterity* (Princeton, 1966).

TYERMAN, C., *England and the Crusades 1095–1588* (Chicago, 1988).

VALE, J., 'Law and Diplomacy in the Alliterative *Morte Arthure*', *NMS* 23 (1979), 31–46.

VALE, M., 'New Techniques and Old Ideals: The Impact of Artillery on War and Chivalry at the End of the Hundred Years War', in C. T. Allmand (ed.), *War, Literature and Politics in the Late Middle Ages* (Liverpool, 1976), 57–60, 72.

—— *War and Chivalry: Warfare and Aristocratic Culture in England, France and Burgundy at the End of the Middle Ages* (London, 1981).

VAN MARLE, R., *Iconographie de l'art profane au Moyen Age et à la Renaissance*, 2 vols. (New York, 1971).

VENINI, P., *Ditti Cretese e Omero* (Milan, 1981).

VERBRUGGEN, J. F., *The Art of Warfare in Western Europe During the Middle Ages: From the Eighth Century to 1340*, trans. J. Willard and J. C. M. Southern, The Middle Ages: Selected Studies, 1 (Amsterdam, 1977).

VIARD, J., 'Le Siège de Calais (4 septembre 1346–4 août 1347)', *LMA* 39 (1929), 129–89.

VINAVER, E., *The Rise of Romance* (Oxford, 1971).

WALZER, M., *Just and Unjust Wars: A Moral Argument with Historical Illustrations* (New York, 1977).

WARD, H. L. D., *Catalogue of Romances in the Department of Manuscripts in the British Museum*, 3 vols. (London, 1961), i. 945–56.

WARNER, P., *Sieges of the Middle Ages* (London, 1968).

—— *The Medieval Castle: Life in a Fortress in Peace and War* (London, 1971).

WETHERBEE, W., 'Chivalry under Siege in Ricardian Romance,' in I. A. Corfis and M. Wolfe (eds.), *The Medieval City under Siege* (Woodbridge, 1995), 207–26.

WHITELOCK, D., *The Audience of Beowulf* (Oxford, 1951).

WICKHAM, G., *Early English Stages 1300 to 1660*, 3 vols. (London, 1959–81).

WIGGINTON, W. B., 'The Nature and Significance of the Medieval Troy Story: A Study of Guido delle Colonne's *Historia destructionis Troiae* (dissertation, Rutgers University, 1964).

WILLARD, C. C., 'Christine de Pizan's Art of Medieval Warfare', in R. J. Cormier and U. T. Holmes (eds.), *Essays in Honor of Louis Francis Solano* (Chapel Hill, NC, 1970), 179–91.

WILLIAMS, C. C., 'A Case of Mistaken Identity: Still Another Trojan Narrative in Old French Prose', *MÆ*, 53 (1984), 59–72.

WILSON, R. M., 'More Lost Literature in Old and Middle English', *LSE* 5 (1936), 1–49.

WISE, T., *The Wars of the Crusades 1096–1291* (London, 1978).

WISMAN, J., 'L'*Epitoma rei militaris* de Végèce et sa fortune au Moyen Age', *LMA*, 85 (1979), 13–29.

WOLEDGE, B., and CLIVE, H. P., *Répertoire des plus anciens textes en prose française* (Geneva, 1964).

WOOLF, R., 'The Theme of Christ the Lover-Knight in Medieval English Literature', *RES*, NS 13 (1962), 1–16.

WRIGHT, N. A. R.,'The *Tree of Battles* of Honoré Bouvet and the Laws of War', in C. T. Allmand (ed.), *War, Literature and Politics in the Late Middle Ages* (Liverpool, 1976), 12–31.

WRIGHT, S. K., *The Vengeance of Our Lord: Medieval Dramatizations of the Destruction of Jerusalem*, Pontifical Institute of Mediaeval Studies, Studies and Texts, 89 (Toronto, 1989).

WÜLFING, J. E.,'Das Laud-Troybook', *Eng. Stud.* 29 (1901), 374–96.

—— 'Das Bild und die bildliche Verneinung im Laud-Troy-Book', *Anglia*, 27 (1904), 555–80; 28 (1905), 29–80.

WURSTER, J.,'The Audience', in K. H. Göller (ed.), *The Alliterative Morte Arthure: A Reassessment of the Poem* (Cambridge, 1981), 44–56.

YOUNG, A. M., *Troy and her Legend* (Pittsburgh, 1948).

Index